First Fruits of

FREEDOM

D1453353

The John Hope Franklin Series in African American History and Culture

WALDO E. MARTIN JR. AND PATRICIA SULLIVAN, EDITORS

JANETTE THOMAS GREENWOOD

First Fruits of

FREEDOM

THE MIGRATION OF FORMER SLAVES AND

THEIR SEARCH FOR EQUALITY

IN WORCESTER, MASSACHUSETTS, 1862–1900

The University of North Carolina Press

CHAPEL HILL

Designed by Courtney Leigh Baker and set in Minion Pro with Edwardian Script
and Gotham Display by Rebecca Evans. The paper in this book meets the guidelines
for permanence and durability of the Committee on Production Guidelines for
Book Longevity of the Council on Library Resources. The University of North
Carolina Press has been a member of the Green Press Initiative since 2003.

Library of Congress Cataloging-in-Publication Data
Greenwood, Janette Thomas.
First fruits of freedom: the migration of former slaves and their search for
equality in Worcester, Massachusetts, 1862–1900 / Janette Thomas Greenwood.
p. cm.—(The John Hope Franklin series in African American history and culture)
Includes bibliographical references and index.
ISBN 978-0-8078-3362-9 (cloth: alk. paper)
ISBN 978-0-8078-7104-1 (pbk: alk. paper)
1. African Americans—Massachusetts—Worcester—History—19th century.
2. African Americans—Massachusetts—Worcester—Social conditions—19th century.
3. Freedmen—Massachusetts—Worcester—History—19th century. 4. African
Americans—Migrations—History—19th century. 5. Migration, Internal—United
States—History—19th century. 6. United States—History—Civil War, 1861–1865—
Social aspects. 7. Worcester (Mass.)—Social conditions—19th century. I. Title.
F74.W9G925 2010
305.896′07307443—dc22   2009031107

cloth   14 13 12 11 10   5 4 3 2 1
paper   14 13 12 11 10   5 4 3 2 1

Portions of this work appeared previously, in somewhat different form, in
Janette Greenwood, "Southern Black Migration and Community Building: Worcester
as a Case Study," in *Faces of Community: Immigrant Massachusetts, 1860–2000*, ed. Reed Ueda
and Conrad Edick Wright (Boston: Massachusetts Historical Society, 2003),
and have been reprinted here with permission of the publisher.

IN MEMORY OF MY PARENTS,

Fern and Carl Thomas,

AND MY FATHER-IN LAW,

Isadore Rubin

Contents

Illustrations

Acknowledgments

This book grew out of a seminar on black Worcester that I co-taught my first year at Clark University with my colleague Sally Deutsch, in conjunction with the Worcester Historical Museum. Saadia Wiggins Lawton, one of our students, wrote a fascinating paper on the John Street Baptist Church, in which she discussed the church's founding by black migrants from North Carolina and Virginia. As a historian of the South in the midst of completing a book on North Carolina, I became tantalized by the Worcester–North Carolina connection, as I was unaware of any significant migration of southern blacks to the North before the World War I era. My initial questions soon snowballed, and before I knew it, I found myself deeply immersed in a second book project.

Saadia Wiggins Lawton was the first of many Clark students who contributed to this book over many years as they delved into local research in subsequent seminars and helped me sketch out this story. I am especially indebted to Michelle Reidel for her research on black women's clubs; Alan Damarjian for his work on the city's black activists in the 1890s; and Emily Thomas's research on Massachusetts teachers of freedpeople. Michelle Reidel, Jodie Medeiros, and Ashley Cataldo helped me labor through years of manuscript censuses. Diane Boucher provided a critical reading of this manuscript, and her seminar paper on the Howard Industrial School in Cambridgeport, Massachusetts, supplied valuable context for the Worcester story.

I am deeply grateful to my history department colleagues who have encouraged me in this project from the start and provided me with excellent feedback, especially Sally Deutsch, now at Duke University. Her early encouragement gave me the confidence to move forward with this project. Doug Little, Drew McCoy, Amy Richter, and Nina Kushner all provided much-needed support and enthusiasm. Diane Fenner, our department's administrative assistant, helped me prepare the manuscript.

I am especially indebted to Thomas L. Doughton, who generously shared his own research and vast knowledge of Worcester's people of color with me and my students. He also provided numerous community contacts and made valuable suggestions throughout the course of this long project.

I also greatly benefited from the camaraderie, enthusiasm, and collective knowledge of the Worcester History Group, convened monthly by Ken Moynihan of Assumption College. Ken read early versions of the initial chapters of this book and generously shared his wide-ranging knowledge of Worcester history. As he did his own research on Worcester history, Al Southwick sent me numerous clippings from late-nineteenth-century newspapers that provided me with many valuable leads.

Many Worcesterites shared family stories and documents relating to the migration. Stanley Gutridge, whose grandfather, George Wiggins, migrated from New Bern, shared invaluable information with me over many years. George Blanchard, whose great-grandfather employed and housed contraband Isaiah Allen, provided the "missing link" for Isaiah Allen's years in Worcester when he shared family papers. And Edna Spencer, a twentieth-century southern migrant, shared her personal insights into Worcester's "southern village." Pastor Noel Williamson of the Pleasant Street Baptist Church and the Reverend Roosevelt Hughes and Victoria Camble of the John Street Baptist Church generously shared church documents with me.

I was also fortunate to present various phases of this project at the American Antiquarian Society, the Massachusetts Historical Society, the New England Historical Association, the Worcester Historical Museum, the College of the Holy Cross, and Boston University. I am especially grateful for feedback from Robert L. Hall and Marilyn Halter. Reed Ueda and Conrad Edick Wright prodded me to place black Worcester within the city's larger ethnic context, and for that I am grateful.

Without financial support and time to write, I would never have completed this book. Clark University provided me with invaluable sabbatical time to complete this project. The Higgins School of Humanities at Clark granted me funds to research in Washington, DC, and North Carolina. A National Endowment for the Humanities Summer Stipend made it possible for me to travel to libraries and archives in eastern North Carolina. The Clark University history department also granted me research money for travel to various archives. A Clark University Logan Fellowship also provided me with research support and the chance to create a Reconstruction research seminar in which my students explored Reconstruction's impact in the North.

Many librarians and archivists aided me along the way. I am especially indebted to Mary Hartman and the research librarians at Clark University; Nancy Gaudette, now retired, of the Worcester Room, Worcester Public Library; the archivists at the American Antiquarian Society, especially Jackie Penny; Robyn Christensen at the Worcester Historical Museum; the Massachusetts Historical Society; the Southern Historical Collection at Chapel Hill; and the Massachusetts Military Museum and Archive.

Working with the outstanding staff at the University of North Carolina Press has once again been a wonderful experience. Lewis Bateman, a former editor at UNC Press, initially encouraged this project. His successor, Chuck Grench, graciously agreed to consider my overdue manuscript and swiftly expedited its publication. I am especially grateful to Katy V. O'Brien, assistant editor, for helping prepare the manuscript and to editor Mary Caviness, whose sharp eye saved me from many embarrassing errors and who generally made this a better book. My outside readers at UNC Press, Elizabeth Pleck and Sydney Nathans, provided insightful critiques of the manuscript and helped me sharpen my argument in a number of key places. I am also deeply indebted to fellow UNC Press author Leslie V. Schwalm, who generously allowed me to read the proofs of her book, *Emancipation's Diaspora*, as I completed my own work. Being able to reference her pathbreaking study on Civil War–era migration to the upper Midwest and its many consequences greatly enhanced this book and helped me place the Worcester story in a larger national context.

Finally, I cannot thank my family and friends enough. While they may not have always received the warmest response to their query, "Have you finished that book yet?," I did appreciate their ongoing interest. My husband, Michael Rubin, came into my life as I struggled to complete this project. His love and support made all the difference. My daughters, Elizabeth and Susannah, grew from little girls to young women over the course of this project; they lived with it much longer than they probably wanted to. I'm grateful to them for reminding me what is most important in life and for their incomparable ability to make me laugh. My stepson, Sam, buoyed my spirits with his enthusiastic questions about this project. My parents, Fern and Carl Thomas, passed away in the course of writing this book, as did my father-in-law, Isadore Rubin. All three of them, children of the Great Depression, embodied the strength and character of that generation. And they loved history. I miss them every day. This book is dedicated to them.

Introduction

In June 1862, amidst news from the Civil War battlefront, the *Worcester Daily Spy* announced the "arrival of a 'Contraband'"—a slave who had absconded to the safety of Union lines in search of freedom. The refugee had just come from New Bern, North Carolina, where he had "rendered important service to Gen. Burnside, in the capacity of pilot." In return for his aid, "he was sent north with his wife and child," bearing "recommendations from officers high in rank." The newspaper editor appealed to readers to consider hiring him, as "such a man certainly deserves immediate employment here—a chance for honest labor, which is all he wants."[1]

The arrival of the escaped bondsman and his family to Worcester marked the beginning of a small but steady stream of contrabands and then emancipated slaves to Worcester County, Massachusetts, during and immediately following the Civil War. The contraband's story contains several clues about the origin and nature of this development. Southern black migration to central Massachusetts from the 1860s on was rooted in the experience of the Civil War, first and foremost in relationships built between northern white soldiers and the southern blacks they encountered during the conflict. Fugitives and white soldiers, sharing the experience of the war, forged strong personal bonds that led former slaves to accompany the veterans north to their homes. Missionary teachers from Worcester, following in the paths of county regiments, reinforced military networks of migration, bringing additional freedpeople north with them after their service in the South. Personally sponsored and highly localized, this wartime journey established southern black migration networks to Worcester County evident through the turn of the twentieth century, as migrants brought family and friends north. A third, less personalized network, the Freedmen's Bureau, helped place additional former slaves in Worcester by finding them employment. Seeking a more complete freedom in the North, these men and women were, in the words of Chaplain Horace James, who played a key role in facilitating the migration from eastern North Carolina, "the Children of this Revolution, the promising first fruits of the war."[2]

As the "contraband's" story from 1862 suggests, Civil War–era migration was profoundly different from the massive Great Migration of the twentieth century, with its own unique context, internal dynamic, and networks. Yet this earlier migration has only begun to be studied on its own terms. The Great Migration dominates the literature and, consequently, our understanding of black migration. Great Migration studies generally treat the Civil War–era movements in a cursory way, as mere prologue to the much larger Great Migration. While the Great Migration drew millions of people north, the Civil War–era migration, by contrast, drew approximately 80,000 blacks to free states in the North and West by 1870. Yet, as historian Michael P. Johnson notes, this migration, while much smaller in scale than the Great Migration, constituted "the largest voluntary interstate migration of African Americans in the first century of the nation's history."[3]

But beyond this demographic fact, this migration, a product of the Civil War, emancipation, and Reconstruction, constitutes the powerful story of former slaves who went north, initially with white patrons, believing that "free New England" and Massachusetts provided the most fertile soil for seeding a new life for themselves and their children. Some of them, especially the first wave of migrants, would, indeed, find their hopes fulfilled in the North, as they established new lives with the aid of "benevolent sympathizers," as one fugitive slave to the city explained. But even the antislavery hotbed of Worcester — like the rest of the nation — eventually reneged on the promises made to African Americans during Reconstruction. Despite noble efforts, southern migrants and their children would be frustrated in their attempts to prod white citizens to live up to promises made to black Americans after emancipation.[4]

Worcester County, Massachusetts, provides an outstanding context for telling this dramatic story and for weaving together several strands of the emancipation story usually treated separately: abolitionism; the story of northern white soldiers who helped liberate slaves and the missionary teachers who educated them; and accounts of emancipated slaves claiming their freedom in the chaos of war and shaping their own freedom. Moreover, two additional underexamined narratives — the role of an activist black community in aiding the settlement of ex-slaves and the subsequent chain migration from the South in the wake of the contraband migrants — also become clear in the Worcester example.

With a deep abolitionist tradition, Worcester County had long been in the forefront of antislavery activities that bonded both white and black activists as crusaders against slavery. By the mid-1850s, the city had gained a reputation of being far more radical than its more celebrated counterpart, Boston, roughly forty miles to the east. Worcester prided itself, in the aftermath of the Fugitive Slave Law, as being "Canada to the Slave," in the words of the city's fiery radical abolitionist minister Thomas Wentworth Higginson, and the city continued to act as a refuge for former slaves during and after the Civil War.[5]

In the first two years of the Civil War, Worcester County raised several regiments made up of white men from the county and contributed fifteen soldiers to the famous 54th Massachusetts. Among the most prominent of the white regiments were the 15th Massachusetts Volunteer Infantry and the 25th Massachusetts Volunteer Infantry, both three-year regiments. The 15th spent most of the war engaged in the bloody, protracted campaigns fought in Virginia and Maryland. The 25th was part of the Burnside Expedition that successfully invaded and controlled much of northeastern North Carolina, including New Bern, in the spring of 1862. Under the direction of Chaplain Horace James, the 25th spearheaded efforts not only in protecting refugee slaves from their former masters but also in setting up schools to educate them. James, later appointed Superintendent of Negro Affairs in eastern North Carolina, played an especially important part in facilitating migration, as he forged strong links between New Bern and Worcester.

Missionary teachers and ministers from Worcester County, many recruited by James, enthusiastically followed in the paths of local units serving in the South. Because of the long-term presence of the 25th Massachusetts in New Bern, young men and women eager to teach former slaves flocked to eastern North Carolina. Others established and taught in freedpeople's schools in southeastern Virginia, also in proximity to Worcester County soldiers.

Black migration networks to Worcester County mirrored the specific path its troops and missionaries trod. Runaway slaves from northern Virginia and from northeastern North Carolina all sought refuge and freedom with the county's regiments during the war. Like the contraband family in 1862, they made their way north during and immediately following the war in the company of local soldiers and teachers, paving the way for future migrants from these specific southern locales. Additional migrants came after the war under the auspices of the Freedmen's Bureau, which found them employment in Worcester. Between 1862 and 1870 alone, approximately 370 southern blacks — the overwhelming number from North Carolina and Virginia — migrated to the county, significantly augmenting its African American population and nearly doubling the city's small black community. Civil War–era migrants established patterns of chain migration in which they rapidly facilitated the arrival of additional family members and friends. Moreover, they helped create a migration tradition of men and women from Virginia and eastern North Carolina that lasted at least through the century. By 1900, well over a thousand southerners, mostly North Carolinians and Virginians, migrated to Worcester County, helping to nearly triple its "colored" population while enlarging that of the city of Worcester nearly fivefold, giving it a decidedly southern cast (see Table A.3).[6]

An examination of Civil War–era migration not only sheds light on the bonds of war created between southern blacks and northern white soldiers and teachers but also demonstrates how their interactions profoundly shaped each other. Wartime experiences left deep and lasting impressions that went far beyond the exigencies of the war.

In addition, Worcester County's Civil War–era migration affords a rare glimpse into the lives and strategies of black men, women, and children on the cusp of freedom. Their stories not only reveal the significant contributions that they made to the Union war effort but also show how former slaves negotiated a new world of freedom, the tactics they employed, and the decisions they made to ensure their liberty and that of family and friends whom they subsequently brought north.

Black migration to Worcester in this period also provides a rich case study of a tiny but highly organized and politically active northern black community that played a crucial role in settling southern migrants. Black Worcesterites, in many cases former slaves themselves who had sought refuge in the city before the Civil War, found migrants housing and employment and helped integrate them into a supportive community. Complemented by a solid infrastructure of antislavery and freedmen's relief organizations, the support of patrons — both black and white — eased the transition of former slaves to a more complete freedom in the North. The interest of sympathetic blacks and whites extended beyond the emancipation of southern blacks to the era of freedom.

Finally, this story mirrors the larger national story of Reconstruction's broken promises. Even in Worcester, with its deep abolitionist tradition, the sympathy of Worcester whites did not extend beyond the Civil War–era abolitionist generation. Just as the nation quickly wearied of the "negro problem" and the ideal of equality for all faded from the national agenda with the passing of the "radical generation," sympathy for southern black refugees diminished in Worcester. Especially for those who came north without white patronage, the city and county provided few opportunities for economic advancement, with an unofficial color bar in industry. Reflecting the national trajectory of Reconstruction and its aftermath, "benevolent sympathizers" became fewer in number. In Worcester, as nationally, African Americans found their hopes of full-fledged citizenship dashed, their dream deferred for another century.

OUTSIDE OF STUDIES of Kansas Exodusters, the Civil War–era/Reconstruction black migration has received only minimal attention from historians until recently, and the Midwest continues to garner the most attention. Elizabeth Pleck's *Black Migration and Poverty: Boston, 1865–1900* (1979) is one of the few book-length, in-depth studies of Civil War–era migration to New England. While examining the role of the Freedmen's Bureau in facilitating the migration of southern blacks to post–Civil War Boston, Pleck's study makes no mention of military or missionary sponsorship and is ultimately less interested in migration and its consequences than in examining "the impact of the city and racial poverty" on Boston's blacks. Other historians, including William C. Cohen, Carol Faulkner, and Robert Harrison, have more broadly explored the organized group relocation of freedpeople to the North by the Freedmen's Bureau and relief organizations.[7]

Building on V. Jacque Voegeli's *Free But Not Equal: The Midwest and the Negro during the Civil War* (1967), recent scholarship has focused on the Midwest, where the majority of black migrants headed. Michael P. Johnson and Leslie A. Schwalm have both examined Civil War–era migration to that region. Schwalm's groundbreaking, book-length study, *Emancipation's Diaspora: Race and Reconstruction in the Upper Midwest* (2009), deftly weaves the story of Civil War–era black migration with the vigorous public discourse on race and politics and teases out the ways that this migration extended the consequences of emancipation beyond the South.[8]

Schwalm's examination of the upper Midwest greatly broadens our understanding of the Civil War–era migration and Reconstruction in the North. Yet the migration experience and Reconstruction in New England differed significantly from that of the Midwest, even as it shared some common ground. As Schwalm carefully delineates, regional history, geography, and national events all shaped the reception of black migrants in the upper Midwest. The same is true for New England. In the upper Midwest, as Schwalm shows, "a legacy of bondage" and a tradition of white supremacy — evident in the presence of slavery, exclusionary laws prohibiting black migration, black codes, and violence — all shaped what Schwalm has characterized as "white hostility" to black migrants. By contrast, residents of New England — Massachusetts and Worcester in particular — had long prided themselves on their liberal race relations and their aid in providing refuge for runaway slaves. Even though, as historian Joanne Pope Melish has shown, the narrative of "free New England" was largely mythical as it erased the region's own slave past, it was a powerful story nevertheless, one that informed the behavior of Worcester troops, as they marched south and liberated slaves, and the decisions of scores of preachers and teachers to go south from Worcester to teach the newly emancipated. Moreover, as the home of their liberators and teachers, Massachusetts loomed large as a symbol of freedom in the eyes of ex-slaves who accompanied soldiers and teachers home in the first wave of Civil War migration. Finally, the antislavery heritage of the region, state, and city deeply affected the way that the community received former slaves who made Worcester their home. Worcester's tiny, but highly activist, black community also played a crucial role. Unlike the Midwest, where even established black communities often responded to migrants with hostility, in Worcester the city's blacks and white abolitionists served as patrons to migrants. Having forged bonds with the white abolitionists in the 1850s in response to the Fugitive Slave Law, they stood shoulder to shoulder, first to defend the free soil of Massachusetts before the war and then to ease former slaves into a new life in the North during and after the war. Their alliance and cooperation would prove vital to the successful settlement of former slaves in the city.[9]

Geography also played a part in shaping contrasting migration experiences in the upper Midwest and New England. With its close physical proximity to slave states and with the Mississippi River providing a natural conduit, the upper Midwest became a magnet for thousands of fugitive and emancipated slaves who made their way to Iowa, Minnesota, and Wisconsin. Whereas Union soldiers and officers there, as in Worcester, provided one avenue for migration as they returned with former slaves or made arrangements for their relocation with friends or family members, "self-liberation" in the midst of wartime chaos, as Schwalm argues, served as a second primary pathway to freedom. In addition, organized, government-sponsored relocation efforts transported hundreds of blacks, mostly women and children, from overcrowded Mississippi Valley contraband camps to the upper Midwest. The large scale of migration set off fears of black inundation and the loss of white privilege among white midwesterners. It also fostered resentment of the federal government, leading to the politicization of the migration issue in the Midwest, where it became a "vigorously debated matter of public policy." Between 1860 and 1870, over 6,000 black migrants streamed into the upper

Midwest, with Wisconsin's black population increasing by 80 percent, Minnesota's by 193 percent, and Iowa's by 439 percent.[10]

By contrast, Civil War–era black migrants to New England faced a longer, more difficult journey from the South to the North, one that often required the aid of patrons. As a result, they came in much smaller numbers. Unlike midwestern migrants, Worcester's first wave of migrants tended to arrive individually, in the company of returning soldiers and teachers. Worcester and Massachusetts received contrabands in small numbers, compared to the Midwest, and most came through personal sponsorship. Only after the war, for a brief period, did former slaves arrive through government sponsorship (the Freedmen's Bureau), and then only in modest numbers. From 1860 to 1870, Massachusetts experienced only a 45 percent net increase in its black population, from 9,602 to 13,947, the largest of any New England state. At the same time, Worcester's black population doubled, from 272 to 524 in the city, and from 769 to 1,136 in the county.[11]

The small scale of the migration and the fact that the first migrants arrived largely through personal sponsorship likely tamped the fears of those who worried, as many white Massachusetts residents clearly did, that emancipation would unleash a disruptive mass migration of blacks. Like their midwestern counterparts, many whites in the Bay State feared throngs of blacks streaming into their state as a result of emancipation; they were not immune to the same race-based concerns. For a brief moment in the fall of 1862, controversy raged when the army requested the relocation of several thousand impoverished contrabands to the Bay State. Notably, abolitionist Republican governor John Andrew, with overwhelming public support, rejected the request. Slamming the door on the mass relocation of former slaves to Massachusetts extinguished the controversy for the most part — unlike in the Midwest, where government-sponsored mass relocation efforts stoked the fires of white hostility — leaving space in cities such as Worcester to accept small numbers of contrabands without a harsh backlash. While occasional violence flared, the first generation of black migrants to Worcester generally found a receptive community.[12]

Despite regional differences, in many ways migrants to New England and the Midwest shared common ground. Catalyzed by the Civil War and shaped by the experience of emancipation, migration represented the deeply felt desire of former slaves to forge and define freedom on their own terms. Creating new lives in the North, migrants in both places established vibrant communities brimming with churches, clubs, and organizations reflecting a rich civic life. And even though Worcester's Civil War–era migrants initially

[handwritten margin note: Fear of Mass Migration]

enjoyed the support of a generally sympathetic community and did not experience the hostility suffered by their midwestern counterparts and patrons, they soon found that white sympathy and support faded with the passing of the abolitionist generation. The advantages enjoyed by the first generation of migrants did not continue. As the descendents of white abolitionists ignored their historical heritage, migrants to Worcester, like those in the Midwest, soon faced unofficial Jim Crow and a color bar in local industry that relegated them to low-paying jobs. Compared to European ethnic groups that flourished in the city, Worcester's black community languished, small and resource-poor.[13]

Like their brothers and sisters in the Midwest, black migrants and their children responded with political and social activism in asserting their civil rights. Fighting for respect and the Radical Republican vision of equality promised them after emancipation, southern migrants and their children shaped a politics and community in Worcester informed by their southern roots. As southern migrants continued to flow to the city in the era of Jim Crow, they built and nourished their own cultural enclave within the city's small African American community. Drawn together by the profound historical experience of slavery and emancipation, family ties, and a shared southern culture, they established a distinctive neighborhood, centered on their own southern-style Baptist church, and celebrated and cultivated an identity apart from the older established community — even as they participated in common community events and social organizations. In the process, they infused the city's small black community with a distinctive southern flavor. In the end, though, the dreams of migrants and their children for full-fledged citizenship and equal opportunity would be dashed as white Worcester, like much of the rest of the North, chose white supremacy over equality and conveniently forgot the promises of Reconstruction.[14]

CHOOSING THE PARAMETERS of any historical study has obvious trade-offs. As a micro-history, this study contains many limitations. But a tight focus on one northern city has enabled me to tease out details of the migration dynamic that would have been nearly impossible to detect with a wider aperture. Using a powerful lens on a small place has also allowed me to see personal relationships at the heart of the migration story and to trace individuals and families in greater depth. Focusing on Worcester has allowed me, to use Charles Joyner's apt and elegant phrase, "to ask big questions in small places." At the very least, by studying one place in great detail I hope I have opened another window on this understudied phase of black migration and have encouraged additional research elsewhere. Finally, in exploring the detailed story of Worcester's sponsored migration, I hope I have presented a story that complements and complicates the narrative of midwestern migration.

As a community study, this study begs an important question: how representative is this story? A city with a deep abolitionist tradition, Worcester was probably more liberal than most northern cities of the era. The 25th Massachusetts Regiment, which played a key role in the migration, also was not "typical," being made up largely of middle-class men with some exposure to antislavery and unusual in its sympathy to runaway slaves. Other historians have painted a far darker portrait of the interactions between Yankee soldiers and the contrabands in the South. Rather than the tales of benevolence that dot the landscape of the Worcester story, these narratives emphasize overt racism and violence between northern soldiers and the southern blacks they encountered.[15]

What is more fruitful, I believe, is to move beyond the question of "typicality" and instead look at Worcester as a revealing study of a community's transition from an antislavery hotbed to a refuge for freedpeople to a community that ultimately abandoned that mission. Despite its tight focus, this study reveals a great deal about race and power in the late nineteenth century, about the deep desire for self-determination among those liberated from slavery and their struggle — and that of their children — to attain "full manhood and womanhood." It also reveals a worsening racial climate nationally and the consequences of the passing of the white abolitionist generation in the North, and the subsequent generation's rejection of its heritage. Worcester was a small stage on which the larger national drama over the meaning of freedom played out.

This study also raises a second obvious question. Was the migration dynamic that brought southern blacks to Worcester replicated elsewhere? I think it is likely that similar migration networks existed, especially in other parts of New England and northern towns and cities with a similar antislavery tradition. Both historians Voegeli and Schwalm note "pockets" of sympathy in the upper Midwest, in Quaker settlements and antislavery Ohio towns, such as Oberlin. The 1870 census of the United States cites a significant jump in the "colored" population in the decade of the Civil War; the North's black population grew by 50 percent overall in the 1860s, as Michael Johnson notes, "more than three times faster than it had grown in the 1850s." In Massachusetts, as noted, it grew by roughly 45 percent. The remaining New England states also showed considerable gains, especially Vermont (over 30 percent); Rhode Island (26 percent); and Maine (21 percent). Several urban studies that cover this period point out a significant southern black migration north following the Civil War, but most attribute it to racial oppression, the crop-lien system, or crop failures and do not explore networks of migration. Perhaps on closer examination, personal networks, built on military and missionary networks, might be revealed.[16]

I have been deeply influenced by Eric Foner's monumental work *Reconstruction: America's Unfinished Revolution, 1863–1877*, especially his challenge to historians to learn more about how Reconstruction shaped the North. This study, a modest effort in that direction, reveals not only the ways that southern migrants shaped and transformed New England but also that the meaning of freedom in post–Civil War America proved to be highly contested, even in "free New England."

Chapter

1

THE GUNS OF WAR

As chattering telegraphs relayed the news of the Confederate attack on Fort Sumter to towns, villages, and cities across the nation, many Americans, both North and South, seemed to welcome the news with a sense of relief. In retrospect, their reaction seems an odd way to greet the opening of what would be the bloodiest war in American history. But for those who had experienced crises that had threatened to rip the Republic apart for decades, the coming of war offered a long-awaited denouement that would finally settle issues fundamental to the future of the United States.

While many welcomed a resolution to sectional conflict, little consensus existed about the meaning of the war in April 1861. Some white southerners saw the war as a necessary fight for independence, a requisite step to protect a distinctive southern way of life built on slavery. Like their Revolutionary forefathers, they viewed a war for independence as a last resort, instigated by years of mistreatment. Others rejected the overblown rhetoric of "fire eaters" and instead viewed the war simply as a defense of hearth and home, especially after Lincoln called for troops to quash the rebellion in the aftermath of the Confederate attack on Fort Sumter. Slaves, drawing on intricate networks of communication that kept many of them abreast of national developments, saw the war as the long-expected and divinely promised vehicle of their liberation.

In the North, most citizens viewed the war as a defense of the Union against wretched traitors who would tear the young nation asunder by arrogantly proclaiming their independence. Abolitionists, on the other hand, while a distinct minority of the northern population, saw the war as a chance to rid the nation of its most egregious sin — slavery. While they disagreed among themselves about how to achieve that goal, they, like slaves in the South, envisioned the end of slavery as the purpose of the war, imbuing the conflict with deep moral purpose and meaning.

"The storm burst and the whole community awakened"

News of events at Fort Sumter catalyzed Worcester County, Massachusetts, as it did the rest of the nation, setting off a frenzy of activities. Thomas Wentworth Higginson, radical abolitionist and minister of Worcester's Free Church, remembered that "on the day that Fort Sumter was fired upon, the storm burst and the whole community awakened." As local citizens read the first sketchy reports of the Confederate attack on the morning of 13 April 1861 — and two days later learned of Lincoln's call for 75,000 volunteers to suppress the rebellion — they quickly organized to show their support for the Union cause. Fort Sumter dominated the thoughts and actions of nearly all Worcesterites. The *Worcester Daily Spy* noted, "The subject is the one controlling, absorbing theme of conversation in all ranks and classes."[1]

By the time of the Civil War, ranks and classes proliferated in the city of Worcester as well as in the towns that dotted the county. Situated on the central corridor running from Boston to the east and Springfield to the west, Worcester had emerged, in the words of historian John Brooke, "as a powerful vortex of population, commerce, and public culture, exerting an overwhelming influence on the surrounding region." Worcester was for many years, as Brooke notes, "only one of a mosaic of towns of roughly equal size" that characterized Worcester County, even though it had been established as the shire town in 1730. But Worcester's location, combined with its forward-looking town leaders, soon propelled it to the heart of the nation's budding industrial revolution. Embracing advances in transportation, Worcester merchants forged a link with Providence, Rhode Island, by constructing the Blackstone Canal, which opened in 1828. Only seven years later, the Boston and Worcester Railroad, the first in the nation, accelerated the city's growth. Other railroads soon followed, elevating Worcester to a regional railroad hub by the 1840s. Whereas many New England towns focused on one industry, particularly textiles, Worcester developed a variety of industries, ranging from textile and boot and shoe production to machinery production and wire works. In 1860, approximately 25,000 people resided in the city, its population exploding by nearly 18,000 in twenty years, as smaller towns in the county declined in population. On the eve of the Civil War, the city boasted 170 manufacturing firms, employing well over 4,000 people, and many Worcester County towns claimed mills and manufactories as well. The war would only accelerate industrial growth as the number of the county's manufacturing enterprises grew from 1,358 to 1,863 between 1860 and 1870 and capital investment ballooned from roughly $14 million to $34 million. Whereas old Yankee families dominated industrial ownership and politics in Worcester, two waves of Irish immigrants, the canal builders of the 1820s and the famine Irish of the 1840s and 1850s, also called Worcester home. Roughly one of four Worcester residents — approximately three-quarters of them Irish — had been born outside of the United States.[2]

A day after Lincoln's call for troops, citizens crowded into city hall to respond to the president's request. Enthusiastic applause greeted Mayor Isaac Davis's announcement that two companies of Worcester militia would take up arms immediately in defense of the Union. Other city leaders promised financial support for soldiers and their families, and local ministers and dignitaries addressed the unfolding national events. Unitarian minister Alonzo Hill "caused a deep sensation" when he challenged his listeners to "defend our dear mother country, now so grossly assailed." With the nation's capital "threatened by selfish traitors, our young men should . . . defend it to the death."[3]

Hill's interpretation of the war seemed to summarize the prevailing sentiment in Worcester County in April 1861. The war, most seemed to agree, was not about slavery but aimed at maintaining the Union against the treasonous actions of arrogant, hotheaded southerners willing to commit matricide. Even the *Worcester Daily Spy*, published by abolitionist John Denison Baldwin and one of the most radical daily newspapers in the state, initially framed the nascent war as a war about Union — not about slavery. "It is not the slavery question, in any form," wrote Baldwin in an editorial, "that is now in issue between the administration and the secession conspirators." Instead, slavery was "a mere pretext" to foment "the overthrow of republican institutions and the establishment of a despotism in their place." With the future of the nation at stake, citizens must "forget to discuss the slavery question, and occupy themselves chiefly in discussing treason and traitors."[4]

While this was the predominant sentiment in the county, it was not the only one. The crowd that gathered in city hall on the night of 17 April included abolitionists, one of whom, Thomas Wentworth Higginson, spoke at the behest of the crowd. Lured to the city to head Worcester's radical Free Church in 1852 — founded by "comeouters" who left their traditional congregations because of the silence of their churches on the slavery issue — Higginson had led some of the most radical abolitionist causes of the 1850s, including supplying guns and money for John Brown's attempted slave revolt in 1859. Yet when called upon to speak, the typically loquacious Higginson seemed at a loss for words, explaining that "there was need of no more speaking, after what he heard." Accustomed to creating divisiveness through his controversial and often illegal activities, Higginson, in April 1861, basked in the fact that "to-night we have more than enthusiasm, we have unanimity."[5]

Higginson's conciliatory remarks, made in the flush of the stunning commencement of civil war, masked not only his radicalism but also the deep antislavery tradition cultivated over several generations in Worcester County. Antislavery activism ran deep and wide in Worcester County. The town of Worcester made its feelings clear as early as 1765 when it charged its representative to the General Court to do what he could "to put an end to that unchristian and impolitic practice of making slaves of the human species." In 1781, a Worcester County slave, Quock Walker of Barre, successfully sued for his freedom and ultimately helped win emancipation for all slaves in Massachusetts when Chief Justice John D. Cushing of the Massachusetts Supreme Judicial Court found slavery "wholly incompatible and repugnant" to the state constitution's guarantee of freedom, liberty, and protection of property. In the 1830s, when William Lloyd Garrison helped ignite abolitionist sentiment in the North, antislavery societies mushroomed throughout the county, sponsoring lectures, debates, and meetings all aimed at raising the public's consciousness about the evils of slavery.[6]

From the 1830s on, Worcester played a leading role in nearly every major antislavery endeavor of the era. In many ways, Worcester initiated more groundbreaking and radical antislavery activity than its more glamorous counterpart, Boston. Underground Railroad activity was rampant throughout the county, and Worcester served as the destination for numerous fugitive slaves. The city was the birthplace of the Free Soil Party in 1848 and local Free Soil leaders helped found the Republican Party in 1854. That year, T. W. Higginson and Martin Stowell, a local farmer, led a group of abolitionists attempting to free Anthony Burns, held in a Boston prison under the Fugitive Slave Act. A contingent of ten Worcester citizens, armed with axes, provided most of the muscle for the unsuccessful rescue of Burns.[7]

Also in 1854, after the passage of the Kansas-Nebraska Act, Worcester's Eli Thayer organized the New England Emigrant Aid Company, recruited the first company of settlers intent on securing Kansas as a free state, and contributed several groups of colonizers — as well as guns — to battle the "slave power" in the West. In the midst of Bleeding Kansas and in the aftermath of the *Dred Scott* decision, Higginson, along with some radical Republicans and Garrisonian abolitionists, called a "state disunion convention" in Worcester, even though, he noted in retrospect, few were ready "for a movement so extreme." And when John Brown and his revolutionary band attempted to instigate a slave rebellion at Harpers Ferry in October 1859, Higginson was one of the "Secret Six" who supplied them with arms. Worcester County resident Charles Plummer Tidd of Clinton served as one of Brown's "captains." On the day of Brown's execution in Virginia, several city churches tolled their bells, businesses closed, and citizens held memorial services throughout the county.[8]

Within days of his conciliatory remarks at the rally in response to Fort Sumter, Higginson questioned his personal involvement in a war that, he feared, did not seek the end of slavery as a stated goal. Offered the position of major in the 4th Battalion Infantry, Higginson refused it, citing his lack of military experience and the ill health of his wife. But above all, he declined the commission because "it was wholly uncertain whether the government would take the anti-slavery attitude, without which a military commission would have been intolerable, since I might have been ordered to deliver up fugitive slaves to their masters, — as had already happened to several officers." While Higginson later accepted a captaincy in the 51st Massachusetts, "when the anti-slavery position of the government became clearer"— and would go on to lead the Union's first official black regiment, the 1st South Carolina Volunteers — his initial attitude reflected the ambivalence of many abolitionists at the beginning of the war.[9]

As the ambiguous nature of federal intervention began to dampen the enthusiasm of some antislavery activists after the first flush of Fort Sumter, others, especially Worcester's black community, welcomed the war as the long-awaited chance to obliterate human slavery in the United States once and for all. As the white sons of Worcester County and the North rushed to volunteer to fight in the army, the federal government soon made it clear that blacks were not welcome. Nevertheless, local African Americans, like their compatriots across the North, committed their services to the Union cause in a variety of ways. As Worcester's volunteers readied themselves to depart for Washington, two local black barbers, William Jankins and Gilbert Walker, invited "members of the military companies to call at their hair dressing salons and get trimmed up, without charge, before leaving."[10]

Jankins and Walker were among numerous ex-slaves who found refuge in Worcester in the 1840s and 1850s, some of them smuggled into the city "at midnight" by T. W. Higginson himself, where they found refuge at the

Tatnuck farm of veteran abolitionists Stephen and Abby Kelley Foster. Like most of their refugee compatriots, they had been born into slavery in the upper South. Jankins had made his way to Worcester after absconding from his master in Virginia. Walker, born a slave in Maryland, secured his freedom through the heroism of his father, whose grateful master freed him after he had saved his master's son from drowning. Walker's father subsequently managed to purchase his family members, and Gilbert and his brother Allen Walker ultimately made their way to Worcester. Others, like Isaac Mason, a fugitive from Maryland, and his wife, Anna, came to Worcester via Boston through abolitionist networks linking the two cities. Mason worked as a ditch digger, a farmhand, and a woodcutter on the estates of several prominent white Worcesterites.[11]

By 1850, Worcester was home to approximately 200 people of color, in a city of about 17,000 people. The community consisted of a mix of northern-born African Americans, people of both Native American and African American descent, and southern-born fugitives. Jankins had already established a flourishing barbering business in Worcester by 1850. Walker, who initially worked as a coachman for a manufacturer, married a local woman of Native American descent and parlayed a state land grant that she received into a thriving barbering business at the prominent Bay State House.[12]

But in 1850, even the seemingly safe bubble of Worcester was punctured by the passage of the Fugitive Slave Law that October. Part of the Compromise of 1850, the law was one of several agreements made between North and South aimed at averting disunion over the admission of California as a free state. A major concession to the South, the legislation now placed the weight of federal law, and the aid of U.S. marshals, behind southern slaveholders who wished to recover their runaway property in the North. Whether runaway slaves or free born, blacks accused of being runaways — based on a physical description — and taken to court were forbidden to testify on their own behalf or show any documentation to prove their identity or status. Moreover, the law threatened fines and imprisonment to those who aided runaways. The Fugitive Slave Law, in the minds of many northerners, now made all of the nation's citizens complicit in the institution of slavery.

Worcesterites responded angrily, and the city's black residents felt especially incensed as the law severely diminished their already fragile freedom. Local citizens jammed into city hall "almost to suffocation" to denounce the Fugitive Slave Law in October 1850. "White and colored, bond and free," residents of all backgrounds and positions rallied to "preserve the Soil of Massachusetts, sacred to freedom." While prominent whites attempted to take charge of the meeting, electing their own to draw up resolutions, two un-named African Americans, both fugitive slaves, insisted on addressing the assembly and enlightening the overwhelmingly white audience about the brutal personal assault that the law represented to them. They recounted their escape from slavery to freedom, one giving "expression to his out-raged feelings" over the law. While the assembly initially appointed a vigi-lance committee to secure the safety of "our colored population," a week later the committee decided that hostility to the fugitive law "was so deep and universal" in Worcester that "a vigilance committee of the whole" seemed unnecessary.[13]

Worcester's black population felt far less confident about their security than their white counterparts. According to Isaac Mason, who came to Worcester just before the passage of the Fugitive Slave Law, the "hunting slave fever got so high that our sympathizing friends advised me to leave at once and go to Canada," which he did for several months. While other Worcester refugees undoubtedly followed Mason's lead, those who remained dug in their heels to defy the law. With radical white allies such as Martin Stowell, they formed the Worcester Freedom Club as well as a local vigilance committee. Featur-ing the goddess of liberty, the club's banner reflected the heartfelt, political sentiments of its members. "Warm Hearts and Fearless Souls — True to the Union and Constitution," the banner proclaimed on one side; on the reverse, "Freedom National — Slavery Sectional! Liberty! Equality, Fraternity!"[14]

In the spring of 1854, Worcester's vigilant resisters entered the fray when they rallied in support of the imprisoned Anthony Burns. Summoned for support by T. W. Higginson, who, with several compatriots, had attempted to free Burns from a Boston prison several days earlier, the Worcester Freedom Club, 500 strong, descended upon Boston. They processed to Court Square, two by two, in a dramatic show of support for the incarcerated Burns. Mani-festing Worcester's radical tradition and activism, the Freedom Club's appear-ance "from the rural districts created some excitement among the outsiders, who cheered them with a will." Although angry opponents destroyed their stunning silk banner, the Worcester delegation nevertheless made a bold and impressive showing. The delegation included many black men from Worcester, and, given their slave backgrounds and leadership positions in the commu-nity, William Jankins and Gilbert Walker were probably among them.[15]

About six months later the battle over fugitive slaves came to Worcester, as a direct consequence of the Burns incident. In late October 1854, Deputy U.S. Marshal Asa O. Butman arrived in the city, allegedly seeking witnesses for the impending trial of Higginson for his attempted rescue of Burns in

May. Butman was notorious for his role in the capture of both fugitive slaves Burns and Anthony Sims, and his appearance set off a wave of terror among the city's black residents. They were sure that he had come to Worcester to apprehend one of their fugitive brethren; some believed that he bore a warrant for the capture of barber William Jankins, who had been pursued by his Virginia master only months before. Handbills appeared, passed along in the streets, warning local black residents to "Look out for Kidnappers!"[16]

Sensitized and bitter about the Burns kidnapping and trial, Worcester's citizenry, black and white, mobilized instantly. The government-sanctioned kidnapping of Burns and his return to slavery, in their view, had granted the "Slave Power" sovereignty even over Massachusetts; now they intended to fight back. They "welled up" with a "spontaneous rising of the spirit of humanity and self-protection of our people," wrote one observer; "our people could not feel safe while his [Butman's] presence polluted our air." A vigilance committee kept an eye on Butman at his hotel on Main Street. Then Worcester police arrested Butman for carrying a concealed weapon. Butman was taken to court in city hall, and a judge granted him a continuance of his trial and released him on $100 bail. But as an angry crowd gathered outside city hall and the common, it soon became clear that Butman would be lucky to exit Worcester unscathed.[17]

As radical white citizens such as Stephen S. Foster helped mobilize the local citizenry to keep an eye on Butman, Worcester's blacks reacted with an extraordinarily vocal and physical response to the deputy marshal. As a local newspaper reported, "The colored men especially were almost beside themselves in their desire to convince him that it was a dangerous mission upon which he had come to the city." The crowd outside city hall included about twenty black men. They unconditionally called for Butman's death, demanding that he be released to them. Butman asked for refuge in the city marshal's office. But even the marshal could not protect Butman from the wrath of the city's angry African Americans. Three black men managed to land several blows to Butman, knocking him to the floor.[18]

Fearful of an impending riot from a mob that had grown to a thousand people, several leading white abolitionists — including Higginson and George Frisbie Hoar, a future Republican congressman and senator — may have saved Butman's life. Amidst a shower of eggs, rocks, tobacco juice, and occasional kicks and punches, Butman ultimately made his way to the train station, ushered out of the city by Higginson, Hoar, and several others. Worcester's violent reaction to Butman, popularly known as "The Butman Riot," guaranteed that no one ever attempted to recapture runaway slaves in the city again.[19]

William Jankins, who many believed was Butman's quarry in Worcester, subsequently managed to secure his liberty by purchasing his freedom from his ex-master. But the Fugitive Slave Law continued to haunt and anger Jankins and his fellow ex-slaves in Worcester and across the North. They fought boldly to circumvent the law and to make it irrelevant by abolishing slavery. For former slaves, especially, securing freedom in the North did not absolve them of responsibility to their enslaved brothers and sisters in the South. Gilbert Walker, for example, who contributed to the New England Emigrant Aid Society to settle Kansas with antislavery citizens and local blacks in defiance of the Fugitive Slave Law, continued to offer food and shelter to fugitive slaves.[20]

In addition, the Fugitive Slave Law bonded the city's blacks and white abolitionists in powerful new ways. They stood shoulder to shoulder to combat the Slave Power and defend the free soil of Massachusetts. The law also bonded black Yankees, former slaves, and those still in bondage. As historian Joanne Pope Melish notes, in New England, the Fugitive Slave Law "effectively reunited the interests of the free and the enslaved, making them one 'whole people' again," reinforcing the region's identity as "free New England," ground zero in the fight against bondage.[21]

The struggle of free northern blacks to end slavery also encompassed a second front: gaining equality as full-fledged American citizens. Even as people of color, as Melish notes, "continued to identify New England as the site of the original experiment in liberty," that liberty was far from perfect. Comprising only 2 percent of the northern population at the time of the Civil War, blacks nonetheless generally confronted a rigid color line and the contempt of many whites, as slavery cast its long shadow across the Mason-Dixon line. Only five northern states — all of them in New England — allowed black men to vote. Moreover, racial segregation characterized northern urban life. Even though Massachusetts had a reputation for racial liberalism, black residents nevertheless suffered myriad forms of racial discrimination. John S. Rock, a northern-born black doctor and lawyer who resided in Boston, summed up the lot of American blacks, free and slave: "We are oppressed everywhere in this slavery-cursed land." Although Massachusetts "has a great name and deserves much credit for what she has done," Rock explained, "the position of the colored people in Massachusetts is far from being an enviable one." Enumerating the daily insults suffered by Massachusetts blacks, Rock noted the "embittered prejudices of whites"; exclusion from many eating houses, churches, and places of amusement; and problems finding housing and employment.[22]

To address these concerns, northern African Americans mobilized, especially in the 1850s, establishing numerous organizations and holding conventions to address the problem of racial discrimination. Targeting labor issues, education, political rights, and segregation, the black convention movement reflected an ethos of political activism and self-help, the determination of northern blacks to take matters into their own hands to improve their condition. Not surprisingly, given their activism, Worcester's blacks embraced the convention movement, and, in 1859, sent thirty-four-year-old Jacob E. Mowbray as their delegate to the New England Colored Citizens' Convention. Mowbray, a paperhanger and later a minister, was a fitting representative of Worcester's black community. A Maryland-born migrant, he came to Worcester in the 1850s with his wife and child, seeking, like so many of his compatriots, refuge and opportunity. Along with more famous, nationally known delegates to the convention, such as Lewis Hayden, William Wells Brown, and William C. Nell, Mowbray was part of a delegation that passed resolutions repudiating migration of American blacks to Africa and condemning the "deep-seated hostility" against "our complexion."[23]

By the time of Fort Sumter, black Worcester, a community that had grown to about 300 people, was a tightly knit circle led by veteran activists. Baptized in the sectional fires of the 1850s, it had established secure connections to other activist communities in New England, especially Boston. A letter from a proud member of the community to a black newspaper in New York in April 1861 pointed out that "in the heart of the Commonwealth of Massachusetts we are moving onward through the tide of oppression to which our race is subject." He noted the "painters, shoe-makers, three or four upholsterers, job cart men, . . . white-washers, paper-hangers, house-cleaners, etc.," along with hairdressers and a music teacher, who formed the community, which even boasted "a kind of literary society" of twenty members who met weekly. Through their efforts, and those of their white abolitionist compatriots, Worcester had risen to Thomas Wentworth Higginson's challenge, made in the gloomy days following Anthony Burns's return to slavery in Virginia: "Hear, O Richmond! and give ear, O Carolina! henceforth Worcester is Canada to the slave!"[24]

In light of their activism in the 1850s, black Worcesterites faced the prospect of civil war in 1861 with great expectations. Not only did they believe that Union victory would certainly bring about the demise of slavery, but they also anticipated that the war might provide an unprecedented opportunity to end their own compromised citizenship in the North.

"War is coming, them birds singing is a sign of war"

As the guns of war reverberated throughout the nation in April 1861, slaves also began to sense that the conflict between North and South could portend enormous changes. Forbidden from learning to read and write, slaves nevertheless managed to develop intricate networks of communication. Free blacks, who often lived and worked in towns and cities, helped their enslaved counterparts keep abreast of national events. House slaves also contributed knowledge to the communication grapevine, by eavesdropping on and overhearing conversations of their masters and mistresses. While many masters did what they could to minimize their slaves' knowledge of the outside world, fearing that such information would foster rebellion, most slaves, ironically, probably learned about the outbreak of the Civil War from their masters. Consumed with fears of a Yankee invasion, southern whites spoke incessantly about the war, piquing the imaginations of those who heard them. Hattie Rogers, a slave in eastern North Carolina, learned about the war listening to her mistress remark on the birds singing around her well: "the Missus would say, 'War is coming, them birds singing is a sign of war; the Yankees will come and kill us all.'"[25]

In order to ensure their slaves' loyalties if Union soldiers should appear, masters and mistresses told frightful stories about the Yankees. One North Carolina slave recalled that his master told him that the Yankees "would bore holes in our shoulders an' wurk us to carts" and that "we would be treated a lot worser den dey wus treating us." Another master told his slaves that they could not possibly be happier in heaven than they were with him "an' dat the Yankees better keep outen his business."[26]

Masters and mistresses also denounced, in the strongest possible terms, the North in general and Abraham Lincoln and the "Black Republicans" in particular. By doing so, they assigned Lincoln and the Republican Party a depth of antislavery sentiment that simply did not yet exist. As scholars from the Freedom and Southern Society Project have noted, "Masters with no doubts about the abolitionist intentions of the North inadvertently persuaded their slaves of the ascendancy and pervasiveness of antislavery sentiment in the free states." Thus, many slaves concluded that given their masters' hatred of the Yankees and Lincoln, the president and northerners were, in fact, allies of slaves long before Lincoln or the Republicans even championed emancipation.[27]

Moreover, as a people steeped in biblical stories and songs of emancipation and deliverance, many slaves framed the impending Yankee invasion as a cataclysmic event ordained by God to liberate His people and to bring enslavers to the bar of justice. Just as God had sent plagues upon the Israelites' Egyptian captors, and had sent Moses to deliver them from bondage, so too did the guns of war promise destruction of their captors and emancipation. But only time would tell. Most slaves watched and waited, with vigilance and circumspection, until events unfolded to reveal more clearly the meaning of the battle between North and South.

"Our country shall be rescued or the Worcester boys will die"

Only a week after the Confederate attack on Fort Sumter, even more electrifying news reached Worcester: Massachusetts troops, en route to Washington to defend the nation's capital, had been brutally attacked by a rebel mob in Baltimore. After a bloody riot, in which soldiers were pummeled with rocks, bricks, and pistol shots, four soldiers from the 6th Massachusetts lay dead.[28]

If Fort Sumter seemed a distant, almost abstract incident, the attack on the 6th Massachusetts brought the incipient war home to the men and women of Worcester County. "It would be difficult," wrote John Denison Baldwin in the *Spy*, "for any occasion to create a more general and intense excitement in this city than was roused here yesterday, by the news from Baltimore." The "secession rowdies," concluded Baldwin and many of his fellow citizens, had shown their true colors with their "dastardly attack on Massachusetts troops." One Worcester County veteran recalled the Baltimore attack as the actual beginning of the Civil War for local residents: "In every town from Blackstone to Winchendon, the Saturday and Sunday which followed were days of patriotic fever never before equalled." Resolutions from hastily convened town meetings condemned the miscreant South. On Sunday morning, 20 April 1861, ministers "proclaimed in no doubtful tones that the voice of patriotism was the voice of God." Several days later, Worcester's first volunteers, three companies of the 3rd Battalion Riflemen, left the city for Maryland, amidst a "thronging and eager multitude" of townspeople, the Baltimore attack adding poignancy and urgency to their departure.[29]

In the small, prosperous shoe manufacturing town of North Brookfield, huge placards relayed word of the violent attack on the 6th Massachusetts. Proclaiming "War! War!! War!!!," the notices announced, "Our Massachusetts citizens have been murdered in the streets of Baltimore, while marching on their way to Washington to protect the capital of our country." The signs announced a town meeting "to see what can be done." North Brookfield's town meeting drew "men eager for action" and resulted in the nucleus of what would eventually become Company F of the 15th Massachusetts Volunteer Infantry, a three-year unit of Worcester County men, formed in response to Lincoln's call for additional, long-term soldiers in June 1861.[30]

The 15th Massachusetts organized, recruited, and trained against the backdrop of deepening southern resistance and Union battlefield disaster. In mid-June, local residents learned of the "blundering failure," in the words of the *Worcester Daily Spy*, of the Union forces at the battle of Big Bethel in Virginia. A little over a month later, even more disheartening news reached Worcester County concerning "a great battle fought near Manassas Junction" in northern Virginia. While early reports declared a Union victory, subsequent accounts from Bull Run soon confirmed a calamitous Confederate rout of Union forces. Declaring the battle "a bad disaster" that "saddens a great many hearts," *Spy* editor John Denison Baldwin articulated the feelings of many northerners when he admitted, "It may be that we were beginning to under-rate the difficulties of the struggle." The following Sunday, Worcester ministers attempted to find meaning in the defeat at Bull Run. Using a well-known verse from Ecclesiastes as his text, Congregational minister Merrill Richardson reminded his flock, "The race is not to the swift, nor the battle to the strong; but time of chance happeneth to them all."[31]

Despite the disaster at Bull Run, Worcester Countians, like many northerners, refused to succumb to despair, responding instead with steely determination. In Worcester, the rapid recruitment of the 15th Massachusetts reflected this attitude. According to prominent attorney Charles Devens, who headed the 15th and was already a veteran of three months' service in the immediate aftermath of Fort Sumter, the 15th was a "peculiarly Worcester County regiment." Composed of young men from the villages and towns of Leominster, Fitchburg, Clinton, Oxford, the Brookfields, Grafton, Northbridge, Webster, and Blackstone, along with the city of Worcester, the regiment quickly filled its ranks with a cross section of young men, recruited from "farms, factories, mills, shops, and stores." Most members of the 15th had at least a minimal, district-school education, and many had attended local high schools and academies, while a handful had earned college degrees. Summoned quickly after the Bull Run fiasco to defend Washington, the men of the 15th left Worcester in early August 1861 amidst soaring speeches comparing their service to that of their Revolutionary ancestors.[32]

As the 15th regiment established camp in Maryland in September 1861, another Worcester County regiment, the 25th Massachusetts Volunteer Infantry, also a three-year unit, organized. Although the 25th was the third regiment recruited from the county, after the 15th and 21st, it was popularly referred to as "The Worcester County Regiment," as all ten companies had been recruited from the city of Worcester and three county towns — Fitchburg, Templeton, and Milford. Headed by A. B. R. Sprague and Edwin Upton, two veterans who had been among the first volunteers to heed Lincoln's call for troops after Fort Sumter, the 25th, even more so than the 15th, attracted an unusually high proportion of well-educated sons of Worcester County's middle class. As the unit formed, the *Daily Spy* commented constantly on the "well appointed" composition of the 25th, made up of "young men of merit and intelligence." While the 25th had both an Irish and a German company, the unit consisted largely of "men who leave young families and large business interests." Many "abandon permanent and valuable situations in banks and elsewhere." Because of the social standing of its members, the 25th received unusual attention in the press and elsewhere. The regiment was even the subject of a widely disseminated poem penned by Henry S. Washburn. The poem's grim refrain echoed the somber, darkening mood of the community in mid-1861: "Our country shall be rescued or the Worcester boys will die."[33]

Many members of the 25th were associated with antislavery churches and were heirs to Worcester's radical antislavery tradition. The Salem Street Society, a Worcester Congregational church, provided a large contingent of young men to the 25th, as its minister, Merrill Richardson, recruited for the regiment throughout the county. While not as radical as T. W. Higginson's Free Church, the Salem Street Society staked its claim as an abolitionist church under Richardson's leadership, unanimously adopting resolutions condemning slavery in 1859. When war broke out in April 1861, the minister played a key role in mobilizing local citizens. His "winged words," wrote an officer in the 25th many years later, "electrified, not alone his congregation, but echoing through the public press from week to week, resounded throughout the country, and touched the hearts of many true men all over the Commonwealth."[34]

As a popular preacher and public speaker, the Reverend Richardson helped frame the meaning of the war for both local citizens and the young men he recruited to the 25th. Delivering vigorous jeremiads before his congregation, public war rallies, and the recruits of the 25th, Richardson saw the war as God's judgment: "Doom's day has come." The American nation, so richly blessed by God, had squandered its inheritance through a series of national sins, the most egregious of which was slavery. Richardson roundly rejected those who would fight to save the Union by preserving slavery; such a position was "an insult to Heaven" and "rebellion itself, and the man who does it should be shot as a traitor." While most Worcesterites in the spring and summer of 1861 claimed that the war was about preserving the Union, Richardson insisted on portraying the war as a righteous war, an opportunity to expunge the sin of slavery and return the nation to God's fold.[35]

As young men "of merit and intelligence" responded to Richardson's call and joined the 25th, the Reverend Horace James, one of Richardson's Congregational colleagues in the city, made the momentous decision to accept the chaplaincy of the 25th. Pastor of the Old South Congregational Church, James believed, much like Richardson, that the war provided an opportunity to renew the nation spiritually, to rid the country of slavery, and to remake the South in New England's image. As James later put it, he "left the 'Old South' to help make a *new* South."[36]

Like many New Englanders, James had grown increasingly militant about slavery as sectional conflict grew shrill in the 1850s. At first the minister advocated gradual emancipation and merely opposed the expansion of slavery. To that end, he and his congregation enthusiastically contributed funds to Eli Thayer's New England Emigration Aid Company in its attempt to people Kansas with antislavery New Englanders. But by the end of the decade, James had embraced abolitionism, the Old South Church being one of four Worcester churches whose bells tolled to memorialize John Brown's execution in late 1859.[37]

James viewed his election as chaplain of the 25th as "the Voice of the Lord." As such, it was "plainly a duty to obey the summons." In a letter tendering his resignation to his congregation, James noted that not only would service with the 25th "accord with the spirit of my public teachings," but it would also be "so fitting a sacrifice in the hour of our nation's danger and distress." Since the 25th consisted of "the flower of our youth" and "takes not a few from our churches and congregations," the minister implied that he would take particular care to provide moral and spiritual guidance as Worcester's fine young men marched into the South, far beyond the reach of family and community.[38]

Chaplain James would indeed help imprint the 25th regiment not only with his antislavery sentiments but also with his social ideals. He would play a crucial role in enforcing middle-class Worcester's mores and notions of community and social reform when the 25th was far from home. He would also prove to be an influential overseer and effective enforcer of community values, and consequently shape the lives of both Worcester's white soldiers and the African Americans who fled to them seeking their freedom.

In his last sermon at Old South, attended by members of his regiment, James boldly declared that "it should be our aim in the war to strike a deadly blow at the root of evil, at the heart of the destroyer, slavery." As the young men of the Worcester County regiment departed Massachusetts in December 1861 with "the heart of the city more deeply touched by its departure than by that of any previous one"— the abolitionist sermons of James and Richardson ringing in their ears — few saw themselves as righteous liberators of slaves. Like young men who volunteer to fight in any war, Worcester's volunteers joined with myriad goals and expectations; some simply had yet to make up their minds about the war's purpose. Many undoubtedly shared the sentiments of David L. Day, who, upon his enlistment in the 25th, confided in his diary, "I should never feel quite satisfied with myself if I did not go" as "the Union must and should be preserved." Yet, he wrote, it would be "useless for me to claim that I have enlisted from purely patriotic motives, as no one would believe it" and "surely no one would believe that I would enlist for the plain thirteen dollars a month." He admitted that "the love of adventure" also influenced his decision. While the antislavery culture of their home communities may have predisposed many of them ultimately to commit to abolitionism, most soldiers did not become abolitionists until they experienced slavery firsthand, particularly through their interactions with the "contrabands of war."[39]

The war dislodged Worcester County's young volunteers from parochial, comfortable surroundings and launched them on a southern sojourn that many would remember as the defining experience of their lives. Thomas Wentworth Higginson vividly captured the formative moment of commencing army life. "It was," he wrote, "a day absolutely broken off from all that had gone before it . . . ; the transformation seemed as perfect as if, by some suddenly revealed process, one had learned to swim in air, and were striking out for some new planet. The past was annihilated, the future was all." Not only would soldiers be changed by combat and carnage, but the men, women, and children fleeing slavery would also transform many of them, the people who were looked upon as the answer to their prayers, the deliverers they had long awaited.[40]

2

THE PRETTIEST

BLUE MENS I HAD EVER SEED

In the fall and early winter of 1861, the 15th Massachusetts Volunteer Infantry regrouped at Poolesville, Maryland, veterans of the disastrous battle at Ball's Bluff. The unit had sustained well over a hundred casualties in what would prove to be a mere taste of the bloodshed they would suffer during the course of the war. On Christmas Eve 1861, Isaiah Allen, a slave in Leesburg, Virginia — across the Potomac from Poolesville — took advantage of his owner's holiday revelries. With a fellow slave, he swam across the river and escaped to the safety of the Worcester County regiment.[1]

Similarly, Allen Parker, a slave in Chowan County on the plantation Martinique, heard of the Yankee invasion of eastern North Carolina in 1862 through the slave grapevine. "Although our masters tried to keep all matters relating to the war from their slaves," he remembered, the slaves nevertheless "managed to get hold of a good deal of news, and the idea was fast gaining ground, that in some way they were soon to be free." Despite "every effort" of masters to keep slaves on the plantations, fearing their escape to the Yankees, Parker and several of his fellow slaves managed to meet and plot their escape. Pledging to flee to the next federal vessel that came up the Chowan River, Parker and three compatriots soon got their chance before dawn on a morning in August 1862. Absconding in a crude cypress dugout, the four slaves made their way to a Union gunboat. Many years later Parker recalled the moment that freedom came into his grasp: "Pushing out from the shore we bid goodbye to the old plantations and slave life forever."[2]

Mary Barbour remembered being awakened in the night by her father. Imploring his children to keep quiet, he guided his wife and children to a wagon he had stolen from his master. Barbour recalled that her father explained "dat we is goin ter jine de Yankees." Yankee soldiers in Chowan County directed the family to New Bern, where they would be taken care of, "so ter New Bern we goes."[3]

Five years old when the Yankees came to North Carolina, Sarah Harris vividly recalled the thrill of seeing Yankees for the first time. "I wuz not afraid of 'em," she remembered. "I thought dey were the prettiest blue mens I had ever seed."[4]

Throughout the South, slaves sought to free themselves from their bondage by escaping to the invading Union army. Despite the efforts of masters to move and hide them, to frighten them into submission with horror stories, and to keep them ignorant of the Yankee invasion, tens of thousands of slaves absconded anyway. And even though the Lincoln administration insisted that the war was not about slavery but about the preservation of the Union, the arrival of the Yankees signaled the commencement of slaves' freedom. Neither the most exhaustive efforts of slavemasters nor the carefully articulated conservative war aims of the federal government could quench the slaves' thirst for freedom or shake a fundamental tenet of their faith: God had finally sent the Yankees to deliver them. As one North Carolina runaway explained to a Worcester soldier, "de Lord is come *now!*"[5]

Some fugitives and soldiers from Worcester County, sharing the experiences of war, forged strong personal bonds that formed the foundation of migration networks to the North during and after the war. The interactions of runaway slaves and their Yankee liberators profoundly shaped each group. Wartime relationships left deep and lasting impressions that went far beyond the exigencies of war.

"Bress de Lord and Massa Lincoln!"

Soon after its formation in Worcester, the 15th Massachusetts Volunteer Regiment made its way south in August 1861, setting up camp near Poolesville, Maryland, on the Potomac, to keep rebel soldiers across the river in Leesburg at bay. At Poolesville, members of the 15th Massachusetts had their first encounter with slavery when they came into contact with "contrabands of war," runaway slaves seeking their freedom with the Union army. "There are plenty of 'Uncle Toms' out this way," wrote W. J. Coulter, a member of the 15th, "and it is amusing to hear them talk." For Coulter, the contrabands provided "amusing incidents . . . which help to remove the monotony clinging to camp life."[6]

Other soldiers, however, embraced the role of liberator, inducing slaves to run away by offering them refuge and employment. Coulter wrote home about a young slave who, with the aid of Company C, swam across the Potomac to his freedom. "He is a boy of about seventeen years of age," wrote Coulter, "and is what they call out this way 'a right smart nigger.' He says he would not go back 'for nothing in this world.'" Incidents such as this occurred with such frequency that General Stone issued an order to soldiers in his command not "to incite and encourage insubordination among the colored servants in the neighborhood of the camps." Stone's order "was bitterly attacked by some ardent antislavery men," who indignantly criticized the general's directive.[7]

The army's engagement with absconding slaves in the first year and a half of the war created division among Union troops. As soon as Federal forces penetrated slave territory, thousands of blacks took the opportunity to free themselves, running to the Union army for refuge. The Lincoln administration, insisting that the war was about saving the Union — not ending slavery — ordered that the army could not free those who sought refuge. But runaways severely complicated official policy, especially as some soldiers rebuffed masters seeking their slaves. In May 1861, when a Virginia master demanded the return of his slaves who had escaped to the Union army at Fortress Monroe, General Benjamin Butler refused. In a highly publicized reply, the general explained that since Virginia had left the Union, the Fugitive Slave Law no longer applied. Referring to the runaways as "contrabands of war," a term thereafter widely used to describe slaves who absconded to the Union army, Butler put them to work. The Lincoln administration, with ambivalence, allowed Butler's policy but in August 1861 passed the Confiscation Act, permitting Federal troops to seize all property used in aiding the rebellion. Notably, the law affected only slaves directly employed by the Confederacy.[8]

Contrabands poured into the Yankee lines in the fall and winter as the 15th moved from Poolesville to southeastern Virginia to participate in McClellan's Peninsular campaign in an attempt to capture Richmond. Some blacks, like Isaiah Allen, who swam to his freedom on Christmas Eve, found employment with officers of the 15th. Newly minted officer Thomas Spurr of Worcester hired Allen as his personal servant, the beginning of a relationship that would bond Spurr and Allen through Spurr's slow and painful death in the aftermath of Antietam and connected Allen with the city of Worcester for decades to come. Similarly, David Porter Allen, a slave near Harrison's

Group of contrabands, Cumberland Landing, Virginia, 1862.
Courtesy of the Library of Congress.

Landing, Virginia, escaped to the 15th and found employment with Sergeant Francis Amasa Walker, beginning a long journey with the soldier that would take him to North Brookfield, Massachusetts, before the end of the war.

Virginia slaves would continue to escape to the 15th Massachusetts for their freedom as the Army of the Potomac marched to the peninsula in the spring of 1862. As the 15th readied itself for the Peninsular campaign, two other Worcester County regiments, the 21st and the 25th, helped establish New Bern, North Carolina, as the Promised Land for thousands of eastern North Carolina slaves when the Burnside Expedition captured the city and placed much of northeastern North Carolina under Federal control by the spring of 1862.

The city became the site of especially intensive personal interactions between Worcester soldiers and "contrabands of war." Due in part to the missionary zeal of Chaplain Horace James as well as the long-term encampment of the 25th Massachusetts in the New Bern area, soldiers and "contrabands of war" established long-term relationships that linked New Bern with the city of Worcester for years to come.

In January of 1862, an armada under the command of General Ambrose Burnside — consisting of naval vessels, gunboats, and transports holding 13,000 soldiers — embarked from Fortress Monroe and bore down on the Carolina coast. Burnside's division consisted of regiments chosen "mainly from states bordering on the northern sea coast," made up of many soldiers "familiar with the coasting trade." Five regiments of Massachusetts Volunteers, including two from Worcester County, the 25th and the 21st Massachusetts, were among them. Approximately 900 men from the city of Worcester alone participated in the expedition.[9]

The Burnside Expedition at first seemed destined to the failure predicted by many military and naval officers who deemed it a foolhardy venture. It took months to procure vessels for the expedition. Those available, which included everything from river barges, passenger steamers, tug and ferry boats, and sailing ships — "a motley fleet" of eighty vessels, according to Burnside — had to be outfitted not only to withstand the infamously hazardous waters of Cape Hatteras but also to accommodate 13,000 troops and all of the food and equipment required by an invading army. After numerous delays, the expedition left Annapolis, Maryland, on 8 January 1862, "with bands playing, colors flying and men cheering and singing from lightness of heart." The vessels then rendezvoused at Fortress Monroe, Virginia, on 12 January, with sealed orders given to all vessel commanders to be opened at sea: their destination, Hatteras Inlet.[10]

Burnside planned to reach Roanoke Island five days later. But tossed about by treacherous seas, winds, and gales, the expedition did not reach Roanoke for another twenty-three days. At Cape Hatteras, numerous vessels ran aground, "driven from their anchors and grounded on the swash and bar." The delayed arrival placed the expedition in a precarious situation, dangerously short of food and water. Worcester's A. B. R. Sprague, a colonel in the 25th Massachusetts, recalled "the entire fleet was many days on short rations of ropy water, barreled in Baltimore two months before, and passing through its first stage of fermentation. There was 'water, water everywhere, but not a drop to drink.'" Worcester's William Green, a private in the 25th, documented the "floating hell," as he put it, in letters to his parents vividly describing unbearably cramped quarters in the steamer *New York*, the stench of unwashed bodies, the hunger and thirst of the desperate soldiers, and above all "what would seem to be an almost inevitable fate, my death by starvation, exhaustion, or drowning." A passing rainstorm saved the expedition from complete disaster as soldiers managed to catch enough water on deck to sustain them a little longer.[11]

Finally, on 6 February, thirty days after their departure from Annapolis, the haggard soldiers received orders to land on Roanoke Island. Grounding their boats in shallow water, and covered by artillery, 4,000 troops disembarked in less than twenty minutes. Building upon the Union capture of Hatteras on the Outer Banks in December 1861, which provided Federal forces a foothold on the Carolina coast, the Burnside Expedition captured Roanoke Island in four hours, despite its weakened state from the tortuous voyage to eastern North Carolina. Within a week, the determined expedition forces also captured Elizabeth City and Edenton and commanded the coastal sounds. Roughly a month later, on 12 March, New Bern, a prosperous port located on the Trent and Neuse Rivers and North Carolina's second largest city, fell to northern forces after weak resistance from seriously outnumbered Confederate troops. In another ten days, Union forces seized Havelock Station, Carolina City, Morehead City, and Beaufort, and in April, Washington, on the Pamlico Sound, fell to Federal forces as well.[12]

A nation hungry for victory after months of setbacks happily greeted the news of Union victory. The *New York Times* reported "Overwhelming Success of the Burnside Expedition," "The Brilliant Successes in North Carolina," and "The Great Victory in North Carolina," complete with battlefield maps documenting the Union's firm foothold in northeast North Carolina. In Worcester, the *Daily Spy* reported, "Newbern in Our Hands: Glorious Victory of Our Troops!" One of the few bright spots in the first year of the war, the Burnside Expedition seemed to herald a turning point in northern fortunes.[13]

The Worcester County regiment was among the first units to march into New Bern, and its soldiers soon beheld scenes of total chaos. "A black pall of smoke" hung over the city, recalled signal officer William F. Draper of the 25th Massachusetts, making it appear "as though the whole city was in flames." Colonel A. B. R. Sprague recalled, "I could think of nothing but Sodom and Gomorrah." Although Confederate forces provided enough resistance to kill 90 of the invading troops and wound another 380, they soon retreated, setting fire to military stores, several buildings and wharves, and a railroad bridge as they withdrew. And despite bluster that Burnside's troops would be picked off "like . . . black-birds in a snow storm" if they ventured up the Neuse River to New Bern, panic-stricken white residents rapidly fled the Yankee invaders, many attempting to board a departing train as they juggled hastily packed boxes and trunks of household goods, leaving half-cooked dinners in their kitchens.[14]

Draper, Sprague, and other members of the 25th marched through a largely deserted city peopled by a handful of obstinate whites and hundreds of slaves abandoned by masters and mistresses. New Bern's blacks "were in ecstasie [*sic*] at our arrival," wrote Private John W. Partridge of Boylston, Massachusetts. Displaying a familiarity with whites forbidden in slavery, blacks approached Partridge, "shaking me by the hand and saying 'Lord bless you I was afraid you would not come.'" Others lined up along the streets as the 25th advanced through the city. Touched by their exuberant welcome, Chaplain Horace James described how "they jumped up, they clapped their hands, they laughed aloud, they cried for joy, they said 'God bress you,' 'We's bin prayin' for you, dis long time.'" James explained that "they seemed too happy for expression, and were actually wild with delight." A New Bern slave euphorically greeted Massachusetts soldiers upon their arrival, shouting, "Bress de Lord and Massa Lincoln! Hallelujah!" While some blacks pillaged the city, joined by Yankee troops in some cases, Union forces restored order after about twenty-four hours. General Burnside reported to Secretary of War Edwin Stanton that on 14 March, New Bern was "now as quiet as a New England village."[15]

As word of the Yankee invasion spread throughout the countryside and Union soldiers made expeditions into the surrounding interior, slaves throughout eastern North Carolina escaped to New Bern. Only a few days after seizing the city, General Burnside reported to Stanton that the city was "being overrun with fugitives from the surrounding towns and plantations," which was "a source of very great anxiety to us." Given the volume and determination of the runaways, Burnside explained, "it would be utterly impossible, if we were so disposed, to keep them outside of our lines, as they find their way through woods and swamps from every side." As an example, Burnside noted the case of two runaways who "have been in the swamps for five years," awaiting a chance to seize their freedom.[16]

By mid-1862, approximately 7,500 eastern North Carolina blacks had made their way to the city, more than doubling its population. Another thousand had made their way to Federal forces on Roanoke Island, and roughly 1,500 more congregated in Washington, Hatteras, Carolina, and Beaufort. Dr. R. R. Clarke of Whitinsville, Worcester County, a surgeon with the 36th Massachusetts, marveled at the waves of runaway slaves "continually coming in, in squads from one to a dozen — wending their way through the swamps at night, avoiding pickets — they at last reach our lines." One runaway confided to the doctor that his master had told him "that the yankees will harness them to their carts & if they don't draw they will *bayonet* them — that they will sell them in Cuba." When Clarke asked the runaway of his response to such stories, he replied, "I said *yes sir* at the same time I was making preparations to leave *him*." Summing up the sentiments of many hopeful runaways, he explained, "I *Knowed* that you was our friends because they told such stories about you."[17]

The runaways' unshakable faith that the Yankees had come to free them far outstripped the official policy of the federal government in the spring of 1862. President Lincoln, still hoping for a surge in southern Unionist sentiment to break the rebellion, continued to define the war in narrow terms as a war to save the Union — not as a war to end slavery — and, under the Confiscation Act, permitted federal troops to free only slaves directly employed by the Confederacy. Such legal niceties mattered little to the thousands of men and women who made their way to New Bern. God, as He had promised, had finally sent the Yankees to grant their freedom.[18]

"An impression . . . not easily effaced"

The runaways' narrative of Yankee deliverance and their perception of the Yankees as their God-sent liberators forced many Worcester County and other northern soldiers to recast their attitudes about the war and slavery. Vincent Colyer accompanied the Burnside Expedition to New Bern under the auspices of the Christian Associations of New York and Brooklyn. He observed, "The calm trustful faith with which these poor people came over from the enemy, to our shores; the unbounded joy which they manifested when they found themselves within our lines, and *Free*; made an impression on my mind not easily effaced."[19]

As slaves — many in rags and in poor physical condition — approached the Yankees and divulged their stories of bondage, many were shocked by what they heard and saw. Most northern soldiers knew of slavery only in the abstract. Abolitionist lecturers, national political debates, and popular literature, particularly *Uncle Tom's Cabin*, had all shaped their perceptions. Yet few were prepared for what they saw and heard firsthand in New Bern as absconding blacks gave slavery a concrete, human face. Contrabands made a huge impression on Yankee soldiers; letters home teemed with descriptions of contrabands, reconstructions of conversations held with them, and bold commentary on the horrors of slavery. Even in regimental histories written years later, contrabands figured prominently and were key figures on the landscape of war memory.

John Cross of the 25th Massachusetts conveyed his impressions of slaves and slavery in a breathless letter he wrote to a friend in Worcester County "to let you no about the Southland Slavery it is a sad sith [sight] to beholde."

Cross found it "horibel [to] her [hear] the tails that some can tell" and "to see such a state as I behold men wimen and children and so degreaded." Even though Cross made a point to "talk avery opertunitey that I get I cant begin to pitcer the state of things heer with Ears." His conversations with slaves convinced him that "the god of haven is anhgrey with the Nation and I hop and pray that the peepul may put away this grait evel fare from them."[20]

Moved by personal contact with slaves, some Worcester County soldiers became ardent abolitionists. While some members of the regiment marched off to war with soaring abolitionist rhetoric ringing in their ears, not all volunteered with the intent of freeing the slaves. Letters written home by members of the 25th reveal that many did not become abolitionists until they witnessed slavery firsthand, particularly through interactions with the "contrabands of war."

Just weeks after the successful Burnside invasion, Lieutenant Thomas Earle of the 25th Massachusetts described his abolitionist conversion to the New England Anti-Slavery Convention. He explained that he "had listened from his boyhood to anti-slavery lectures but only after his enlistment as a private in this war had he realized what it was to be an antislavery man." Their initial experience in North Carolina, explained Earle, "had abolitionized the young men of Worcester county in that regiment." Many of his comrades had "been proslavery from Worcester to Hatteras, but their eyes were opened on the island."[21]

Captain J. Waldo Denny of the 25th was one such soldier whose experiences in North Carolina radically shifted his beliefs. Although highly familiar with abolitionist sermons and speeches, as his family attended Merrill Richardson's Salem Street Society, Denny did not consider himself an abolitionist until his experiences in North Carolina turned him into one. In April 1862, soon after the capture of New Bern, Denny penned a series of letters to the *Worcester Daily Spy*, reporting to a community thirsting for information about the Worcester County regiment. In one missive, he described the arrival of a group of around seventy contrabands at a wharf near his residence in New Bern. Denny engaged one of them, a five-year-old boy, in conversation, asking him why he fled, "not thinking," Denny wrote, "that the little fellow *could* realize anything." The boy promptly remarked, "'Kase I don't want to be a slave — I'se want to be free.'" Denny "talked with many of the slaves" and, to his surprise, "found that they understood affairs pretty well." Although their masters had told them terrible tales about the Yankees, the contrabands explained to Denny that "'we knowed dey lied — we'd been praying to de Lord dat you Yankees *might* come.'" Another runaway slave greeted Worcester's

Major Pickett of the 25th as an answer to prayer: "'Tank God, massa, now I *do bleve de Lord is come for sure*! Yes, de Lord is come *Now*! We've been praying and praying dis long time dat de Lord *come*, and I *knowed* he would.'"[22]

Denny's interaction with runaways altered his fundamental beliefs about the meaning of the war. "The more I think of this matter," he wrote home to Worcester, "the more I see of the white people here . . . the more I see the joy of the slaves as they flee to us for protection, the more satisfied I am that a *deadly blow* must be struck at the *cause* of this rebellion." Ending slavery, he wrote, "is a just punishment to them [the rebels] . . . and a war measure of vital necessity." Denny noted that this sentiment represented a major change of heart, admitting that the folks back in Worcester "may be surprised" by his new opinions. "But I am sure that other men of the north," he explained, "who have thought differently, as I have heretofore, would be satisfied to adopt my views, if they could see the devil of rebellion with his cloven foot as I have seen him."[23]

Notably, Denny remarked that he had witnessed a similar change of heart among other members of the 25th Massachusetts. This occurred especially among those "who have been known as conservative men"— even some of whom "I know to have been Breckinridge [southern] democrats" in the 1860 presidential election. Another Worcester soldier wrote in May 1862, "I have always been a very stiff advocate for southern rights, as you well know; but I have become so far 'educated up,'" proclaiming only a "little strip of land between Charles Sumner's views and mine."[24]

Not only were Worcester County soldiers in New Bern deeply impressed with the slaves' understanding of the war and their deep desire for freedom, which was demonstrated continuously through their perilous journeys to Union lines, but the devotion of runaways to the Union also genuinely moved them. In eastern North Carolina, where northern soldiers resided among resentful, openly defiant whites and seemed particularly vulnerable to Confederate attack, blacks appeared to be their only true friends. Worcester's soldiers repeatedly contrasted the devotion of African Americans with the disloyalty of white North Carolinians. In a letter published in the *Worcester Daily Spy*, a soldier admonished a Worcester letter writer for complaining that the war was "'all about the nigger,'" making it clear that blacks "are the only Union men we have here." W. P. Derby of the 27th Massachusetts, also stationed in eastern North Carolina, recalled the enthusiastic greeting conferred on the Union troops by runaways after the battle of New Bern. By contrast, he noted, "there was not the least demonstration of loyalty or Union sentiment with the whites, but a sullen moroseness, indicative of intense disloyalty." Another

"Headquarters of Vincent Collyer, superintendent of the poor at New Berne N.C. —
Distribution of captured Confederate clothing to the contrabands." From *Frank Leslie's
Illustrated Newspaper*, 14 June 1862. Courtesy of the North Carolina Collection,
University of North Carolina Library at Chapel Hill.

Worcester soldier labeled the white "'secesshers'" as "a disgrace to the nineteenth century," while praising the blacks in his midst.[25]

Runaway slaves proved the depth of their loyalty to the Union by providing invaluable and highly dangerous service. Almost immediately after
seizing control of New Bern, General Burnside, like Benjamin Butler before
him, put contrabands to work for the Union army, paying men ten dollars
a month to work as laborers and women four dollars a month as servants.
Burnside soon appointed Vincent Colyer of the Christian Association of New
York as "Superintendent of the Poor" to enroll contrabands who wished to
work for the federal government, disburse wages, and provide food, clothing, and shelter to the most desperate poor — both black and white. While
some slaves seemed to the white soldiers "bewildered in their freedom" and
unsure of what to do next, many showed an enterprising spirit, as they "val-
ued their freedom with its opportunity," in the words of soldier W. P. Derby.

Another Bay State soldier noted that every returning expedition to New Bern "was accompanied by stalwart darkies who were glad to pay for protection and rations by 'toting' the arms and equipment of tired and lazy soldiers."[26] Women and children eased the lives of white soldiers by washing and ironing, cooking, and baking pies and cakes. Men worked as laborers, unloading and loading government ships, and as crew members aboard steamers. Union authorities sent some into the countryside to forage and to observe the movements of Confederate forces. Skilled contrabands also lent their expertise to the Union cause, working as blacksmiths, coopers, ship-joiners, and bridge-builders. Contrabands were chiefly responsible for building a large railroad bridge over the Trent River and the docks at Roanoke Island.[27]

In addition, a group of about fifty contraband men worked continually for the Union army as spies, scouts, and guides. Spies ventured as far as several hundred miles behind Confederate lines to bring back valuable information to Federal forces, some chased by bloodhounds and barely escaping with their lives, others captured as prisoners and shot. An officer wrote from New Bern that having observed "large numbers of 'contraband' negroes . . . my respect for the black race has been greatly increased thereby," since "in the operations of the Union armies, the contrabands have been of inestimable value. They obtained important information when white men could not; they have acted as spies when white men could not be hired to risk their necks."[28]

Not all northerners were impressed with the contrabands. To some, like James Emmerton of the 23rd Massachusetts, they were a burden, "like the poor, always with us." Emmerton scoffed at their seeming lack of foresight: "Possessed with the single idea of personal freedom, they took no thought of how they were to be supported." Some, he wrote, had only the vaguest notion of freedom, anticipating only "a new and, they hoped, a kinder master." Similarly, W. P. Derby of the 27th Massachusetts insisted that contrabands did not fully understand the concept of freedom: "Freedom to many of them consisted of nothing to do." Few soldiers sympathized with blacks who wished to define their freedom as autonomy from whites and white control.[29]

Many soldiers also attempted to analyze what they viewed as distinctive racial characteristics of the blacks in their midst. Emmerton noted that contrabands came in "all shades of color" and was convinced that "mental development was, as a rule, in direct ratio of the proportion of white blood." Yet, he admitted, the blacks he met behaved far less savagely than he had expected. Emmerton concluded that "the brutishness of the black field-hand was rare in our part of North Carolina."[30]

Expectations about blacks could also lead to incidents of cruelty. Envisioning them to be the happy, dancing figures of minstrel shows — especially popular among white working men in cities like Worcester before the war — Yankee soldiers expected to be entertained by them. Thomas J. Jennings, a Massachusetts soldier from Fall River, wrote home that while "bats and balls" helped pass the time during the day, "at night we gather together a few contra-bands and have a Negro performance," which "rather beats Christy's," the world-famous black-face minstrel troupe. Samuel Putnam of the Worcester County regiment recalled how, during an expedition to nearby Washington, North Carolina, "for amusement, squads were sent out to pick up negroes and bring them to the quarters" where "they were made to show their agility in dancing." At least several blacks refused to be part of the soldiers' fun, one claiming that as a Methodist he was forbidden to dance and another "strug-gling violently with the soldiers" before breaking through the crowd and run-ning away. Contraband children, especially, were often viewed by Yankees as pets and objects of amusement. Putnam described a foray to Plymouth, North Carolina, where soldiers of the 25th "picked up . . . as soldiers will, many pets — a curious lot — squirrels, owls, raccoons, birds, and little dar-kies, the latter quite useful in blacking shoes and such jobs."[31]

"What shall we do for them?"

Chaplain Horace James of the 25th had far grander plans for the contrabands of war. Whereas military officers such as Burnside viewed the contrabands as a burden, and some soldiers saw them as cheap labor or a diversion from the monotony of camp life, James deemed their presence a providential opportu-nity. In a letter penned to the *Congregationalist*, written only a week after the successful invasion of New Bern, James answered the question that "comes up" as "thousands of black people" fled to New Bern: "'What shall we do for them?'" To James the answer was obvious: "[L]et us give them all the new ideas we are able."[32]

For James, educating the contrabands was the key way to "make a *new* South." Idealistic and committed to radical social change, James focused his chaplaincy on preparing the contrabands for freedom. While distributing food and clothing to contrabands, James, as a middle-class New Englander, sought above all to arm former slaves with self-sufficiency based on literacy. He believed, as did many northerners, that ex-slaves would experience true freedom only through economic independence.

Working closely with Vincent Colyer, General Burnside's "Superintendent of the Poor," James immediately recruited approximately thirty soldiers from

Horace James, chaplain of the 25th Massachusetts Volunteer Infantry, Superintendent of the Poor, and Superintendent of Negro Affairs for Eastern North Carolina. From J. Waldo Denny, *Wearing the Blue.*

the 25th Massachusetts to serve as volunteer teachers for the contrabands; white children and adults were also welcome, although few attended. James found that young men from his regiment were "intensely interested in this work" and those "who could not attend in person were ready to be taxed for the support of these schools." Establishing free schools seemed like a natural first step in the North's conquest of the South. As James wrote, "Coming here as a conquering army, from a part of the country where free schools are an essential and very powerful element of its civilization, we naturally desired to establish similar institutions here." James also enthusiastically enlisted soldier-teachers from other units, the 23rd and 27th Massachusetts, as well as the 10th Connecticut, to "teach them to read the English language, so that they may study their own bibles, and find out for themselves the will of God." James found many New England soldiers "glad to give an hour in the evening to this delightful work." Some of them, Colyer bragged, "were graduates of the first colleges in the North." Over 800 contrabands attended two evening schools, held in the rooms of New Bern's two black churches. Some learned to read from a homemade banner, made of a cotton sheet and suspended over the pulpit, upon which Colyer wrote passages of scripture, such as "love your enemies, bless them that curse you."[33]

James's work with the contrabands served an additional, crucial purpose. Not only was it a tool, as James believed, for social reform and the spiritual regeneration of the South, but the chaplain's educational activities and his engagement of Worcester County soldiers as teachers also enforced northern middle-class community values. The chaplain imbued the soldiers of the 25th Massachusetts with a sense of moral purpose; their service in New Bern, he made clear from the start, involved much more than simply vanquishing rebels. When James organized the regiment's first church service after the invasion of New Bern, he chose to preach from the text "He that keepeth his spirit is greater than he that taketh a city." Noting "the general ignorance" of both southern blacks and whites, James adamantly instructed the soldiers "that we had come among them as friends to declare to them a *free education* for all classes of the population." Historian Reid Mitchell has argued, "The community never entirely relinquished its power to oversee its men at war." Chaplain James oversaw and enforced community values as the sons of Worcester County were far from home, in a strange land, confronting new and often disturbing circumstances. In addition to attending the regular Sunday church services in New Bern where James presided, teaching in the contraband night schools prodded soldiers to recognize their responsibility to the less fortunate while reinforcing a sense of the war's noble purpose to end slavery.[34]

James also forged vital links between New Bern's contrabands and his home community of Worcester. Returning to Worcester briefly in May, the chaplain immediately collected funds to support the contraband schools from the Sabbath school of the Old South Congregational Church. With the money, James purchased "a large quantity of primers and elementary books," which were immediately put to use by hundreds of students upon his return to New Bern. This would be the first link in what would become a long chain of associations connecting New Bern's black population with Worcester.[35]

Private John W. Partridge, a member of the Worcester County regiment, was among the soldiers recruited by James to teach New Bern's contrabands. A graduate of Westfield Normal School and a teacher in West Boylston when the war broke out, Partridge was an ideal enlistee for the teaching corps. Writing to his grandfather in Boylston in May 1862, Partridge assured him, "We are doing the right thing by the Contrabands," explaining that he and a friend "are going tonight to give our aid in the good work." Three hundred contrabands regularly crowded the Methodist Church, eager to learn how to read, even though "the secessionists are very wrathy about it."[36]

The World Turned Upside Down

To New Bern's contrabands, the first few months of Yankee occupation initiated the dawn of a new era. While the arrival of Union troops seemed to offer emancipation, contrabands often served as the architects of their own freedom, constructing its meaning and imbuing it with purpose. Enthusiastically offering themselves to the Union cause in a variety of capacities, they made themselves active participants in the war itself, warriors against slavery, would-be liberators of those still in bondage.

As diligent students taught at night by Yankee soldiers, contrabands armed themselves with the power of literacy, a weapon so feared that white authorities in the South made teaching a slave to read or write illegal. Vincent Colyer witnessed "colored refugees" who "evinced the utmost eagerness to learn to read." Crowding into makeshift classrooms, they "seized spelling books and primers with great avidity."[37]

Seismic shifts in New Bern's social order were also evident to contrabands — as well as to remaining white southerners — in other ways. Ransacking the homes of wealthy whites who deserted the city on the day the Yankees invaded, some blacks dressed themselves in the finery of masters and mistresses, a striking symbol that the world had indeed turned upside down. In occupied New Bern, blacks even found themselves at times treated better than native whites. Mrs. Frederick C. Roberts, a white resident of the city, recalled that when her father attempted to buy fish at a local market, he was ordered by a Union officer to "'stand back, soldiers first, negroes next and rebels last.'"[38]

The use that contrabands made — or refused to make — of their labor was a significant way that they defined what it meant to be free. After years under the lash, some contrabands exercised their freedom by simply refusing to work at all, to the chagrin of northern soldiers who viewed such behavior as irresponsible and childlike. White New Bern residents also seemed appalled by the behavior of blacks. Roberts was astonished that although some blacks remained "constantly in the yard" of her family's home in New Bern, "not one of them offered to do a hand's work for their master and mistresses." Others lent their labor to the Yankees only. John Partridge of the 25th Massachusetts wrote home that while local whites remaining in New Bern "complain that the negroes will not do anything," the fact was, "they will not lift a finger for any one except the Yankees."[39]

With schools, paid employment opportunities, and sympathetic Yankees providing a barrier between them and their former masters, New Bern's contrabands generally felt safe, convinced of the inexorable march of their God-ordained liberation. But events transpiring in both Washington and North Carolina soon shattered their sense of security.

"Are we bound to sustain the proscriptive
statutes of a slave state?"

On 26 May 1862, Edward Stanly arrived in the occupied city of New Bern, newly appointed by President Lincoln as the military governor of North Carolina. A native of Beaufort County who had represented the state in Congress as a Whig before the Civil War, Stanly returned to the Tar Heel State from California, Lincoln's emissary to North Carolina. Still holding out for a surge of Unionist sentiment, Lincoln hoped that Stanly would rally Tar Heel Unionists and crush the rebellion there. Stanly's defined mission was "to re-establish, and maintain, under military form, the functions of civil government, until the loyal inhabitants of North Carolina shall be able to assert their constitutional rights and privileges." Secretary of War Edwin Stanton informed General Burnside that the president expected "cordial co-operation" between the military and the newly appointed governor, "for the restoration of the authority of the Federal Government." But Lincoln sent Stanly to North Carolina with no specific instructions regarding his duties, which immediately led to confusion and turmoil.[40]

Meeting with Vincent Colyer in the first days of his administration, Stanly informed him that while he had no problem with the material aid Colyer provided the city's poor, he could not abide the schools that Colyer, James, and Union soldiers ran for the contrabands. The governor explained to Colyer that he "had been sent to restore the old order of things" and that "his Negro-school, if approved by me, would do more harm to the Union cause." Moreover, he had been appointed by Lincoln to administer the laws of the state, which clearly "forbade slaves to be taught to read and write."[41]

After unsuccessfully appealing to General Burnside, Colyer immediately closed the schools. Explaining to his students that he did so "by the necessity laid upon me by Governor Stanly," he requested that they "submit patiently to the deprivation like good, law abiding people, such as they had always proved themselves to be." Vowing that their suffering would ultimately be redeemed, Colyer promised that "the Saviour" would not only restore the schools but bring about even greater blessings.[42]

Shattered by the announcement, the pupils could not contain their grief. A *New York Times* reporter witnessed this "sad and impressive spectacle" as old people "dropped their heads upon their breasts and wept in silence" while "the young looked at each other with mute surprise and grief at this sudden termination of their bright hopes." Colyer later confided to Horace

James, "Such sobbing and weeping I hope I may never see again" and admitted that he himself "could hardly conceal his emotion." After a few moments of silence, "[as] if by one impulse, the whole audience rose and sang with mournful cadence, 'Praise God from whom all blessings flow.'" They then shook hands with each other and departed. As students found the news of the school closings heartbreaking, so, too, did the soldiers who taught in them. Daniel Reed Larned wrote home, "It seems as if all we had accomplished was being undone. What the effect will be on the blacks I cannot tell."[43]

To make matters worse, Governor Stanly also made it clear that he would support the return of "fugitive slaves" who had found refuge with the Federal army to masters who took the oath of allegiance. As soon as Stanly arrived in New Bern, slave masters called upon the governor, appealing to him to restore their absconded property. Stanly gave permission to Nicholas Bray to reenslave two sisters who, Bray claimed, had been "enticed away" and held behind Federal lines against their will. Locating one of his slave girls sick in bed in New Bern, Bray "dragged her forth and drove away with her to the plantation." The second sister eluded her master by escaping "with lightning speed," concealing herself "in an out-building almost under the eaves of Gen. Burnside's headquarters." The *New York Times* reported that four additional contrabands had been ordered "captured and carried out of our lines yesterday."[44]

Governor Stanly's new policies sent a wave of terror through New Bern's contraband settlement, initiating a "stampede in all directions." Dr. R. R. Clarke of Whitinsville, Worcester County, who was well-acquainted with many contrabands, having, with the aid of Colyer, opened a hospital for their care in New Bern, noted that fear of reenslavement led many to take "themselves to the woods" to hide from former masters. Clarke encountered a man who told him that "Gen Burnside may take him out and shoot him if he pleases, but he will never go back to his Master." *New York Times* reporter Elias Smith wrote that many of New Bern's contrabands "scattered like a flock of frightened birds" as "a perfect panic prevails among them." Some "have taken to the swamps, and others concealed themselves in out-of-the-way places." An old man of sixty bluntly explained that "he would rather be placed before a cannon and blown to pieces than go back. Multitudes say they would rather die."[45]

But not all hid or ran away. Many defended their newfound freedom with the support of incensed Yankee allies. According to Dr. Clarke, "[T]he feeling is deep and bitter among the soldiers and many of the officers." A Worcester County officer, whose letter was published in the *Worcester Daily Spy*, remarked that "the acts of Gov. Stanley [*sic*] is working up a mighty revolutionary feeling in the city, *and in the camps, too.*" The correspondent for the *Times* concurred: "Prominent officers, from colonels to quartermasters down to the humblest soldiers in the ranks, speak in terms of the most vehement indignation of the course which the new Governor is pursuing, and I have not met an individual, either officer or soldier, and I have seen a large number, who does not condemn, in the plainest language, the course which has been adopted." The reporter noted, however, that no disloyalty would be tolerated among the soldiers, and he predicted that "Massachusetts as well as New York troops, it is assumed, will conquer their prejudices and execute the behests of the Government."[46]

But some soldiers simply could not contain their outrage and they made their unhappiness known. Several days after Nicholas Bray managed to capture one of his two runaway slave women, the 21st Massachusetts regimental band mocked Governor Stanly during his review of the troops by playing "John Brown's Body." Another officer wrote home of his frustration that "we are playing war" as "we treat rebels with absurd leniency." Instead of conciliation, "they must be beaten, slavery abolished, and their country held with an iron hand until the next generation has grown up educated to antislavery ideas."[47]

Some soldiers moved far beyond exasperation and passive resistance, taking action that boldly defied the law — both civil and military. Reflecting a growing political consciousness and a deepening alliance with African Americans, Union soldiers lent their support to "an indignation meeting" organized by New Bern's blacks to protest Stanly's policies. Six white soldiers attended the meeting, probably the teacher-soldiers James recruited. One unidentified white soldier made a speech, exceptional not only for its fiery content but also for its blatant insubordination. Radicalized by the developments in New Bern, the soldier told the gathered audience that "they were free" and that he and thousands of others had enlisted in the army "for the sole purpose of freeing them." But, he warned, New Bern's blacks "must not leave it all to their friends" and instead must take matters into their own hands to secure their freedom. If Stanly insisted on returning them to their masters, "they must strike down every one who stood in the way to freedom." He boldly declared, "It would be better for every house to be burned, and the land made desolate, that they should be made slaves again, etc. etc. etc." The speech, according to a witness, left the audience "in a state of high excitement."[48]

The "indignation meeting" provides insight into the dynamic of budding black-white alliances. While blacks instigated the meeting, the support of some white soldiers undoubtedly affirmed and provided impetus to their cause. Prime movers for their freedom, blacks nonetheless had created powerful allies to help them fight for their freedom and negotiate the new terrain of liberation. Moreover, the incendiary words of the white soldier and the participation of others suggest that support for blacks was more than a pragmatic attempt to undercut the southern cause but represented a radical stance in favor of black rights.

Several New England soldiers went even further in their resistance to Stanly and Lincoln's policies. After Bray kidnapped his female slave from the safety of Union lines, "a party of our men," according to Dr. Clarke, made their way to his plantation. There they "held a pistol at the head of Bray and his wife," placed the slave girl in a carriage, and returned her to New Bern. As a parting touch, they burned down one of Bray's houses and a fence. Although the outraged Bray protested to Stanly, the slave master "concluded that it was best to let the matter drop."[49]

In the audacious and illegal act of liberating a kidnapped slave girl, the soldiers reenacted, in a new context, New England's famous slave rescues of the 1850s. Like their forebears, the soldiers purposefully broke the law, appealing to "higher law" that recognized the sanctity of individual freedom. Galvanized by their personal interactions with the contrabands and moved by the former slaves' deep desire for freedom and their devotion to the Union cause, Yankee soldiers willingly defied federal policy and military law, risking charges of mutiny and insubordination, to enforce the freedom of the contrabands. The soldiers' immediate and dramatic show of force, according to Dr. Clarke, ensured that "this kidnapping game has been played out in a brief and summary fashion — It will not be attempted again." He surmised that New Bern's contrabands were safe as "the Negroes friends are vastly more numerous than the masters."[50]

Letters such as those written by Dr. Clarke, with vivid and sympathetic descriptions of the plight of New Bern's blacks, coupled with news reports from New Bern, created an outcry in the North regarding Lincoln's wartime Reconstruction policy. The Stanly affair became a national cause célèbre. From the most prominent pulpit in the country, Henry Ward Beecher lashed out at both Stanly and Lincoln. In Washington, Senator Charles Sumner spearheaded the assault on the military governor. Accompanied by Colyer, Sumner demanded a meeting with President Lincoln, but after several testy exchanges between the senator and president, Lincoln refused to renounce his military governor. Sumner then attempted to remove Stanly through a Senate vote, which failed. The House of Representatives also joined the fray by passing a resolution demanding an explanation from Lincoln regarding the extent of Stanly's power and authority.[51]

In Worcester, Lincoln's North Carolina policy seemed like a personal affront, with Horace James and the sons of Worcester County playing a key role in the contraband schools. James publicized the crisis in his regularly published column in the *Congregationalist*. He challenged his readers: "Will not the north ask the question: are we bound to sustain the proscriptive statutes of a slave state? . . . are we to be told, as a basis of pacification for rebels and traitors, that we must not teach a black man . . . under pain of imprisonment?" John Denison Baldwin, the fiery editor of the *Worcester Daily Spy*, acidly criticized Stanly, labeling him "a usurper" who had "execute[d] the worst and most odious features of a villainous state code, against the constitution and every instinct of humanity and justice." The governor, a representative of the corrupt slave South — Union man or not — had attempted to undo all of the good works of Worcester County's young men and deserved the harshest criticism. But Worcester's citizens would soon get their chance to aid the cause of the contrabands of war. As a result of Stanly's policies, they soon welcomed the first contraband family into their community.[52]

THESE ARE THE CHILDREN OF

THIS REVOLUTION,

THE PROMISING FIRST FRUITS OF THE WAR

Worcester's incensed soldiers and citizenry soon responded to the crisis in New Bern with more than words of moral indignation. The calamity precipitated by Governor Stanly resulted in the first of what ultimately would be hundreds of New Bern's former slaves resettling in Worcester. Their story reveals intricate networks of support that the city's tiny, but activist, black community provided southern refugees. In addition, from the spring of 1862 forward, New Bern became a focal point for Worcesterites — both black and white — who wished to aid the plight of freed slaves. The arrival in New Bern of another Worcester County regiment, the 51st Massachusetts Volunteer Infantry, in late November 1862, only strengthened the bonds between the two cities. Responding to the effective fund-raising efforts of the Reverend Horace James and his wife, Helen, local citizens provided money, machinery, and barrels of clothing. In addition, Horace and Helen James also inspired many civilian residents of Worcester to follow in their footsteps; they practically inundated eastern North Carolina, fanning out to teach freedpeople in Washington, Plymouth, Beaufort, and Elizabeth City. At the same time that the first contrabands began to trickle into Worcester, Worcesterites made their way to North Carolina to help Horace James and others "make a *new* South," as the minister pledged in 1861. So many Worcesterites — soldiers, missionary teachers, and occasional businessmen — converged in New Bern that a soldier remarked in a letter home, "Newbern abounds with Worcester faces."[1]

"A chance for honest labor, which is all he wants"

In June 1862, editor John Denison Baldwin announced, on the first page of the *Worcester Daily Spy*, the "arrival of a 'Contraband'" directly from New Bern. The contraband had "rendered important services to General Burnside, in the capacity of pilot." In return for his aid, according to Baldwin, "he was sent north with his wife and child," bearing "recommendations from officers high in rank." Baldwin appealed to readers to consider employing the contraband, as "such a man certainly deserved immediate employment here — a chance for honest labor, which is all he wants." In announcing the arrival of the contrabands in Worcester, Baldwin managed to insert an editorial comment regarding the crisis in North Carolina. That they felt the need to relocate to Worcester, argued Baldwin, only proved the failure of Lincoln's Unionist strategy in North Carolina. "It certainly seems a singular state of things," the editor wrote, "when our army cannot protect its own benefactors, the only loyal men whom it finds in secessia."[2]

The contrabands were probably William and Mary Bryant and their child. The Bryants married in Worcester in January 1863. Their marriage record not only listed their places of birth as New Bern, but a city official carefully wrote "contraband" after their names in the marriage registry.[3]

The Bryants were among the thousands of eastern North Carolina slaves who sought refuge with the Union army as the massive Burnside Expedition descended upon eastern North Carolina. William Bryant was one of the fifty "of the best and most courageous," as described by Vincent Colyer, who worked for the Union army as spies, scouts, and guides. Boat pilots such as William Bryant provided indispensable assistance to Union officers through their knowledge of eastern North Carolina's intricate waterways.[4]

William Bryant's service to General Burnside must have been especially exemplary to warrant the attention and reward that he received. The Bryant family's choice to parlay William's service to the Union army for a new life in the North reveals the bonds forged between some contrabands and Yankee soldiers. But his relocation to Worcester also provides a concrete example of the dynamic, synergetic, and benevolent relationship built between some white soldiers and refugee slaves during the Civil War. Whereas Worcester soldiers provided both the encouragement and means through which the Bryants could secure their freedom in the North, the family's willingness to migrate to a strange and distant location reflects their deep-seated desire to seize and define their freedom, which was tenuous at best in New Bern.

Many questions surrounding the family's relocation to the North cannot be answered with certainty. For example, it is unclear whether Bryant or Union officers hatched the idea and why Worcester became their destination. Arriving in Worcester with "recommendations from officers high in rank," Bryant likely got to Worcester through the influence of the Reverend Horace James, whose work among the contrabands had drawn the attention of Union officers. Several weeks before the Bryants' arrival in Worcester, James had been in Worcester and may have helped make arrangements for them. Lieutenant Thomas Earle may also have played a part in the couple's relocation. Earle was on leave in Worcester in June 1862. In a speech before the New England Anti-Slavery Convention that month, in which he described the abolitionist conversions that swept over the 25th Massachusetts in North Carolina, Earle recalled that the night before the landing at Roanoke Island, "A Negro came out to Gen. Burnside in a boat and gave him essential information about the landing place, the force of the enemy, etc." This "Negro" may well have been the contraband who editor Baldwin had described as having "rendered important services to General Burnside." He and his family may have accompanied Earle to Worcester that June.[5]

"Worcester is Canada to the Slave"

When the *Spy* announced the arrival of the contraband Bryant family and appealed to Worcesterites to give Bryant a "chance for honest labor," the newspaper urged potential employers to contact "R. H. Johnson, truckman." Johnson's involvement in settling the Bryant family reveals the crucial role that Worcester's black community played in facilitating the Civil War–era migration of southern blacks from its earliest days. While white military officers served as the Bryants' initial patrons, Worcester's black community subsequently settled the contraband family in the community, providing shelter and employment. Unlike the upper Midwest, where Leslie Schwalm found hostility toward recent migrants from long-established black residents, Worcester's black community — both "black Yankees" and southern fugitives — united in aiding southern migrants.[6]

Robert H. Johnson belonged to a community of blacks consisting of approximately 272 people in 1860, roughly one percent of the overall population in a city of 25,000 residents. Approximately 500 additional African Americans resided in the county, making Worcester County's black population less than one-half of one percent of the county's total population. Unlike Boston, where nearly half of the black residents were northern-born, the overwhelming majority — approximately 80 percent — of Worcester's black residents were born in the North. A full 60 percent had been born in Massachusetts, compared to Boston, where only 40 percent of the black population was born in the Bay State. Many were "black Yankees," with deep roots in the area extending to colonial times, many having intermarried with Nipmuc Indians, claiming a dual heritage. Whereas approximately a quarter of Boston's black population was southern-born, in Worcester only about 17 percent (or forty-six people) had been born south of the Mason-Dixon line. An overwhelming majority, 78 percent (thirty-five people), like Johnson and his wife, Mary, had been born in Maryland, most likely as slaves. Four, the Jones family, had been born in North Carolina, and the city claimed single representatives from the District of Columbia, Delaware, Florida, and Virginia (William Jankins). Three listed birthplaces as unknown, two claimed English birth, and one designated himself "African."[7] (See Appendix.)

Johnson was one of a number of former slaves who had found refuge in Worcester before the Civil War. Worcester had risen to Thomas Wentworth Higginson's challenge to become "Canada to the Slave." Along with barbers Gilbert and Allen Walker and William Jankins and carpet and window cleaner Isaac Mason, R. H. Johnson was an ex-slave from the Upper South who had become a well-known personage in the city. Arriving in Worcester in 1856, Johnson established a family and a business in Worcester as a job truckman. Of the 49 black men over sixteen who were listed in the census as having occupations, over a quarter (14) worked as barbers, most likely in the shops run by Gilbert Walker and William Jankins. Three reported working as upholsterers, including black Yankee William Brown, who owned and operated his own business, which catered to Worcester's elite. The relatively large numbers of barbers and upholsterers attests to the ability and willingness of those black-owned businesses to provide employment to fellow African Americans in the city. Whereas 11 adult males (or 22 percent) reported no occupation, the remainder listed a scattering of occupations, including laborer (11), whitewasher (2), shoemaker (2), farmer (2), and single listings for machinist, paperhanger, teamster, and waiter. Given the overall occupational structure of black Worcester in 1860, Johnson, as a self-employed truckman, had done well in his adopted city.[8]

Perhaps remembering his own migration north from Maryland and his transition from slavery to freedom, Johnson assumed the role of employment agent for the Bryants. Former slaves such as Johnson who had arrived

Isaac Mason. From *Life of Isaac Mason as a Slave*, 1893.
Courtesy of the Manuscript Archives and Rare Books
Division, Schomburg Center for Research in Black
Culture, The New York Public Library, Astor,
Lenox, and Tilden Foundations.

in Worcester in the years before the Civil War fought boldly to end slavery
and to aid ex-slaves seeking a new start in the North. As members of the
city's Vigilance Committee and Freedom Club, they built alliances with black
Yankee families, like the William Brown family, as well as with radical whites,
such as T. W. Higginson and Martin Stowell; they guarded their community
from slave catchers; and they fought for an end to slavery and for equal rights
in the North.[9]

The contraband Bryant family — and subsequent Civil War–era black migrants — greatly benefited from Worcester's tightly organized black community and well-established interracial networks of aid and support. By 1863,
through the efforts of Robert H. Johnson and other members of Worcester's
black community, William Bryant obtained work as a laborer and resided
with his wife at 62 Union Street, a house previously occupied by Johnson.
Their residence placed them on the outskirts of the city's largest black residential cluster and reveals an intricate web of support provided by Worcester's southern-born blacks to migrants.[10]

Isaac and Anna Mason owned the Bryants' residence at 62 Union Street,
which stood next to their own home at 64 Union. The Masons played an especially central role in assisting the Bryants and other southern migrants in
the era of the Civil War. Like the Bryants, the Masons knew what it was like to
elude a grasping master. Born a slave in Kent County, Maryland, Isaac Mason

escaped with several companions to Philadelphia around 1848. After a close brush with his master's son, who attempted to recapture him in 1850, Isaac Mason fled to Boston, where he resided with black abolitionist Lewis Hayden for several weeks. Despite its reputation as a safe haven for fugitive slaves, the city offered few jobs and Mason struggled to find employment. Through antislavery networks that linked Boston and Worcester, Hayden solicited the aid of radical white abolitionist Martin Stowell and African American abolitionist and upholsterer William Brown to relocate Mason to Worcester. Through their efforts, Mason and two fellow fugitives found work and shelter in Worcester. His wife, Anna, eventually joined him.[11]

Isaac Mason chose to make Worcester his permanent home. The city proffered two key benefits for fugitives: in Mason's words, "plenty of good employment and benevolent sympathizers." Isaac Mason soon established himself as a carpet and window cleaner. In 1856, the Masons purchased what would become 62 and 64 Union Street.[12]

That Mason, a fugitive slave, and his wife became property owners within six years of their arrival in Worcester was highly unusual and reflects the importance of property ownership to former slaves, evident in the South as well as in Worcester, in the decades following emancipation. Only about 20 percent of all Worcesterites owned any real property. That the Masons managed this acquisition attests to their work ethic and reputation, as well as the support of the city's "benevolent sympathizers." In his first years in Worcester, Mason established a reputation for industry and "an honest and truthful life," according to George Frisbie Hoar, one of several prominent white antislavery advocates who befriended Mason when he came to the city. Several other white sympathizers, industrialists George T. Rice and George Barton, and a black citizen, Delaware-born Robert Wilson, who worked in a city crockery shop, enabled the Masons to purchase the Union Street properties by capitalizing a mortgage.[13]

As Isaac Mason had been the recipient of aid from Worcester's "benevolent sympathizers" in the decade before the Civil War, he, in turn, became a benefactor to southern migrants who made their way to Worcester during and after the war. According to his friend George Frisbie Hoar, a Worcester lawyer and politician, Mason "did his best always for his race." Residing at 64 Union Street, the Masons rented the house next door at 62 Union to former slaves, including Robert H. Johnson, the Bryants' "employment agent," who lived in the house with his family in 1861. Johnson likely directed the Bryants to this house.[14]

William Bryant's choice of employment also attests to Isaac Mason's role as patron. In 1864, like Mason, William Bryant listed his occupation in the city directory as "carpet cleaner," a job that included house and window cleaning as well. Isaac Mason probably gave William Bryant his start in this business. Bryant may have been working for Mason and learning the business when he first listed his occupation as "laborer" in the 1863 city directory.[15]

Embraced by an activist and supportive black community, the Bryant family shaped and secured their freedom in the North. They would be the first of many "contrabands of war" and freedpeople who would migrate to Worcester to escape the shadow of slavery in the years during and immediately following the Civil War.

Notably, the city's generally enthusiastic embrace of the Bryants, and subsequent contraband migrants, took place outside the boundaries of general public opinion and the governor's position on black migration to the Bay State. In Massachusetts and across the North, just as the Bryants arrived, Democrats bolstered their constitutional arguments against emancipation by painting fearful portraits of a flood of black migrants to the North, who, they claimed, would compete with white workers, drive down wages, and exacerbate racial tensions. Just as the Bryants settled into the city, in September 1862, General John Dix requested that Governor John Andrew provide temporary asylum for roughly 2,000 desperate contraband men, women, and children who had sought refuge at Fortress Monroe. Given the Bay State's deep antislavery roots and abolitionist-dominated government, Dix figured that Massachusetts would be most receptive to his request. But Andrew and his antislavery "Bird Club" Republican colleagues feared that Dix, a Democrat, only wished to fan the flames of racial anxiety with his request. In the immediate wake of Lincoln's preliminary Emancipation Proclamation, and facing a surging Democratic Party as fall elections approached, Andrew refused asylum for the refugees. He insisted, as many of his abolitionist colleagues did, that blacks remain in the South, their natural home, rather than migrate as "paupers and sufferers into a strange land and a climate trying even to its habitués." Better to secure their liberty and habits of self-help in the South, Andrew argued, than remove them to the harsh and inhospitable climate of the North, where they would likely become helpless dependents. Even the *Worcester Daily Spy*, which had announced the arrival of the Bryants and appealed for aid on their behalf, toed the Republican leadership's line. For the remainder of the war and through Reconstruction, as historian V. Jacque Voegeli notes, most abolitionists and advocates for freedpeople maintained this position — that the nation could best aid emancipated slaves by securing their freedom in the South, a position reflected in Federal policy.[16]

The *Spy* and its white readers probably did not see the two opposing impulses — aiding an individual contraband family in Worcester while rejecting the temporary migration of 2,000 contrabands to Massachusetts — as contradictory. The Bryants had "earned" their relocation to the North through William Bryant's service to the army. He came with references from high-ranking officers who attested to his stellar character. Moreover, his liberty, and that of his family, was at risk during the Stanly crisis. One "deserving" family hardly portended a flood of impoverished and desperate black migrants to Worcester.

The willingness of many white Worcesterites to aid individual migrants such as the Bryants during and immediately after the war reflects the nature of this early migration. Worcester offered refuge to individual former slaves with personal connections to the area — it was not a carte blanche invitation to the South's freedpeople to settle there. As a result, migration remained small and generally nonthreatening to the white population. Worcester never experienced the widespread hostility to ex-slave migrants that was common in the upper Midwest and that was largely generated by government-sponsored mass relocation of impoverished contrabands. Whereas the migration issue grew increasingly politicized and inflammatory in the Midwest — perhaps even stalling Quakers' efforts to aid contrabands — the controversy in Massachusetts over mass relocation quieted quickly, allowing room for sympathetic whites to provide aid to individual blacks who made their way north.[17]

Black Worcesterites, though, undoubtedly viewed migration in a very different light. Informed by their own experiences — either as escaped slaves themselves or as natives who continually fought for equality — African Americans acted as patrons and facilitators for migrants, regardless of the stance of Governor Andrew or Union policy. But as subsequent migration patterns show, neither local blacks nor whites could confine or define migration to Worcester and Worcester County. Migration developed its own dynamic, as friends and family members followed in the wake of pioneer migrants.

"Captives of war . . . forever free"

As the first black migrants settled in Worcester, the crisis in New Bern abated. On 17 July 1862, Congress finally quelled the controversy over fugitive slaves. The Second Confiscation Act unambiguously stated that slaves owned by rebel masters who had escaped to the Federal army, were captured by the army, or were deserted by their masters "shall be deemed captives of war, and shall be forever free of their servitude, and not again held as slaves." In addition, the outcry over his policies ultimately forced Stanly to reach an accommodation with Vincent Colyer on the issue of black education. If Colyer would be more conciliatory to Stanly, the governor would not meddle in the schools. In addition, Colyer agreed to extend more aid to the city's poor whites.[18]

While pragmatic, Colyer's bargain with the military governor only angered many New England soldiers. Radicalized by the events in the spring of 1862, they viewed the accord as appeasement of their hated enemy. Moreover, they especially resented any aid they had to provide to New Bern's whites, whom they viewed as sullen, unrepentant adversaries, especially when compared to the unflinchingly loyal blacks. In the summer of 1862, a Worcester soldier wrote home complaining that "our principle business now is to assist the ——, I mean his excellency Governor Stanley [sic] in protecting rebel property and feeding the poor snuff-dipping, dirt-eating, union-defying, yellow skinned North Carolinians, nine-tenths of whom will stab us the moment they get a chance." He continued, "I hope things will be changed in NC, or else the troops taken out of the state where we can do something." Such sentiments, he assured his readers, were widespread among his compatriots. "Don't think I am alone in these criticisms," he wrote. "It is the universal talk of the army here, and if you could hear others talk you would consider me very *conservative*." Chaplain James also commented on the demoralized attitude of New Bern's Federal troops in the summer of 1862. They were "weary unto death of this way of conducting the war. They want to get out of it. They want to go home. They never came here to save slavery, black laws, bloodhounds, ignorance, tyranny and all." Soldiers were "bitterly disappointed to see the rattlesnake of the South handled with gloves instead of being scotched and crushed." According to James, the "privates in our ranks are even more eager for a thorough policy than the officers, and if they are not soon permitted to 'cry havoc, and let slip the dogs of war,' they will be utterly demoralized."[19]

With the loss of his military allies and his mission in New Bern irretrievably compromised, Vincent Colyer left New Bern in the summer of 1862. General J. G. Foster, who succeeded Burnside as commander of Union forces in New Bern, appointed Chaplain Horace James as Superintendent of the Poor in the spring of 1863, after the death of Colyer's initial replacement. By the time James assumed his new position, he was unencumbered with Governor Stanly and the provisional Unionist government in North Carolina. The

"The effects of the proclamation — Freed negroes coming into our lines at Newbern, North Carolina." From *Harper's Weekly*, 21 February 1863. Courtesy of the North Carolina Collection, University of North Carolina Library at Chapel Hill.

Emancipation Proclamation officially changed the purpose of the war, defining the elimination of slavery as a war aim, finally making policy congruent with the hopes of New Bern's blacks and radicalized soldiers. In response, Stanly resigned his position. Gathered into New Bern's churches on 1 January 1863, the contrabands heard the proclamation read by Union soldiers, who helped explain its meaning and ramifications. Chaplain James noted that for the first time, they now "dare to believe that they are free." James viewed the emancipation as part of God's providential plan: He "is permitting this war to be lengthened out" until slavery "can be utterly destroyed."[20]

While no longer burdened by Stanly and Lincoln's Unionist strategy, James faced unprecedented challenges. Approximately 8,000 freedpeople inhabited New Bern and its vicinity in the spring of 1863. In addition, another 7,000 had settled in Plymouth, Washington, Roanoke Island, Hatteras, and Beaufort, raising the total to approximately 15,000 people for whom James was responsible. Moreover, former slaves continued to flock to Union-occupied towns and cities in eastern North Carolina, often following Union troops who made forays into the surrounding countryside, attempting to keep rebel troops at bay. After an expedition to Pollocksville in late January 1863, a Worcester soldier described the journey of "about one hundred contraband fugitives, men, women, and children" who "came in with us . . . marching several miles to join our outposts and then twenty miles through mud and rain to gain their freedom." George F. Weston, a member of the 43rd Massachusetts, remarked that he found eastern North Carolina's blacks "well informed upon the president's proclamation, at least the portion relating to their own immediate change of condition, viz. freedom." Although they were a burden on Federal authorities, to James these were "the children of this revolution, the promising first fruits of the war, and if the government does not gather and protect them, it will be convicted both of incompetence and brutality, before the civilized world."[21]

One of the consequences of the Emancipation Proclamation complicated James's mission to the freedpeople. In April 1863, Colonel Edward A. Wild of Boston received permission to enlist freedmen in eastern North Carolina for his "African Brigade." Former slaves jumped at the opportunity to serve as full-fledged soldiers in the Union army and fight to end slavery. While their enlistment greatly aided the Union cause, it placed another burden on the Superintendent of the Poor. As black recruits left wives and children behind who desperately required assistance, the responsibility for their support fell to James, who was already challenged with a dearth of resources to aid the needy.[22]

"Let us fight with our right hand and civilize with our left"

James soon surmised that he would need to enlist the aid of sympathetic northerners in order to provide for the needs of such a large population. In late June 1863, he embarked on a fund-raising trip in the North "to collect materials and implements for colonizing the families of colored soldiers upon Roanoke Island." James had formulated a plan that he explained in a circular distributed in advance of his fund-raising visits. Families of eastern North Carolina's black Union soldiers needed to relocate to "places of safety" where they could be taught, "in their ignorance, how to live and support themselves." They would be made "proprietors of the soil" and their labor directed "into such channels as promise to be remunerative and self-supporting." Roanoke Island, like Hilton Head, offered an insular location, free from Confederate attack. James solicited "all the friends of the *New Social Order in the South*, and in particular . . . those who believe that the solution of the Negro question is the turning point of the war." With the planting season already nearly past, James appealed for a steam engine to cut wood and grind corn; construction materials, including boards and shingles; a variety of saws, axes, hammers, and other tools; household items, seeds, and agricultural implements; and clothing and schoolbooks — all the items necessary to establish a self-sufficient village on the model of New England's self-contained towns. "Let us fight with our right hand," implored James, "and civilize with our left, till the courage, the enterprise, and the ideas of the North have swept away the barbarism and reason of the South, and made of this country *One Goodly and Free Land*."[23]

After several fund-raising stops in northern towns and cities, including New York and Boston, James arrived in Worcester in mid-July 1863. On 17 July, accompanied by his wife, Helen, who had joined her husband in New Bern to aid his work, James addressed a large audience at Mechanics Hall and laid out his plans for colonizing Roanoke Island. In addition to supplies, the minister estimated that he needed $10,000 to begin the work. The proposed Roanoke Island colony, he claimed, could provide a model of self-support for the nation's entire slave population and solve "the great problem, what is to become of this unfortunate class of our fellow beings, when endowed with the boon of freedom." He concluded "with an earnest appeal to Worcester to do her duty in this great cause."[24]

Already closely linked to New Bern and eastern North Carolina through the service of their men in the 25th and 51st Massachusetts Volunteer Infantry regiments, Worcester Countians strengthened their ties with New Bern and eastern North Carolina by responding eagerly to the Reverend James's appeal and providing ongoing support over the next several years. Initial contributions for Roanoke Island included a gift of $100 from Worcester industrialist and longtime abolitionist Ichabod Washburn, along with numerous smaller monetary contributions from the local citizenry, all for the purchase of machinery "for the use of colored mechanics at Roanoke Island." The notion of proud and independent "colored mechanics" evolving from the degradation of slavery clearly appealed to the men and women of industrial Worcester, a city built on a deep tradition of self-reliant, skilled mechanics. Mechanics not only manned the city's numerous manufactures but also provided much of the Yankee ingenuity responsible for the city's pioneering industries, such as wire pulling, a process invented by Washburn. Worcester also contributed a steam gong, manufactured by the city's Steam Boiler Company, as well as pipes and fittings for Roanoke Island's steam engine. Local railroads even provided free transportation of these items to North Carolina. Overall, James managed to raise between eight and nine thousand dollars for the Roanoke Island colony during his trip north.[25]

In addition to the funds raised in July 1863, Worcester County's numerous freedmen's relief organizations provided generous and ongoing support for the work of Horace and Helen James among eastern North Carolina's freedpeople. By the time that the Jameses made their appeal on behalf of eastern North Carolina's blacks, Worcester County women were seasoned veterans who had already solicited and sent off hundreds of dollars for freedmen's relief, as well as numerous barrels of clothing and schoolbooks. Worcesterites' personal connections with New Bern and Horace and Helen James only energized and focused their work.

As early as December 1861, as Lincoln and Congress struggled with a contraband policy, prominent white abolitionist women organized Worcester's first freedmen's aid association. Deeply engaged in numerous reform movements before the Civil War, including antislavery and feminism—Worcester hosted the first national women's rights convention in 1850 — the city's women quickly rallied to the cause of contraband aid. Led by Mrs. John Davis, Mrs. Ichabod Washburn, and Mrs. Edward Earle—wives of Worcester's most prominent citizens — white women organized "a systematic effort in behalf of the destitute 'contrabands'" at Fortress Monroe and Port Royal, the first sites of contraband relief. As the dire need of refugee slaves became clearer, the Ladies Committee held its first fund-raising concert at Washburn Hall in the spring of 1862. By the fall of 1862, the committee expanded its efforts considerably by appealing to women in surrounding towns and cities throughout the county "to co-operate with us, form local associations and connect themselves with us, whether by membership or through committee." Throughout the remaining years of the war and into the postwar era, the Association for the Relief of Liberated Slaves, as the organization became known (and later renamed the Freedmen's Relief Society), not only spearheaded relief efforts in Worcester but also coordinated the labors of numerous town-based associations throughout the county.[26]

Nearly every Worcester County town boasted a freedmen's relief society. Regular reports cited contributions from Grafton and Oxford, Leicester and Shrewsbury, Harvard, Millbury, Paxton, and North Brookfield. Petersham in northern Worcester County even organized a "juvenile aid society" to encourage the participation of the town's young people. Relief societies engaged in a wide variety of fund-raising activities, including costume promenades and dress balls, while meeting regularly to sew and mend clothing for the destitute. While the relief societies contributed to needy freedpeople throughout the South, their reports indicate numerous shipments earmarked specifically for the Jameses and freedpeople in eastern North Carolina.[27]

As women spearheaded freedmen's relief organizations in the North, as historian Carol Faulkner notes, these organizations provided them with a political platform and an opportunity to influence Federal policy toward newly liberated slaves. Emphasizing the destitution of newly liberated African Americans and the pressing need to alleviate their situation through contributions of food, clothing, and shelter, women activists often collided head-on with those who feared that their efforts would cultivate the dependence of freedpeople.[28]

In the midst of a flurry of relief activities in the spring of 1862 and just after the Worcester women organized, they faced public criticism that encapsulated what would become an ongoing national debate over how best to aid former slaves. In a letter to the *Worcester Daily Spy*, the Reverend H. L. Wayland, a well-known Worcester Baptist minister serving as a chaplain with the 7th Connecticut in Port Royal, South Carolina, argued vehemently against well-meaning northerners organizing contraband aid, those who would sentimentally "do for them [contrabands] without regard to results." Wayland insisted that providing former slaves with supplies only undercut efforts "to make *men* out of these slaves." In Wayland's opinion, the best course was to plunge them into an ice-cold bath of self-sufficiency to stimulate them to independence.[29]

The relief association swiftly responded publicly. "The only result desired *is* their 'intellectual, social, and moral elevation,'" one member explained in a letter published in the *Spy*. She continued, "As a first step in the educating process, which is to make these people men and women, clean and proper clothing is requisite." Another writer replied, "If there are benevolent persons disposed to aid the government in the effort to raise them from the barbarism and beggarism in which slavery has left them, what can be the harm?"[30]

The debate over contraband relief in Worcester provides insight into two competing freedmen's policies, one that promoted direct aid to alleviate suffering, the other demanding self-reliance, even under the harshest circumstances, to avoid cultivating dependency. These approaches would continue to be in contention during Reconstruction. At the same time, the debate reveals the racial attitudes that southern blacks would confront as they worked with sympathetic northerners in the South and as they moved to the North. Both critics and supporters of contraband aid began with the same racial assumptions: slavery had blunted the development of blacks and had left them in a childlike, dependent condition. Southern blacks needed to be "educated up" to manhood and womanhood, to citizenship and full responsibility. Those on either side of the debate merely differed on the means of uplift, on the tools needed to raise former slaves to responsible adulthood. Both asserted that it was the duty of northern whites to elevate the former slaves — to lead them — to "manhood and womanhood." This elevation, they implied, required aid from sympathetic whites, those who, they believed, knew what was best for them. And, more importantly, they argued that until former slaves received proper clothing and the rudiments of an education, they were not yet fully men and women, and were dependent upon the aid of sympathetic whites.[31]

These racialist notions created a double-edged sword for former slaves in both the South and the North. While sympathetic whites played a crucial role in helping provide for many fundamental needs of the newly emancipated, many nonetheless often failed to see the full humanity of those they wished to aid. And even when they did recognize former slaves' humanity, white patrons imposed their own values and definitions of "manhood" and "womanhood" upon them. Ironically, those who were most sympathetic to ex-slaves, including Chaplain James, often saw whites alone as indispensable agents of "uplift," denying the agency of blacks themselves as adequate to the task.

Not all friends of the freedpeople shared these racialist ideas. Lunsford Lane, a former North Carolina slave living in Worcester, made it his goal to educate local citizens about the slaves and "contrabands," who constituted the most pressing question of the day. Lane had been in bondage for thirty-two years in the Tar Heel State, toiling as a house slave, body servant, and waiter in Raleigh, where he served many members of the North Carolina state legislature. Establishing his own tobacco shops in Chapel Hill, Salisbury, and Fayetteville, the entrepreneurial Lane saved enough money to purchase his freedom for $1,000. However, North Carolina's laws stipulated that slaves could be freed only if they proved "meritorious service." Unable to meet this requirement, he managed to convince his wife's owner to purchase him and then take him to New York and emancipate him. He obtained his freedom in 1835. Lane returned to North Carolina, where he pursued a variety of business interests, all the while saving money to purchase his family in Raleigh. But in 1841, because he was in violation of a state law prohibiting freed blacks to reenter the state, Lane was forced to leave Raleigh, with only one of his children accompanying him north. He joined the abolitionist lecture circuit to raise money to purchase his remaining family members, and in April 1842, he returned to Raleigh to buy their freedom. But authorities immediately arrested him "for delivering abolition lectures in the State of Massachusetts."

Lunsford Lane. From William G. Hawkins, *Lunsford Lane; or, Another Helper from North Carolina*, 1863. Courtesy of the Manuscript Archives and Rare Books Division, Schomburg Center for Research in Black Culture, The New York Public Library, Astor, Lenox, and Tilden Foundations.

Tarred and feathered at the hands of an angry mob, Lane managed, through the help of some white sympathizers, to escape to the North with his mother, wife, and children. Two years later, his father joined them. After seeking his fortune in Philadelphia and Ohio, Lane returned once again to Massachusetts. "To be rocked in their cradle of liberty — oh, how unlike being stretched on the pillory of slavery," he lyrically recalled; he was "determined to settle in Worcester," perhaps because of its reputation for its many "benevolent sympathizers." Lane made a living practicing folk medicine and manufacturing and selling "Dr. Lane's Vegetable Pills."[32]

When the Civil War broke out, Lane emerged as an outspoken advocate for southern blacks, tirelessly addressing the fact that "the wishes of the colored people are much misunderstood by their friends North and South." Lane's "long residence in the South and his extensive acquaintance with persons of his race, made him in some sense representative of their views," according to his biographer, the Reverend William G. Hawkins, a local black minister. Whenever a hall could be obtained in Worcester or in the surrounding towns and villages, Lane spoke on "the big question" of the day: "what to do with four million slaves?" For Lane, the answer was simple and direct: "We desire, in the first place, freedom in its truest and best sense, — not a mere license to do as we please. Having secured this, we wish to be situated so as to be profitably employed, so as to benefit the State as well as ourselves." Lane argued that former slaves like himself did not wish to stay in the harsh climate of the North where "our offspring wither and die." Instead, as soon as the war ended, "we would return to a clime so well suiting our constitutions." Anticipating the later plans of several radical politicians, Lane pointed out that in North Carolina alone "there are thousands of acres of unoccupied lands, which might be made to flourish under the diligent culture of the black man" as either "tenants or owners." Lane also encouraged northern teachers and preachers "to visit the South," to overcome "ignorance and prejudice." Finally, he made it clear that southern blacks had no desire to leave their homeland for Liberia, the West Indies, or any other place: "The South is our home." He concluded by pointing out that the common good could only be enhanced by a free, industrious black race: "There is no branch of business or of commerce which would not be benefited by our elevation and industry. Millions of acres, now worthless, would be made to bud and blossom."[33]

As stories about the contrabands seized the attention of Worcester residents and white Worcesterites debated the best approach to "the question of the day," Lunsford Lane sought "in a very unpretending way, to awaken a renewed interest in the colored race." While acknowledging that former slaves did indeed need the help of sympathetic northerners to aid them in the journey from slavery to freedom, Lane nevertheless emphasized — like his far more famous compatriot Frederick Douglass — the innate manhood and womanhood of freedpeople and their desire and ability to help themselves.[34]

Worcester's black women also made major contributions to the cause of freedpeople. While the head of the first women's relief organization made a point to welcome the participation of African Americans, black women ultimately chose to establish their own separate aid society. In an appeal for membership in 1862, Mrs. John Davis denounced the prejudice against blacks that might hinder relief efforts and explained that "we shall all welcome the assistance of such as may join us in our semi-monthly meetings." Worcester's black women may have been welcome as participants, but they could not have served as leaders, as Mrs. Davis, Mrs. Washburn, and Mrs. Earle already oversaw the organization. As a result, the city's black women created a separate freedmen's aid society, organizing the Colored Freedmen's Aid Society of Worcester by early 1864. Informed by their own experiences as former slaves and second-class citizens in the North, the city's black women created their own society with its own vision, one in which they could exercise their own leadership and set their own agenda. As Carol Faulkner notes, their organizations stressed race pride and self-help and often "challenged white perceptions of race, equal rights, free labor and dependency, drawing on their personal investment in the outcome of Reconstruction."[35]

The Colored Freedmen's Aid Society was another manifestation of the activism of Worcester's black community and the leadership provided by former slaves who shaped community efforts to both end slavery and aid freedpeople. Mrs. Elizabeth Mowbray served as president of the organization. With her husband, Jacob, she had fled Maryland and found refuge in Worcester in the 1850s. By the time of the war, both Jacob and Elizabeth had emerged as leaders in black Worcester. In January 1862, Jacob presented a lecture on "the War and the Safety of the Union" at Brinley Hall. As head of the Colored Freedmen's Aid Society, Elizabeth continued her fight for freedom by rallying Worcester's black community to provide aid for eastern North Carolina's blacks.[36]

The city's black community enthusiastically responded to appeals from New Bern and other Yankee outposts in the South. Proceeds from a community celebration of the first anniversary of the Emancipation Proclamation in January 1864 went to support the Jameses' work in eastern North Carolina. In March 1864, Helen James wrote a moving letter to "the Colored People of Worcester," thanking them for the clothing they had recently sent. Acknowledging the tiny community's dearth of resources, she noted that she was especially touched by their gift, as "I remember how you are forced to struggle along, both for your own support and to keep up the church with which most of you are connected." Mrs. James recognized "how much effort you have made to send these supplies to the naked ones with whom I am surrounded." She noted that their contribution was especially timely, given a recent smallpox epidemic that required the destruction of infected clothing.[37]

"Next to the church I believe in the school-house,
and next to the minister in the school-teacher"

In addition to soliciting money and supplies in July 1863, Horace and Helen James recruited teachers from the North to return with them to North Carolina. The seeds of contraband education, sown by New England soldiers immediately after the occupation of New Bern, had by the spring of 1863 flowered into several schools in eastern North Carolina. Plymouth, Roanoke Island, Washington, and Beaufort, in addition to New Bern, all boasted schools "taught by chaplains, wives of officers, or by soldiers." But they alone could not accommodate the overwhelming numbers of freedpeople who

Yankee schoolteachers in front of their home in New Bern, c. 1863. Courtesy of the North Carolina Collection, University of North Carolina Library at Chapel Hill.

desperately wished to learn to read and write. After all, education, believed James, served as the cornerstone of their freedom and self-reliance. "We are getting as many new thoughts in their heads as we possibly can," he wrote to Worcester's Old South Sunday School in 1863, "hoping to enlarge and furnish their minds, and arouse their manhood to such an extent that they can never again be made slaves." While freedmen who enlisted in the Union army would learn discipline "and valuable culture under military law, nothing short of 'Yankee school ma'ams' will answer for their children." He proclaimed, "Next to the church I believe in the School-house, and next to the minister in the school teacher."[38]

When James returned to New Bern after his northern fund-raising trip in late July 1863, four "Yankee school ma'ams" accompanied him: Betsey L. Canedy, Alice Roper, Mary A. Burnap, and Susan Hosmer, all from Massachusetts. Roper hailed from Sterling in Worcester County, and Burnap and Hosmer taught school in Ashby, Middlesex County. They opened the first full-time schools in New Bern for freedpeople on 23 July 1863. By the summer of 1864, James had massively expanded his teaching corps. Working with the American Missionary Association (AMA), the National Freedman's Relief Association, and the Boston Educational Commission, he had recruited sixty-six northern teachers to eastern North Carolina, who taught in nineteen day schools and eight evening schools, all but two supported by northern missionary societies.[39]

James's responsibilities for eastern North Carolina's blacks continued to expand, and he enlisted several of his Worcester County Congregational church colleagues to assist him. By late 1863, he was appointed "Superintendent of Negro Affairs for the District of North Carolina," which included New Bern, Beaufort, Plymouth, Roanoke Island, and Wilmington. In January 1864, the Reverends Clarendon Waite of Rutland and William T. Briggs of Princeton arrived in New Bern to serve as Horace James's assistants. Waite became Assistant Superintendent of Negro Affairs, and Briggs aided James as Superintendent of Colored Schools in North Carolina. Briggs humorously remarked that the three Worcester County ministers constituted "a stupendous Body of New England Divinity!"[40]

The Jameses were so successful in inspiring Worcester Countians to follow in their footsteps that they practically inundated eastern North Carolina. New Bern, wrote the Reverend Briggs, "is gradually taking on a Northern likeness." Anne P. Merriam and Emily Piper of Worcester taught in eastern North Carolina (Merriam in Washington and later New Bern), under the auspices of the Boston Educational Commission and the New England Freedmen's Relief Association, respectively. Juliet B. Smith of Sutton, Worcester County, taught at the Trent River Camp outside of New Bern, sponsored by the New York National Freedman's Relief Association. The H. S. Beals family, with many ties to Worcester, served as the nucleus of a small corps of teachers in Beaufort. In 1866, due to the Beals's efforts, Worcester industrialist and veteran abolitionist Ichabod Washburn donated $300 toward the establishment of a freedpeople's school in Beaufort. Named Washburn Seminary, in his honor, the school further strengthened ties between Worcester and eastern North Carolina. In the view of northern men stationed in New Bern, an influx of northern women — teachers and officers' wives — greatly improved the atmosphere there. "Wives and daughters find their way hither in increasing numbers," wrote the Reverend Briggs, "and their advent is as welcome as the fall of manna was to the Jews in the wilderness."[41]

New Bern was not the only destination for Worcester's missionary teachers. In January 1863, Lucy and Sarah Chase, Quaker sisters and daughters of prominent Worcester businessman Anthony Chase, arrived in Craney Island, six miles from Norfolk, Virginia, under the auspices of the Boston Educational Commission. A. C. Peckham, also of the city, and Mary Fletcher of Grafton taught in Norfolk as well. Sarah G. Brown of Barre heeded the call to Virginia's eastern shore, and Ellen Lee of Templeton ventured to teach on St. Helena Island, South Carolina.[42]

The Chase sisters spent much of the next three years teaching in the Norfolk area, making regular visits to Worcester friends and acquaintances in New Bern and the vicinity. In January 1865, for example, Lucy visited Roanoke Island and New Bern, where she called on the Reverend Briggs, among others, and noted in a letter to her sister that "Capt James and his wife are at Moorehead [sic] City. We shall try to find them there." The sisters not only forged links between eastern Virginia and fellow townspeople in the New Bern area, but they also established a nexus between Worcester and eastern Virginia, which would influence later migration patterns. Just as local freedmen's aid societies targeted New Bern through the Jameses and local soldiers, aid societies sent barrels of goods to aid the Chase sisters' work in Virginia. The solicitations of the Chases, and their many connections in Worcester County, made Norfolk, along with New Bern, a favorite destination for contributions of books, clothing, food, and money from Worcesterites wishing to aid newly liberated blacks. The Chases' informative letters, some of which were printed in the local press, kept local citizens abreast of developments in Virginia and the dire needs of former slaves there.[43]

*"Like going down into Egypt & dwelling
in the region & shadow of death"*

Like their mentors, the teachers recruited by Horace and Helen James ventured to eastern North Carolina brimming with idealism. Their task, James explained, was "plain enough — We desire to instruct the colored people of the South, to lift them up from subservience and helplessness into a dignified independence and citizenship." In addition, he explained, "We wish to inspire them with all the virtues of individual and social life, and prepare them to enjoy the rights and perform the duties of free men under the law in our great republic." In short, teachers were expected to impart far more than the ABC's to their charges: they were to prepare them for freedom. In addition, many teachers, especially those sponsored by the evangelical American Missionary

Association, viewed eastern North Carolina as a fertile mission field, and they enthusiastically mixed northern Protestant evangelicalism with reading, writing, arithmetic, and civics lessons.[44]

Overwhelmingly female and young, generally in their twenties and thirties, many had experience teaching in the North. "With few exceptions," wrote Superintendent William T. Briggs, "they are experienced, cultivated & most heartily devoted to their work," representing "the very best from our cities & populous villages." Some had as many as ten to fifteen years of experience in "select schools & academies." In addition, many had been involved in the antislavery movement, and leapt at the chance to soldier for freedom in the classroom. Both Horace James and the northern freedmen's aid societies that recruited teachers sought out young women in particular. Female teachers, James noted with New England practicality, "*cost* less & are generally as successful as men." Moreover, many organizations, such as the AMA, contended that women naturally possessed the qualities necessary for the task at hand. As caregivers and nurturers, and as possessors of a superior moral character, women, the aid societies believed, were especially suited to care for the suffering and to uplift the degraded. In addition, teachers who applied to the AMA had to demonstrate "fervent piety" and possess "missionary spirit" as well as "a desire for the salvation of souls." They were expected to be healthy "to insure energy, cheerfulness, and courage for work" and to be able to demonstrate "earnestness of purpose." The New England Freedmen's Aid Society warned that "no mere youthful enthusiasm" could sustain a teacher in the South. Instead, "she must see in the freedmen the representatives of humanity, 'the little ones' whom Jesus told us we serve him in serving." Freedmen's organizations also stressed the gravity of her mission, "that she is forming the people who are to influence very largely its future, for good or evil."[45]

Worcester County resident Ella Roper, who would be assigned to teach in Roanoke Island, summed up the sentiments of many Yankee women who labored among freedpeople in eastern North Carolina and elsewhere during and after the Civil War. In her application to the AMA, Roper explained that she felt called by God to be a "self-denying teacher," knowing full well "that the ease and comfort of home, the society of friends will be withdrawn, but this is nothing to the consciousness of giving a cup of water to *one* of His little ones." Moreover, she endorsed the conventional wisdom that "a lady might have more direct influence than a gentleman."[46]

Despite their deeply held convictions, both religious and political, many teachers simply were not prepared for the suffering, danger, and deprivation they encountered. As Superintendent Briggs wrote, "At that early period, being in the enemy country & amid the desolation of war, it seemed like going down into Egypt & dwelling in the region & shadow of death."[47]

The profound misery of many former slaves shocked the teachers. Soon after her arrival to teach on Roanoke Island in late 1863, Elizabeth James of Medford, Massachusetts, a cousin of Horace James, wrote to the head of the American Missionary Association of being overwhelmed by "scenes of suffering . . . which baffle description." She described children dying of exposure in the Carolina winter while others shivered in rags, circumstances so painful to observe that, she wrote, "I can hardly eat or sleep." She found relief, she explained, only in doing "what the disciples of John the Baptist did, when their master was beheaded. They went and *told Jesus*." Teacher H. S. Beals wrote from Beaufort that "[l]ittle know the multitude at the North, the Significance of that word, 'poor.'" Beals was especially struck by the physical toll that slavery had taken on the blacks he encountered in eastern North Carolina. "None but those who labor among them," he contended, "can understand how Slavery has reduced them physically." In practically "every other cabin may be found the crawling, scrawny forms of victims whose constitutions have been wrecked amid toils and stripes."[48]

Teachers themselves also lived and labored in trying circumstances. While those in New Bern generally found decent facilities for their schools and comfortable housing, teachers in the hinterlands struggled in makeshift settings. Teachers also regularly faced threats of violence from angry southern whites who resented their presence. At Clumfort Creek, outside of New Bern, local whites "tried to extort a promise from the teacher that she would never again teach 'niggers' to read." The threats only strengthened the determination of the teacher and her students "that a church & school house should stand."[49]

Missionary teachers received reminders in other ways that they were indeed in the South. In 1863, a yellow fever epidemic closed the schools in the city of New Bern soon after they had opened. They did not open again until December, and "then it was virtually commencing the enterprise anew," wrote Superintendent Briggs, and "our task seemed about as impossible as that of the ancient Jews, compelled to make bricks without straw." In 1864, another attack of yellow fever once again closed the schools, killing several teachers and incapacitating many others, including Horace James. The oppressive southern heat and a limited diet contributed to a variety of illnesses as well; teachers often complained of fatigue, fevers, and diarrhea, and occasionally they succumbed to disease. As were dead Yankee soldiers, they were memorialized as martyrs for freedom. Upon the deaths of Worcester County teacher M. Louise Boyden, who died at her home in Leominster in June 1865, and

Salem native Sarah Lakeman, the *Freedmen's Record* described the women as "soldiers in the army of the Lord." They were "raised up on high, where they may rejoice in the triumph of the holy cause for which they labored."[50]

To make matters worse, Confederate attacks regularly interrupted school, sometimes sending teachers and students fleeing for safety. In January 1864, rebel troops launched an all-out offensive in an attempt to push the Yankees out of eastern North Carolina. In February 1864, Sara Pearson, who ran the Russell School in the Trent River Camp near New Bern, reported "another broken month" as school had to be closed due to "the continuous firing of cannons from the neighboring Forts." In April 1864, the sounds of Confederate cannon forced teachers to abandon their work in New Bern, Plymouth, Washington, and Roanoke Island, as they sought safety in Beaufort. While failing to recapture New Bern, rebel forces nevertheless managed to regain Morehead City and Plymouth in the spring of 1864. Frustrated, the Reverend William T. Briggs questioned God's purpose in the continual interruptions. "It is a dark mystery," he wrote to the secretary of the American Missionary Association, "that our schools, never so flourishing as the last month should again be interrupted & some permanently broken up."[51]

In addition to the frustrations of war, climate, and sickness, some teachers complained about the "degraded" behavior and culture of their students. Their middle-class values and expectations about "proper" and "respectable" behavior often clashed with the culture of their charges. It is likely that most teachers brought with them the "romantic racialist" notions elucidated by historian George Fredrickson that accepted indelible differences between blacks and whites while rejecting a clear-cut racial hierarchy. They viewed blacks as childlike, emotional, highly spiritual, and affectionate while whites, by contrast, were mature and rational. Such racial notions led many teachers to view freedpeople with condescension; they often dismissed black culture as primitive and foolish; their mission of "uplift" equaled an attempt to replace it with the white, middle-class Protestant values they deemed superior.[52]

The shock of encountering a truly alien and often incomprehensible culture is woven throughout the teachers' correspondence. Some students, they reported, did not know how to hold a book or how to write on a slate. Unaccustomed to the discipline of the clock, an object as foreign to former slaves as books and slates, students seemed to have no concept of time and regularly showed up late for class; others arrived at any time of the day, in hopes of "catching a lesson." According to the teachers, younger students, especially, often grew restless in hot, overcrowded classrooms, talked incessantly, and giggled at the slightest provocation. New Bern teacher Oliver Howard wrote,

"Habit makes them talk aloud; lack of elbow-room makes them impatient at times." Outside of the classroom, evangelical teachers tried to eradicate "their rude forms of worship," replacing them with the decorum of a New England congregation.[53]

Despite a plague of hardships and frustrations, Superintendent Briggs noted in 1865, "From the first there has been no lack of competent & accomplished teachers, ready to take the risk of a malarious climate — meet the annoyances & privations of a military post & cash in their lot with the poor." Many teachers found that the joy of teaching freedpeople more than offset the vicissitudes of their daily lives. The Reverend E. J. Comings reported from Beaufort, "Such eagerness to learn, and such unbounded gratitude for help in so doing, make the teacher's burden light." Teacher Oliver Howard exclaimed, "The wonder is that they do so well under the circumstances."[54]

Other teachers maintained that black students seemed more teachable than the white students they had taught in the North; and many argued that black students learned just as quickly, some comparing them favorably to the Irish immigrants they taught in Massachusetts. After several years of experience as a teacher and Superintendent of Schools in North Carolina, the Reverend B. W. Pond concluded, "I believe it is a common sense lesson, which many friends of the negro have yet to learn, that while there is no positive proof of his far inferiority to the white race, there is no more proof of his superiority to the Saxon, but only that on the whole he is *very much like* all the rest of mankind."[55]

Whereas white Worcester Countians dominated the teaching corps recruited by Horace and Helen James, a prominent representative of black Worcester also sojourned to eastern North Carolina immediately after the war ended. Former slave Lunsford Lane, who had spoken on behalf of freedpeople to numerous white audiences in and around Worcester after the Civil War broke out, returned to his home state in 1865 to establish a manual labor school for the benefit of former slaves. Lane, who with his wife and two daughters cared for sick and wounded soldiers during the Civil War at Worcester's Wellington Hospital, surely knew of Horace James's labors in eastern North Carolina. Not only would he have been aware of James's fundraising visits to Worcester, but he also had a personal connection to James. Lane's father, known as "Uncle Ned," followed his son north to Boston in 1844. Overwhelmed "by the strange sights and sounds of civilized life" in that city, he sought refuge in the surrounding countryside. Lane managed to find his father a job as a gardener — for the Reverend Horace James, then a pastor of a Congregational church in the town of Wrentham. Lane may have returned to eastern North Carolina because of James's influence.[56]

Lane's return created "a stir" among New Bern blacks. According to Reverend Pond, Lane's dramatic story of his difficulties escaping the bonds of slavery in North Carolina was well-known among the state's blacks and had "enlisted the sympathies of the entire black population here. So that they whisper the name and memory of Lunsford Lane as the name of a banished favorite." More than a "martyr," he "had been a sort of leader and prince among them." When Pond announced Lane's return to his native state, "strong men and women shook with intense feeling, and that day brought great rejoicing to many."[57]

In June 1865, Lane reported that he, along with Edward Hill of New Bern, had established a manual labor school and farm twenty-five miles west of New Bern, near Rouse Depot. The school, according to Lane, "is now in working order, with thirty hands, including men, women, and children." Returning to Worcester in 1866 to raise money, he recounted the resourcefulness necessary to establish such a school "almost totally without funds." Unable to purchase land for the school, he made arrangements to work the land for shares, paying the owner one-fourth of the crop. With parents working in the fields to raise the crop, their children attended school during the day and the parents managed two hours of schooling at night. Despite the death of the farm's only mule, and no animal to pull a plow, the farmers nonetheless managed to raise 375 bushels of corn and 100 bushels of sweet potatoes, samples of which Lane brought back to Worcester as evidence of the skills of his farming students. Just as Horace James and his corps of teachers and ministers cemented ties between white Worcester and eastern North Carolina, so, too, did Lunsford Lane establish networks to black Worcester. Mrs. William Brown, head of the colored Freedmen's Aid Society and the wife of a prominent black upholsterer, helped coordinate Worcester's contributions to Lane's school.[58]

"1st, They believe in 'de good Lord.'...
2d, in Abraham Lincoln.... 3d, In Massachusetts,
and everything that comes from it"

Like the soldiers who preceded them, and who were transformed by their contact with the "contrabands of war," teachers in eastern North Carolina found themselves deeply moved by interaction with their students. Similarly, freedpeople found themselves profoundly shaped by their contact with northern teachers. Former slaves flocked to the schools established by their northern benefactors and responded enthusiastically to the teachers and ministers who converged on eastern North Carolina. "The colored people seem to understand," Superintendent Briggs wrote in 1865, "that knowledge is power." To that end, children and adults filled day schools, night schools, and Sabbath schools; between 1863 and 1865, the number of pupils in freedpeople's schools jumped "from a few hundred to nearly three thousand." Fervently embracing the education denied them in slave times, students showed "a genuine love for school," Briggs noted. "Repeatedly the vote has been unanimous to dispense with holidays for the sake of attending." Even children, Briggs pointed out, "will part with their pennies for a book sooner than for candy, and men will come short of food and clothing for the sake of learning to read." Those who learned how to read requested books so that they could teach others. Freedpeople willingly made sacrifices over and over to secure educational opportunities, "denying themselves little comforts." Although money was scarce, at least one New Bern school was self-supporting as early as 1865, with pupils paying one dollar per month for tuition. To support the newly established Washburn Seminary in Beaufort, named after benefactor Ichabod Washburn of Worcester, freedwomen organized a festival that highlighted "speaking," singing, and "tables filled with good things," raising over $100 for the school. One Beaufort freedwoman even "gave up a dress last week she greatly admired," wrote Sarah Beals, in order to make a donation to the school; and a freedman successfully appealed to his Sunday school class to contribute toward the $500 needed to keep a teacher over the summer, arguing, "we must help him all we can. We can all of us do something." In addition to financial contributions, freedpeople helped build the school with their own hands.[59]

Yankee teachers were impressed with the freedpeople's unquenchable desire for knowledge and their assiduous support of their schools. Superintendent Briggs admitted that he came to North Carolina with "certainly no extravagant view of the Negro race — their capacity for improvement or ability to take care of themselves." But, he wrote, a year of work with freedpeople "has inspired me with unbounded hope." In their reports to sponsoring missionary societies, numerous teachers wrote glowingly of the perseverance, abilities, and progress of their students. Ellen M. Jones of North Woburn, Massachusetts, who taught in Washington, North Carolina, wrote to the *Freedmen's Record*, "I wish that some of these southern unbelievers who talk of the dull and stolid Negro, could see my evening scholars hastening to the schoolroom after a long, hard day's work," many of whom stayed for hours, "although some are so tired that they drop asleep in their chairs." She stressed that "their zeal and patience have quite astonished me." Teacher Helen Dodd confessed that "one feels incapable of ever dealing out enough to satisfy the longing, craving appetite for knowledge."[60]

Freedpeople embraced the Yankee teachers, as they did the soldiers who preceded them, as God-sent liberators. As soldiers had freed them from the bonds of slavery, teachers emancipated them from the "mental darkness," in the words of Frederick Douglass, imposed by slavemasters. Worcester County's Ella Roper reported how an elderly man, learning to read the Bible, "grew more and more earnest, till at last, one day, he dropped his book, and with uplifted hands cried out 'oh how you do let the light in!'" Another pupil told Worcester native Lucy Chase, who was visiting friends in New Bern on a break from teaching freedpeople in eastern Virginia, "The North Carolina folks have kept us in the dark, but you folks want to put some light into us."[61]

By bringing "light," the missionary teachers only reinforced the freedpeople's identification of Massachusetts with liberty. As the home of abolitionism, their liberators, and their schoolteachers, the Bay State soon took on mythical proportions to former slaves. A teacher of contrabands in New Bern related the "creed" of her students there: "1st, They believe in 'de good Lord,' who has heard their prayers; 2d, in Abraham Lincoln, who has broken their chains; 3d, In Massachusetts, and everything that comes from it." Similarly, former South Carolina slave Susie King Taylor, who served as a laundress for Thomas Wentworth Higginson's 1st South Carolina Volunteers (33rd U.S. Colored Troops) and migrated to Massachusetts after the war, explained, "Old Massachusetts" stood for "liberty in the full sense of the word."[62]

Taking their lessons to heart, freedpeople expected their teachers — especially those from Massachusetts — to live up to the principles that they imparted to their pupils. And when they did not, former slaves did not hesitate to take them to task. A controversy over separate schooling for whites and blacks in Beaufort reflected the willingness of ex-slaves to challenge their teachers when their actions fell short of the ideals they preached. The freedpeople's schools in Beaufort, sponsored by the American Missionary Association, welcomed poor white pupils, until they were, according to H. S. Beals, "subjects of persecution" and "driven away" by local citizens. Arguing that "we pursue our honest work till God should convert those, whom we cannot," Beals and his fellow teachers set up a separate, "prospering," white school. But African Americans, feeling excluded, responded angrily. The separate school created "much excitement and hard feeling among the colored people," according to teacher S. J. Whiton, who sympathized with them. Freedpeople, he explained, "said we were making distinctions between them and the whites," and as a result they demanded "a public declaration" from the AMA "that the school for white children, was open for the reception of colored children."[63]

Much to the chagrin of the black community, the AMA upheld the separate schools. In a letter published in the *Missionary*, the organization justified educational segregation. Freedpeople obtained a copy of the periodical, which "was passed round among those who could read, with the taunting remark, 'See there, they *pretend* to make no distinctions, but they *act* directly contrary.'" Local whites also seized on the controversy. According to Whiton, they mocked their "'Northern friends,'" who "came down here with loud professions of love" and were willing to "make greater distinctions than we would if we had free schools."[64]

In March 1867, the "Col'd. citizens of Beaufort" sent a memorial, signed by "ten and hundred more" to the American Missionary Association criticizing their "separate but equal" policy. What seemed especially galling to them was that "Mr. H. S. Beals claims he is from Mass and he is the man that is Building up the wall of Separation between the two races."[65]

Local blacks would not let the issue die. In a letter to AMA chief George Whipple, Hyman Thompson, one of the signers of the memorial to the AMA, wrote, "Mr Beals says he makes no distinction on account of color, yet he turns colored folks away from [the white school]." Beyond the insult to Beaufort's blacks, Thompson saw more insidious consequences, anticipating arguments against "separate but equal" schools that would be made in *Brown v. Board of Education of Topeka, Kansas*, nearly a hundred years later: "It makes the poor white children feel above the colored, and helps build up the old prejudice." He pleaded, "I wish you would open that school to colored children. The people will not be satisfied with anything short." Thompson concluded, "We believe you are our true friends, and mean to do right" but that the matter had been misrepresented. He added, after his signature, "pleas [sic] excuse my poor writing I am a new beginner."[66]

Despite the fact that the AMA would not budge on its policy, African Americans boldly stood up to their white benefactors. In the view of some teachers, they had learned their lessons too well. Having been delivered from slavery and encouraged by their mentors to demand equality, they refused to compromise on fundamental issues of justice. Especially outrageous in their eyes was their betrayal by a Massachusetts man, H. S. Beals, who erected walls of racial separation in postwar North Carolina. Unfortunately, this incident would hardly be the last in which the promises of Reconstruction and a truly reconstructed South would disappear before their eyes.

As teachers and their students labored in tandem to prepare for freedom — and even as they struggled over the meaning of freedom — strong emotional bonds grew between them. That many white southerners hoped for their failure only hardened their determination and strengthened their attachments. One teacher explained, "As an incentive to good conduct I try to impress upon my pupils the idea that they are closely watched by enemies who wish this experiment to fail." A comment in a letter from George W. Jenkins of Beaufort to his teacher Sarah Comings during her summer break in 1864 in New England summed up the affection that many freedpeople felt for their teachers: "We neve[r] will forget the kind teachers for bringing Light to our land, when she was dark as night." The teachers "came in spite of rebs. Their reward is not in this world, but a World to come."[67]

"A prophecy of the future!"

The year 1865 dawned cold and clear in New Bern as freedpeople celebrated the anniversary of their emancipation and, with their teachers, anticipated the end of the war. A "grand procession," led by the Union League and accompanied by the Brigade Band, featured scholars from nine of the city's schools who proudly wore badges and flew banners with the words "Freedom reigns To-day" and "Rally round the Flag." As the students passed Horace James's residence and the homes of their teachers, they broke out in cheers. A northern observer, overwhelmed by the sight, remarked, "What a commentary on the past and what a prophecy of the future!" He wished to photograph the scene, to enlighten "the skeptical Northerners who think the negro incapable of receiving our civilization." The observer continued, "Could the barbarous laws of North Carolina be enforced, no one could teach these people a letter of the alphabet with impunity; much less put into their possession that key of knowledge which is fast bringing them upon a level with their Saxon oppressors!" The day concluded with students of the Palmer School presenting a flag to the 1st North Carolina Heavy Artillery (Colored) and an afternoon and evening of orations and speeches. The witness concluded, "Thank God that to-day the year opens in which this terrible revolution, which has wrenched society from its civil moorings, and sacrificed upon the altar of Freedom the best blood of the nation, is likely to terminate with the more than compensating blessings of a true republic, and freedom for *all* its citizens, of whatever cast or color. . . . The voice of Justice . . . has at length, through the retributive sufferings of war, been heard and heeded."[68]

Soon Sherman's army cut a swath through the Carolinas and the Confederacy, as anticipated by the Emancipation Day revelers, crumbled. The *North Carolina Daily Times*, New Bern's newspaper, now controlled and edited by former Massachusetts soldiers, exclaimed, "The Old Flag More Than Welcome. . . . Welcome! Welcome!!" Sherman's March "delivers North Carolina from a thralldom which she has scorned from the beginning." With "North Carolina having become the theatre of war . . . being almost within hearing distance of the thunder of cannon and the roar of artillery," Worcester native and teacher Anne P. Merriam wrote, many "evidences of our proximity to the field of battle are continually accumulating." Makeshift hospitals accommodated the wounded soldiers arriving in packed railroad cars. In addition, rebel deserters "have been escaping and coming into our lines." One day 900 Confederate prisoners "were marched in a body through our street, and drawn up into a line just in front of the Teachers' Home." Black refugees of war poured into the city. "Our streets are literally thronged with colored refugees," reported Merriam. "They come in by hundreds, — men, women, and children." They are "frequently seen in families. The father ahead, bearing all his effects in a bag thrown over his shoulder, the mother behind, 'toting' the baby, and the ragged children in the rear." Most, she wrote, were "in a state of *appalling* destitution." Despite the demands of caring for the basic needs of the refugees, Merriam reaffirmed her commitment "to make education follow closely in the rear of our victorious armies; 'planting a schoolhouse behind every cannon,'" in order "to strengthen that element which, in North Carolina, as in all other hitherto slaveholding States, is destined to constitute the *base* of the social fabric, and to make 'the stone which the builders rejected to become the head of the corner.'"[69]

The Reverend Horace James echoed Merriam's commitment to education as the key to protecting the freedpeople's newly gained freedom. In his annual report for 1864, James made an appeal for more teachers, as "the tyranny under which they [ex-slaves] have been ground was nursed by ignorance." He wrote, "Send out teachers then, and especially female teachers. Let them follow in the track of every conquering army. Let them swarm over the savannahs of the South. Bring hither the surplus of females in New England greatly increased by the bereavements of war; for here it can essentially contribute to the national wealth and honor. . . . *The negro made free* is the great fact of this century; and its vouchers are a national debt of two thousand millions of dollars, and the graves of half a million of young men!"[70]

When news reached New Bern in April 1865 of Lee's surrender, "the whole city," according to the *North Carolina Daily Times*, "became aglow with enthusiasm and excitement." In addition to celebrations featuring an impromptu procession and the fandango, "the bars were opened, and an indiscriminate getting tight ensued."[71]

As Yankees and freedpeople celebrated, New Bern's white refugees slowly trickled back to the city from the interior along with Confederate soldiers "plodding wearily toward their homes," as one of the refugees put it, to face a world turned upside down. Refugee Mary Norcutt Bryan summed up the demoralization of the returning whites: "The War seemed to derange every part of society, death and carnage in the army, sickness and losses at home." Mrs. Frederick C. Roberts, a white New Bernian who fled to Warren County after the Yankee invasion in 1862, remembered, many years later, her return to the city in the fall of 1865. Arriving penniless, Roberts refused to call New Bern "home," as "I had no such place. Not even the ashes of my old home remained" since "the provident Yankees had gathered them up with bricks from chimneys, basement, wine cellar, and even from the pavement of the street." Even "the very earth had been carried off, so that where flowers and shrubs once grew was stagnant pond." In addition, her husband's law office "had been gutted" and only the bare walls remained. "All our household possessions were gone." Speaking for many like her, Roberts faced an uncertain future with steely resolve: "With bowed heads and aching hearts we began the battle of life again, this time without the sinews of war."[72]

As white southerners began to fight "the battle of life again," African Americans stood in the dawn of their freedom. Roberts remembered calling her slaves together to tell them "the tie was broken, we now had no longer any claim on them, and at that moment they were free to leave." Such scenes occurred repeatedly across eastern North Carolina and the South, characterized by a range of reactions and feelings. While Roberts recalled that her "servants" asked to stay on with the family another year, others immediately left the plantations and all that they symbolized, seeking a new beginning in towns and cities, such as New Bern, where, many felt, "freedom is free-er."[73]

Sherman's March, the end of the war, and emancipation precipitated a new influx of blacks to New Bern and Beaufort. "Their destitution," wrote William Briggs, "is extreme." Refugees deeply taxed the already stretched resources of the Superintendent of Negro Affairs. Several months before the war's end, Horace James noted in his 1865 annual report that overcrowding and dependence on the Federal government continued to plague both the contraband camps around New Bern and the Roanoke Island colony. James's vision for a self-supporting, permanent freedpeople's colony on Roanoke seemed especially jeopardized: most of the able-bodied men had been enlisted into the Federal army, first recruited in the summer of 1863, "converting [the colony] into an asylum for the wives and children of soldiers, and also for the aged and infirm." Unable to support themselves, these women and children remained dependent on the Federal government for food and clothing. Still, James remained optimistic about the abilities of former slaves to make a successful transition to freedom. Around 1,200 freedpeople, supporting roughly 5,000 family members, successfully worked cotton and turpentine plantations on lands abandoned by their former owners and now parceled out into individual plots. "When this process can be carried out *in extenso*," James wrote, "the 'negro question' need give political economists no more perplexity." The answer was simple: "Make them lords of the land, and everything else will naturally follow."[74]

Horace James's well-laid plans, experiments, and visions for creating a New South soon foundered on the rocks of military and political expediency. Congress established the Bureau of Freedmen, Refugees and Abandoned Lands in March 1865 to aid ex-slaves make the transition to freedom. It distributed food, clothing, and fuel to the destitute and oversaw "all subjects" relating to both freedpeople and white refugees of war. While granted expansive oversight, the Freedmen's Bureau was meant to be a temporary institution, to operate for one year only. In addition, Congress appropriated no money for its operation. The bureau had to rely on staff and funding from the War Department as well as the goodwill of northern aid societies.[75]

James agreed to stay on under the Freedmen's Bureau as superintendent of the Eastern District of North Carolina, which covered the territory within which he had labored since the spring of 1862. But the Federal government's indifference to eastern North Carolina's freedpeople damaged both his reputation and his plans. On Roanoke Island, the site of his ambitious, New England–style freedman's village — to which many Worcesterites had contributed financial support and industrial equipment — freedpeople angrily blamed James for the fact that they had never been paid for their labor on behalf of the Federal government. Some had toiled for as long as three years and had never been compensated, leading to terrible suffering for their families. Appealing to President Lincoln and Secretary of War Edwin Stanton, they also complained about being impressed into military service. Not only did lack of compensation poison the relationship between James and the Roanoke colonists, but it also undercut all of his efforts to make freedpeople self-supporting and independent.[76]

The final blow to James's experiment at Roanoke occurred when the Federal government, at President Johnson's behest, returned the colony's lands to the whites who had abandoned them in the spring of 1862. James even traveled to Washington and tried to convince the president that the colony's inhabitants owned the land based on the improvements they had made. But Johnson turned a deaf ear. Thrown off the land that they thought was theirs, Roanoke's freedpeople faced a final insult when the bureau decided to dispense with them by reducing their rations, forcing them to leave the island for employment on the mainland.[77]

With his Roanoke dream in shambles, James focused his attention on New Bern's freedpeople and their transition to freedom. The Trent River Settlement (known as James City by the end of the war in honor of the Worcester clergyman), one of three freedmen's villages in New Bern, was a model freedmen's village. James City contained 790 cabins, numerous stores, a blacksmith shop, a hospital, churches, and individual gardens. Whereas some freedpeople, especially skilled tradesmen, prospered in the new system of free labor, with some "becoming rich," according to James, many others, unable to find work and dependent on government rations, languished. The *North Carolina Daily Times* reported that many refugees who had fled to New Bern during the war were now too poor to move on and the local economy was too depressed to absorb them all. The war had shattered the area's economic base, leaving mountains of debt, declining property values, and eviscerated agricultural and manufacturing enterprises. In the summer of 1865, approximately 150 desperate freedpeople moved into "tents recently vacated by [Union] soldiers" at a local farm. The newspaper reported that "they are dying at a rate, we learn from reliable sources, of about a half dozen a day."[78]

"These are the times foretold by the Prophets,
'when a Nation shall be born in a day'"

Despite the desperate conditions faced by numerous freedpeople in the New Bern area, the city's African Americans wasted no time asserting themselves and defining the meaning of their freedom. African Americans established their own churches and organizations, such as fire companies. They also organized politically, throwing off their slave past and declaring their intentions to become full-fledged citizens of the United States. As armed black soldiers relieved a Massachusetts regiment and began guarding the city in June 1865, and New Bern's blacks celebrated the Fourth of July by marching through the streets with "a colored band and banners flying," black leaders organized for a statewide "colored convention" to be held in Raleigh in September. The circular advertising the New Bern meeting and encouraging freedmen in other parts of east Carolina to organize to send delegates from their towns and cities captured the exhilaration of political leaders: "These are the times foretold by the Prophets, 'when a Nation shall be born in a day,' the good time coming." Another circular clearly articulated their activist posture and the demand that African Americans play a central role in defining the meaning of their freedom. "Let us not, by our silence," the circular implored, "give our consent to remain where slavery left us, and where pro-slavery men would keep us, but let us appeal, protest, remonstrate and agitate, till justice and right be done unto us and every obstacle that impedes our progress is removed."[79]

New Bern's black political leadership knew that nothing short of organization and agitation would lead them to political equality. Even before the war's end, they began their fight for black suffrage; A. H. Galloway and John Goode had been part of a delegation of North Carolina blacks who had personally called upon President Lincoln in 1864 to argue for their political rights. The end of the Civil War only meant the start of the next campaign to be waged: the battle for political rights. In August 1865 New Bern's blacks met in Andrew Chapel to choose delegates to a statewide convention to be held in Raleigh in September 1865.[80]

New Bern's black leaders powerfully articulated their understanding of freedom and their place in postemancipation society. A. H. Galloway stated, "In the first place we want to be an educated people and an intelligent people," and he demanded the education of former slaves as the necessary first step to "enable us to discharge the duties of life as citizens." And "in the second place, we want to be allowed the privilege of voting." The vote, he argued, had been earned through the sacrifice that black men had made in the service of their country: "If the Negro knows how to use the cartridge box, he knows how to use the ballot box. If he is capable of handling the one, he is capable of handling the other." Galloway also rejected the title "freedman": "It is not right, sir; we are free men now, and should be called 'Freemen.'" Acknowledging inevitable white resistance to black political activism, Galloway nonetheless responded with a steely resolve: "We will agitate, and agitate, and agitate the question, sir, till we gain the freeman's privilege of voting and giving evidence in court."[81]

The assembled body then unanimously passed several resolutions supporting the convention in Raleigh and demanding "our earnest efforts by education, virtue, industry, and economy to qualify ourselves for the higher stations of life, and by appealing to those in authority to extend to us those rights and privileges of which we have heretofore been deprived." The meeting also addressed "the many atrocities committed upon our people in almost every section of the country" that "clearly demonstrate the immense prejudice and hatred on the part of our former owners toward us." Specifically, they condemned black codes, put into effect by whites across the South, that attempted to control blacks in a kind of pseudo-slavery: "The enforcement of the old code of slave laws that prohibit us from the privilege of schools, that deny us the right to control our families, that reject our testimony in courts of justice, that after keeping us at work without pay till their crops are laid by and then driving us off, refusing longer to give us food and shelter, the whipping, thumb-screwing and not infrequently murdering us in cold blood on the high-ways, in our judgment, comes far short of being a republican form of Government and needs to be remodeled." The assembly concluded, "[W]e shall insist for nothing more than what we conceive to be our rights as Freemen, and disclaim any intention of stirring up strife or engendering a feeling of hostility towards white citizens of the State."[82]

Notably, the New Bern assembly called upon Horace James to speak. The assembly's choice was a sign of the minister's influence and the respect and trust — despite controversies on Roanoke Island — that he had engendered among the area's blacks laboring in east Carolina. James gave the delegates "the greatest encouragement," advising them "to be prudent, zealous and determined." His speech also demonstrates that his new position as an officer of the Freedmen's Bureau for eastern North Carolina did not inhibit him from publicly espousing his radical political beliefs that blacks should be given the rights of full-fledged citizens. While he continued to work diligently to provide for the physical needs of freedpeople, he openly supported and encouraged New Bern's black political leaders in their next step, to fight for their political equality.[83]

Blacks' assertiveness, often encouraged by James as well as the area's missionary teachers, took other forms beyond formal political meetings and conventions, much to the chagrin of their white neighbors. Blacks opened their own schools with their own teachers. And they did not hesitate to take their grievances to the Freedmen's Bureau for adjudication, angering the area's whites, who felt that the bureau was biased against them. Social interactions provided the most visible and dramatic symbol of the new state of things. White residents claimed that blacks transgressed racial boundaries, that black men harassed white women and that black women forced white women off of the sidewalks. Blacks also infuriated whites when they gathered in the city to socialize.[84]

African Americans' deep aspiration for equality inevitably clashed with the obstinacy of whites who wished to maintain as much of the Old South as possible in postemancipation society. The *Daily Times*, edited by Yankees who were nonetheless supportive of white supremacy, warned blacks not to "mistake freedom of person with political independence" and "in a moment of exuberance and joy overstep the bounds of their true position." A "reaction will soon take place . . . and it is well that the colored people should gravely consider this fact." Whites regularly made it clear in more forceful ways that they would use any means necessary to maintain their superiority and to keep blacks in their place. Jesse Lassiter, "a wealthy citizen," shot and killed one of his former slaves, Jack, after Jack visited a relative on the Lassiter plantation. When Lassiter asserted "that all Negroes were ordered to return to their former masters" and demanded that he go to work, Jack refused and received a severe caning. When Jack reported this act of violence to the Freedmen's Bureau, Lassiter responded by shooting him, "three slugs entering his body, inflicting severe and dangerous wounds." In December 1865, rumors flew that blacks planned an insurrection on Christmas, and whites armed themselves in preparation for a race war. Blacks easily saw the purpose behind these trumped-up charges. As the Reverend J. W. Hood of New Bern's AME Zion Church wrote in a letter to the daily paper, his community "almost universally" agreed "that the rumors are the work of designing men, for the purpose of exciting hatred against the colored people." Whites were "especially displeased" that the government allowed discharged black soldiers to retain their sidearms. "The time has come," noted Hood, "when they could cane a colored man off the sidewalk with impunity." But now "they fear that it would not be quite safe to amuse themselves in that way while the colored man is permitted to have the means of self-defence."[85]

The attempts of African Americans to "shake off the bonds, drop the chains, and rise up in the dignity of men," as one local convention put it, would be continuously thwarted by local white violence and the often disastrous Reconstruction policies of the Federal government. As early as 1866, a northern observer noted that "civil order is generally restored, and the control of local matters has fallen in great measure into the hands of the white residents." While black men would get the right to vote and cast their first ballots in the fall of 1867, freedpeople soon found that a lack of economic independence undercut the power of the vote. President Johnson's overt hatred for the Freedmen's Bureau and his sympathy for southern whites punctured the dreams of political equality and economic independence that so many freedpeople harbored and their northern missionary allies encouraged. James's solution to the "negro question," to make African Americans the "lords of the land"—a plan readily embraced by freedpeople—foundered on the shoals of Reconstruction politics. Although James pleaded with the

Federal government to buy the land at James City so that freedpeople might purchase it in the future, Johnson instead did everything in his power to discredit the Freedmen's Bureau and, as he did elsewhere in the South, returned confiscated and abandoned lands to their white owners. In December 1865, James wrote in a letter to the *Congregationalist* that "abandoned plantations are being restored to amnestied rebels as fast as the orders can be issued." At that rate, "By January 1, 1866, there will probably not be a foot of them left." Even though James City had been a remarkable success — a colony of approximately 3,000 freedpeople, 90 percent of whom were self-supporting in the fall of 1865 — its once-proud and independent inhabitants soon found themselves reduced to dependency, working as farm laborers or sharecroppers for the white Evans family, who had owned the land before the war. Despite their "intense desire to own their own land" and their demonstrated ability to support themselves, African Americans found themselves once again dispossessed. James noted their disappointment and the fact that few freedmen willingly made labor contracts with white planters because, "to use their own expression, 'We have been fooled by them all our lives; and we do not mean to be fooled again.'"[86]

In response to President Johnson's attacks on the Freedmen's Bureau, agents began to wind down their activities, convinced that the bureau had no future. Bureau agents did all they could to reduce rations and clothing allowances in order to force freedpeople to return to plantations in the countryside and work once again for their former masters. As the Federal presence declined and local white authorities once again assumed control, the situation of black citizens worsened. Many complained of being cheated out of their wages or their portion of the crop but had little legal recourse in white-controlled courts. The waning Federal presence in New Bern and President Johnson's outright contempt for freedpeople provided carte blanche to whites who wished to return blacks to "their place." Violence against blacks heightened, and although Freedmen's Bureau officials requested aid from local authorities in protecting blacks and prosecuting cases of white on black violence, they generally refused to help. Within a shockingly short period of time, African Americans fell from the heady days of "the Prophets," standing at the brink of what seemed to be a future of unlimited possibility, to what must have seemed a halfway return to slavery.[87]

By 1868, the Freedmen's Bureau had closed its operations and left the state of North Carolina. Most northern missionary teachers vacated eastern North Carolina soon after. Horace James had left the state two years earlier, in 1866, after experimenting with "model plantations" as another answer for the "negro question." With labor relations poisoned by mistrust, James argued that the solution to the labor problem lay in the migration of northerners to the South: "Northern men, who know what free labor is, and who understand how to treat hired men, must lease or buy the southern lands and show the people here how the thing is done." With several partners, James did just that, leasing two plantations in Pitt County, outside of Washington, North Carolina, that he hoped to turn into profitable cotton plantations by employing approximately 200 freedmen at fair wages, providing them decent housing with garden plots, and educating them in a school run by a missionary teacher. He would prove that "while negroes will not work for their old masters or under the overseers who used to drive them to their tasks with the lash, they will cheerfully work for men who treat them like human beings, and pay them reasonable wages." Harassed by local whites, James got a taste of the kind of terror regularly visited upon blacks, leaving him convinced that should the "Freedmen's Bureau and the military garrison be withdrawn . . . there is no longer safety for negroes, or even for Yankee settlers." He believed that "the gangrene of slavery and dry rot of treason" had left public sentiment "without vitality, putrid, offensive" and could only be turned around with "an infusion of northern life" that could "set new forces in motion."[88]

James soon left the state — and the South for good — under a cloud of controversy. In a highly publicized case, he was accused of a myriad of offenses, including ordering the shooting of a black employee who was trying to escape an overseer, and of systematically mistreating his workers. The incident placed James in the crosshairs of a highly publicized investigation of the Freedmen's Bureau ordered by President Johnson. Generals James B. Steedman and J. S. Fullerton, who headed the investigation into alleged bureau malfeasance, featured the incident in an attempt to damage the reputation of the Freedmen's Bureau, blaming James for the shooting and charging him with conflict of interest for running a plantation that employed freedpeople while he was a bureau agent. James and several others were court-martialed. While a military commission ultimately exonerated James, this final chapter of his mission work, coupled with the destruction of both the Roanoke Island and James City colonies by the Federal government, must have been an especially bitter pill to swallow. Embittered, James returned to Massachusetts and a Congregationalist pulpit in Lowell. He died in Boylston, near Worcester, in 1875. At their next regimental reunion, in 1876, veterans of the 25th Massachusetts memorialized the chaplain, "whose voice and pen, and arm were ever ready in the cause of loyalty and human rights."[89]

DESPITE A BITTER FINAL CHAPTER, Horace James's labors established a lasting legacy. Amidst the wreckage of the failed experiments and political gamesmanship of Reconstruction, James and his compatriots forged a permanent connection between New Bern and its environs and Worcester, Massachusetts. Following the pathway established by the first contraband migrants who fled New Bern in the midst of the Stanly crisis, hundreds of east Carolina blacks would make their way to Massachusetts, capitalizing on the relationships they had made with Worcester soldiers and teachers. Others would come north from Virginia and several other states through similar military/missionary connections. As the South lurched into a future fraught with violence and uncertainty, many southern blacks, following the Bryant family, turned north as they sought a more certain freedom.

Chapter

4

A NEW PROMISE

OF FREEDOM AND DIGNITY

The morning of 4 July 1865 was greeted in Worcester with an anticipation and excitement not experienced in years. For the previous two months, towns-people — from schoolchildren to captains of industry — had prepared for a celebration worthy of the momentous Union victory. The city commemo-rated Independence Day "in a manner worthy of the new glories that cluster around the natal day of the republic from the trials, sacrifices, and victories of the last four years," wrote *Worcester Daily Spy* editor John Denison Baldwin. The celebration was "commensurate with the new promise of national free-dom and dignity assured by the overthrow of our country's enemies."[1]

Between 1862 and 1870, over 330 newly freed black Americans sought the new promise of national freedom and dignity in Worcester and Worcester County in the aftermath of the Civil War. This pioneer generation of migrants significantly augmented the county's African American population, from ap-proximately 769 to 1,136, and nearly doubled the city's black community, from approximately 272 to 524. Virginians and North Carolinians accounted for the lion's share of migrants, making up over 60 percent of those who came North. While the census shows that only 46 southern-born blacks, 35 of them from Maryland, lived in the city and county in 1860, as early as 1865, 128 southerners lived in the city and county, many hailing from states previously unrepresented in 1860. (See Appendix.)[2]

Black migration patterns to Worcester County mirrored the specific paths the county's troops and missionaries trod. Birth, marriage, and death records, unlike the census, often specified the towns where southern migrants were born, and these often were the same towns and cities Worcester soldiers and missionary teachers traversed. For North Carolina–born transplants, New Bern appears frequently, along with Kinston, Washington, Beaufort, and Elizabeth City — all within the orbit of the activities of the 25th and 51st Massachusetts regiments and Worcester's missionary teachers in the era of the Civil War. Likewise, Leesburg, Culpeper, Norfolk, and Fredericksburg natives replicate the trails of Worcester County regiments, including the 15th Massachusetts, as well as local missionary teachers, such as the Chase sisters, who went south to teach in Virginia. A handful of young Louisianans appeared in northern Worcester County, having returned with the 53rd Massachusetts, a regiment largely raised from the northern part of the county that served in Louisiana in 1863–64.[3]

Whereas many migrants made their way north during and immediately after the war in the company of local soldiers and missionaries, beginning in 1866, another group of migrants came to Worcester and Worcester County under the auspices of the Freedmen's Bureau. Inundated with unemployed and desperately poor ex-slaves who had made their way to the nation's capital, the Freedmen's Bureau in Washington established an employment agency to find jobs for them, providing transportation. Washington-area blacks, from Virginia and Maryland, as well as the District of Columbia, came to Worcester and Worcester County through this network, swelling the number of migrants from those locales.

Pioneer Civil War–era migrants soon established patterns of chain migration, wherein they rapidly facilitated the arrival of additional family members and friends. Moreover, they helped create a migration tradition for men and women from eastern North Carolina and Virginia that lasted at least through the end of the century. Notably, by 1870, southern-born Worcesterites made up almost half of the city's black adult population. Young and vigorous, they would leave their imprint on the city's black community.

An examination of Civil War–era migration not only sheds light on the bonds created between southern blacks and northern white soldiers and missionaries; it also demonstrates how their interactions profoundly shaped each group. In addition, the study of Civil War–era black migration to Worcester County affords a rare glimpse into the lives and strategies of freedpeople, of black men, women, and children, as they shaped and defined their own freedom. Their stories show the way in which former slaves negotiated a new world of freedom, the strategies they employed, and the decisions they made in an effort to ensure their liberty and that of family and friends whom they subsequently brought north.

Finally, a comparison of migrants who came north through personal connections with missionaries and military personnel with those who came through the Freedmen's Bureau suggests the importance of patronage networks in facilitating opportunities for southern migrants. For those with patrons — especially influential white patrons — who provided networks of employment and, in some cases, even access to higher education, Worcester was indeed a place of opportunity. But for southern black migrants who came through less personalized connections, Worcester proved to be less of a promised land.

"The black man has shed his blood for the Union;
he claims equal rights before the law"

As word of Lee's surrender reached Worcester in the first week of April 1865, its citizens, like their counterparts across the country, had little time to bask in the glow of Union victory. The city celebrated with "joy and hilarity." Bonfires blazed, a hundred guns fired on the common, and the steam whistles of Worcester's numerous industries mixed with the ringing bells of the city's schools and churches in an hour-long revelry. But only a week later, the shocking news of Lincoln's assassination deflated the city's euphoria. "The traitorous creatures of the desperate and dying slave power, insane with malignity," wrote editor Baldwin in the *Spy*, "have assassinated the man from whose clemency they had most to hope." Their actions "show all Christendom how little they deserve mercy, and how much the welfare of this nation requires their extermination." Bells that only a week before accompanied the joyful victory celebration now tolled in mourning for the slain president.[4]

On 19 April, the day of Lincoln's funeral, businesses closed and the entire city wore the trappings of mourning, with city hall, storefronts, private homes, and even horse cars shrouded in black. The bells of the city tolled once again between 2 and 3 P.M., marking the passage of the president's funeral cortege from the White House through the streets of Washington. In overflowing churches ministers solemnly struggled to give meaning to Lincoln's death. The Reverend Cutler of the Union Church on Front Street articulated the feelings shared by many: "President Lincoln has fallen a martyr to the principles of free government." His assassination was not merely the death of one man; it also represented "the attempted assassination of the loyal people of the land." Moreover, "the crime is not the product of one man's malignity" but "the culmination of cowardly treason . . . sown by the Evil One in the hearts of the southern oligarchy." The assassination, according to editor Baldwin, "wrought a great change in public opinion in regard to the treatment of the responsible actors in the rebellion after the war." Reminding his readers of the atrocities at Andersonville and Salisbury prisons and the massacre of black soldiers at Fort Pillow, Baldwin argued that the murder of the president derived from the same source, "the legitimate fruit of the conspiracy to overthrow the government, and secure the garden of the western continent for a perpetual slave market, and traffic in the bodies and souls of men."[5]

By the Fourth of July, the people of Worcester had begun to recover from the shock of President Lincoln's assassination, and they prepared once again to celebrate the end of the war in grand style. Decked out in bunting and flowers, the city physically reflected both the joys and the sorrows that its citizens felt in the aftermath of the war. Decorative arches, some forty feet high, loomed over the city, each conveying its own message. The "Triumphal Arch" across Main Street at Harrington Corner, under which the city's returning veterans would march, bore the names of once-obscure places — now household names — such as Antietam, New Bern, and Cold Harbor, where Worcester soldiers had fought and died for the Union. The "Memorial Arch" somberly honored those who did not return, and the "Rustic Arch," trimmed with evergreen, symbolized the steadfastness of residents and soldiers alike who endured the four long years of conflict.[6]

Civil War veterans kicked off the celebration on Independence Day morning. Led by the city marshal and a platoon of police and numerous city officials and accompanied by five bands, soldiers representing eleven regiments, a battalion, and the Naval Corps marched triumphantly through the city. While the 25th Massachusetts remained in service in the North Carolina Piedmont and would not be officially mustered out until the end of July, eighty veterans of the 25th represented the regiment, the largest single contingent. They proudly bore three Confederate flags captured at New Bern in March 1862. Wounded and infirm veterans from the Dale Hospital, a military hospital established in the city during the war, brought up the rear of the military contingent and served as a grim reminder of the human cost of the war. "Emblematic representations" throughout the parade declared, "Peace Through Victory," "Union," and "the Goddess of Liberty." The emancipation of four million slaves also received considerable emphasis. A banner emblazoned with the words "Pen and Sword" bore the image of Grant's sword and Lincoln's pen that, together, ended slavery once and for all in the United States.

The banner also displayed an image of Lincoln with a black child and the words "Forever Free."[7]

While the parade acknowledged the significance of emancipation, Worcester's black veterans seem to have been absent from the victory parade. While the *Spy* noted that the parade committee attempted to make "the celebration as complete as possible" and invitations had been sent "to all citizens of Worcester and vicinity" who had served or were still serving, African American units, such as the 54th and 55th Massachusetts and the 5th Massachusetts Cavalry, were not represented despite the fact that several dozen local men served in these units. Since these units remained deployed in the South, it is possible that mustered-out black soldiers marched in a catchall group of "unattached companies and members of other regiments." But their low or absent profile may have reflected some ambivalence on the part of white Worcesterites about the place of African Americans in postwar Worcester.[8]

An afternoon parade, featuring the city's numerous industries and business concerns, provided the opportunity for one of Worcester's African Americans to make a bold statement about black rights. Stretching two and a half miles, the parade included major firms, such as wire manufacturer Washburn & Moen, as well as smaller tradesmen and artisans, including a handful of black businessmen, who showcased their products and ventures. Former slave Isaac Mason advertised his house and carpet cleaning business and Maryland migrant J. G. Mowbray "displayed his willingness to attend to orders for wall papering, &tc." But Maryland-born abolitionist Gilbert Walker drew the most attention, seeking to promote much more than his barbershop. Walker, who served as a recruiter for the 54th Massachusetts regiment in 1863, stood on a wagon pulled by a team of horses as he demonstrated his trade by cutting a little girl's hair. A banner flew overhead: "The black man has shed his blood for the Union; he claims equal rights before the law."[9]

While only a small part of the massive victory parade, Walker's banner served notice to the people of Worcester that the war was indeed a watershed. The conflict represented a pivotal moment that had indelibly altered the nation, with implications far beyond the emancipation of four million southern blacks. Having fought and died for the Union, black Americans now demanded full-fledged citizenship. Just a few months earlier, only days before the war ended, Frederick Douglass visited the city and spoke at Mechanic's Hall. There he powerfully articulated a "bold, logical, and eloquent statement" regarding black civil rights before an enthusiastic audience. While the editor of the *Spy* enthusiastically supported Douglass's arguments, he self-righteously hoped that Douglass's message would be "presented in states whose laws are still at fault on this subject," smugly implying that Massachusetts had adequately dealt with problems of racial inequality. Worcester's black citizens likely drew different conclusions, taking heart in Douglass's daring demands. Like Gilbert Walker, they stood ready to apply them locally as well as nationally.[10]

"Gone North"

As the Independence Day victory parade wended its way through the streets of Worcester, William Bryant, the city's original "contraband," may have reflected on the remarkable changes in his life since arriving in Worcester three years earlier. Fearful of being returned to his master amidst the chaos of the Stanly regime, William had headed north through his military connections to Worcester, seeking a more secure freedom. From the very beginning, loosed from the bonds of slavery, he and his wife, Mary, actively defined the meaning of their freedom. Only months after finding a job and home, he and Mary married, a right denied them in slavery, a step that defined, secured, and celebrated their status as free people. A fugitive in 1862, William, by the time the war ended, had established his own housecleaning business. Reflecting his growing status in the city, in 1865, William and Mary Bryant left the house rented to them by their original patron, Isaac Mason, on Union Street and rented a house at 24 Wilmot Street. While their original home in Worcester, next to Isaac Mason, provided supportive southern neighbors, the street was hemmed in by a railroad yard, a lumberyard, and machine shops. On Wilmot Street, the Bryants situated themselves in a more bucolic setting, their house backing up to hospital grounds and a reservoir. Moreover, they now lived only several streets away from prominent community leaders such as Gilbert Walker.[11]

A year after the war ended, Bryant was successful enough to pay for a listing in the Worcester city directory. By 1867 — unlike Isaac Mason, the only other carpet and house cleaner in the directory — Bryant listed a separate business address: a prime location at 248 Main Street. By 1869, he advertised in the *Spy*, another indication of his growing business success; only seven years before, the newspaper had beseeched Worcester citizens to aid the fleeing Bryant. In the advertisement he promised "Windows Washed, Carpets Cleaned, and General Housework Done in the Best Manner." Another testament to his achievement was that William's business was lucrative enough to support the Bryant family without Mary working outside of the home.[12]

While Isaac Mason and other members of the city's black community provided invaluable support in establishing the Bryant family, Worcester's blacks were too few in number to secure Bryant's success in the cleaning business. To establish his own business on Main Street, Bryant needed to develop a large and dependable white clientele. Sympathetic whites, aware of Bryant's story and his service to the Union army, may have patronized him and helped him establish a successful business.

William and Mary Bryant also served as patrons for the black community. As soon as they fashioned a foothold in Worcester, they assisted additional family members in coming north, helping craft the first links of chain migration from New Bern to Worcester. By the end of the Civil War, a second Bryant family, Christopher, Harriet, and Eliza Bryant, appears in the 1865 state census, residing near William and Mary Bryant. Soon after the war, Julia Ann Bryant of New Bern, William's younger sister, resided in Worcester, and in 1868 she married a fellow southern migrant, Henry Johnson of Mississippi. Bryant employed his brother-in-law in his cleaning business.[13]

That family members joined William and Mary in the North attests to the Bryants' success in Worcester. Family ties and economic opportunity combined to pull additional New Bern Bryants north to Worcester. Political instability, with the resurgence of white conservative rule at the end of 1865, and postwar economic problems likely provided a push from North Carolina. New Bern, a magnet for east Carolina freedpeople since the Yankee invasion in 1862, offered little economically for black workers. An excess of unskilled laborers and a dearth of jobs made steady employment almost impossible.[14]

Against this backdrop, William and Mary Bryant's success in Worcester must have stood out in sharp relief to their Carolina kin. By 1870, an extended Bryant family of ten people made Worcester their home. The city would become the long-term home of Julia Ann Bryant Johnson and her family, which blossomed to four children by 1880. Christopher and Harriet Bryant and their growing family also planted roots in Worcester.[15]

William and Mary Bryant did not limit their help to family. Just as Robert H. Johnson and Isaac Mason had aided them in their early years in Worcester, the Bryants perpetuated a tradition of aid to fellow southerners. In 1869, Civil War veteran Allen Parker of Chowan County, North Carolina, resided in the Bryant household. After his escape with three fellow slaves to a Yankee gunboat in August 1862, he immediately joined the Union navy as a landsman and served aboard the USS *Norcum* and the USS *Albemarle*. Discharged in New Bern in December 1864, he moved on to Beaufort, where he worked in a sawmill. But like many of his compatriots, Parker soon turned his sights northward. Serving as a steward aboard a Portland, Maine, vessel that transported timber, Parker disembarked in Portland and, as he noted, never "went south since." After spending a year with a cousin in New Haven, Connecticut, Parker "went to various places, staying but a short time in each" until he "finally drifted to Worcester, where," he said, "I lived most of the time for the past thirty years."[16]

Parker never explained why he "drifted" to Worcester. But it is likely that military and missionary networks that crisscrossed eastern North Carolina influenced his decision. Moreover, in Worcester he immediately found fellow eastern North Carolina migrants who helped find him work and a place to live. The 1869 city directory listed him as a laborer boarding at 24 Wilmot Street, the home of William and Mary Bryant. William Bryant likely employed Parker in his carpet cleaning business. In March 1869, Parker placed a "Card" in the Worcester Daily Spy that exclaimed: "Allen Parker holds himself in readiness to do housecleaning, washing windows, cleaning carpets, and all kinds of chores. Terms reasonable, Orders may be left at the Drug Store, cor. Main and Pleasant sts." After living in Worcester several years, Parker resided in several other New England cities, including New Haven, Meriden, and Waterbury, Connecticut, as well as Amherst, Massachusetts. But he returned to Worcester in 1888 and lived in the city until his death in 1906.[17]

The Bryants aided additional southern migrants in other ways. An indication of the family's growing prominence and financial stability, in 1867 William loaned $150 to Lacy and Ruth Liel to purchase a house and property near the Adriatic Mills. Lacy Liel was a Virginian who came to Worcester during or immediately after the war and worked as a waiter in the city. Bryant's role as a moneylender in the black community proved especially crucial to a young migrant couple such as the Liels who otherwise might have had difficulty financing a house.[18]

William and Mary Bryant, however, left the city under a cloud of scandal in 1870. In 1869, the Bryants' neighbor and fellow North Carolina migrant Lunsford Lane, who had returned from his school-building efforts in eastern North Carolina after the Civil War, accused William of setting his house on fire. Ultimately, a municipal court found William Bryant not guilty for lack of evidence. Because the court records no longer exist, it is impossible to know the nature of Lane's accusations against Bryant and whether they represented more than personal tensions between the two families.[19]

Despite the unceremonious departure of Worcester's pioneer "contraband family," the Bryants had nonetheless broken new paths of migration from eastern North Carolina to Worcester in the era of the Civil War. As early as March 1865 a veteran Yankee schoolteacher noted the migration of her students northward. Writing that "there is much sadness connected with our work" at the Trent River (James City) Camp outside of New Bern, she noted that "all our smartest and most advanced students have settled in New Bern, Beaufort, or gone North, their bright faces and ready answers we miss."[20]

The state census for 1865, taken in June of that year, recorded a number of young North Carolinians residing in the homes of veterans or in hometowns of soldiers who fought in eastern North Carolina. For example, Henry Jones, a seventeen-year-old from North Carolina, lived with the Harrington family in Paxton, just outside of Worcester. Samuel Harrington served as an officer in the 25th Massachusetts and mustered out as a lieutenant colonel in July 1865. Jones likely accompanied Harrington home to Paxton when the war ended. Jane Waples traveled with General and Mrs. A. B. R. Sprague to Worcester at the end of the war. Born in New Bern in 1836, Waples gained her freedom after the Burnside invasion in the spring of 1862 and found employment with Sprague, then an officer in the 25th Massachusetts and later commander of the 51st Massachusetts, which also spent considerable time in the New Bern area. Sprague's wife, Elizabeth, managed to join her husband in New Bern, and Waples worked for the couple while the colonel was stationed there and apparently accompanied them through the remainder of the war. Twenty-five-year-old Cato Brooks, a native of New Bern, lived in the household of the Alonzo Goodrich family in Fitchburg, where he worked as a laborer. Thirteen-year-old Samuel Toombs of North Carolina lived in the Searles household in Templeton, and New Bern native William Beckton, fifteen, resided on the Robertson farm in Sterling. By 1870, approximately seventy North Carolinians — almost all of them from New Bern and vicinity — had migrated to Worcester County.[21]

Black Virginians, along with a handful of Louisianans, expanded the wartime migration. Like their Carolina counterparts, many of them, too, came north through the same kinds of military networks that brought North Carolinians to Worcester, notably through their connections with the 15th and 53rd Massachusetts regiments, which saw service in Virginia and Louisiana, respectively.

Their stories are variations on the themes revealed in the stories of the North Carolina migrants: contrabands of war, many of them found their freedom with sympathetic Worcester County units. Some forged close personal bonds with white soldiers — most often officers — through outstanding wartime service. Exchanging that service for a new beginning in the North, they accompanied these officers back to Worcester County at the end of the war. Soldiers, their families, and sometimes whole communities — many with a tradition of abolitionist activity — served as patrons to migrants. For some, as in the case of William Bryant, their wartime service provided a fund of goodwill upon which they drew to establish themselves in the North.

Midwestern soldiers also played a key role in protecting refugee slaves in the South and helping them relocate to the North. But their efforts yielded sharply different results. Instead of generating public support for the plight of the contrabands, "official and public support evaporated" in the wake of relocation efforts, notes Leslie Schwalm, and "aroused fears of white Midwesterners that Federal authorities would unleash a flood of black migrants in their region." Not only were black migrants targeted in angry public tirades, but their white patrons also suffered abuse. By contrast, Worcester's abolitionist tradition, coupled with the small scale of migration, helped engender support that greatly benefited the first migrants to the city and county.[22]

Contraband David Porter Allen earned the indebtedness of an entire Worcester County community for his aid to Francis Amasa Walker. Walker would go on to a distinguished postwar career as superintendent of the census, commissioner of Indian Affairs, and the third president of the Massachusetts Institute of Technology. Originally a sergeant major in the 15th Massachusetts, Walker ultimately rose to the rank of brevet brigadier general as a staff officer of the Army of the Potomac. Allen was a seventeen-year-old slave on the plantation of William Cole, near Harrison's Landing, Virginia, when the Yankees came in the early spring of 1862. Part of McClellan's massive Peninsular campaign, the 15th Massachusetts helped shake the foundations of slavery in southeastern Virginia.[23]

As McClellan's vast army, overcome by heavy rains, disease, and Confederate resistance, failed in its attempts to capture Richmond, it fell back to Harrison's Landing. David Allen decided that the time was right to flee. Absconding to the Union army with several other slaves from the Cole plantation, he found refuge with the 15th Massachusetts. Sergeant Major Walker hired Allen as his servant, beginning a long journey that would ultimately take Allen to Walker's hometown before the end of the war.[24]

Allen accompanied Walker in nearly every step of his distinguished military career. From the Peninsular campaign to the Second Bull Run, Antietam, and Fredericksburg, Allen assisted Walker as his servant in the field. Promoted to major in August 1862, Walker left the 15th in October to serve on the staff of the Second Army Corps. In May 1863, Walker, by that time promoted to lieutenant colonel, suffered severe wounds at Chancellorsville and went home to Massachusetts to recover for several months, accompanied by Allen. A little over a year later, David Allen returned to North Brookfield under different circumstances. In August 1864, at Reames Station, Virginia, Confederates captured Walker and held him prisoner. Allen dutifully collected all of Walker's belongings and made his way to the Walker family home in North Brookfield.[25]

Allen's devotion to Walker and his contribution to the Union cause deeply moved the Walker family and many of their friends and neighbors in North Brookfield. The small town had been deeply touched by the Civil War, suffering the devastating loss of many of its young men at the battle of Antietam. Moreover, North Brookfield also boasted a deep reform and antislavery tradition, led by Francis Walker's parents, Amasa and Hannah. "With the Walkers," family friend George Frisbie Hoar once remarked, "reform was chronic." In 1853, the Walkers had created a huge rift in the town by walking out of the Congregational church, along with 177 other antislavery church members, in protest of a "gag rule" imposed by congregant and shoe manufacturer Tyler Batcheller. Batcheller, who manufactured cheap slave brogans in the town, insisted that slavery not be discussed in the church. After the walkout, the Walkers helped found an antislavery church directly across the street, later served by the Reverend William H. Beecher, brother of Harriet Beecher Stowe. "Feeling a lively interest in one who had served their friend so faithfully," Walker's parents took Allen into their household, taught him to read and write, and enrolled him in the North Brookfield public schools. Allen then worked as a servant in the home of S. S. Edmands, next door to the Walkers, for at least six years.[26]

Former slave Robert Morse also earned the respect of North Brookfield's citizens. Born a slave in Louisa County, Virginia, Morse ran away to the 36th Massachusetts in search of his freedom. Dr. Warren Tyler of North Brookfield, a surgeon in the 36th, which saw extensive service in Virginia, hired him as his personal servant. Finding Morse "a bright and gentlemanly chap," Dr. Tyler "became so attached to him" that he brought Morse along with him when he returned to North Brookfield. Residing several years with Amasa and Hannah Walker, next door to David Allen, Morse worked for Dr. Tyler for several years and later found employment as a fireman for the Batcheller shoe factory in North Brookfield.[27]

Isaiah Allen was another Virginia migrant whose service in the war earned him the gratitude of local citizens who helped him settle in the city of Worcester. As noted previously, Allen was a thirty-one-year-old slave in Leesburg, Virginia, when the 15th Massachusetts arrived in Poolesville, Maryland, in 1861. Armed only with his faith in the Union soldiers, he escaped across the river on Christmas Eve, 1861, and found refuge with the Worcester County regiment.[28]

While caring for horses in the camp, Allen caught the eye of Lieutenant Thomas Spurr. A member of a prominent Worcester family, the Harvard-educated lawyer, like many of his fellow officers, was on the lookout for blacks to hire as personal servants. Around January 1862, Isaiah Allen began assisting Spurr, who assigned him a variety of duties. For example, he scoured the countryside for fresh food for the officer's dinner table and carried Spurr's blanket on long marches.

Spurr's early descriptions of Allen's service reflect a distant, aloof paternalism. He referred to Allen as "My Nig," sounding more like a possessive southern master than a Yankee liberator.[29] But the relationship between Allen and Spurr deepened during the war and ultimately led to Allen's relocation to Worcester. In September 1862, the 15th Massachusetts participated in the battle of Antietam, the bloodiest single day of fighting in the Civil War. On the morning of 17 September, in less than twenty minutes of fighting, more than half of the unit was killed, earning the 15th terrible distinction of losing the largest number of troops of any regiment — Union or Confederate — in the carnage of that day.[30]

Among the casualties was Thomas Jefferson Spurr. After the fighting ended, Spurr was among the missing, and after a frantic search by his childhood friend Dr. S. Foster Haven Jr., he was found in a farmyard near the battlefield. Spurr's thigh had been shattered by a minié ball.[31]

Allen helped Haven and others carry Spurr from the farmyard and assisted in transporting him to a private home in Hagerstown, where, it soon became clear, that he would not survive his wound. His mother, Mary Spurr of Worcester, along with his brother-in-law, antislavery politician and attorney George Frisbie Hoar, rushed to his bedside to comfort the dying young man. Isaiah Allen also participated in the death watch. According to Hoar, who scribbled notes describing Spurr's final hours, the lieutenant "called for his man Isaiah and said, 'Isey, I hope I have not been unreasonable with you. I've tried not to be.'" Allen responded, "'You've always been mighty good to me, Sir, you've always been mighty good to me.'" Spurr then requested that Allen be given $100 and his silver watch. He then made a final request: "'I should like to have Isey ride in the car with the coffin so that it should not be roughly handled.'"[32]

Isaiah Allen accompanied Spurr's body back to Worcester. On the stormy day of 2 October, "while the heavens were weeping as in sympathy," in the words of Rev. Alonzo Hill of the First Unitarian Church, crowds thronged the home of George Frisbie Hoar to say their farewells. While Hill offered words of comfort, Isaiah Allen provided the most memorable and poignant image of the day. According to Hill, Spurr's "humble friend . . . stood like a bronze statue beside the coffin through the whole service, while the tears silently stole down his cheeks. Set to guard the sacred relics, he did not leave them, from the hour of quitting at Hagerstown, until they were deposited in the place of their rest — the beautiful cemetery in Worcester."[33]

For Worcesterites grappling with the meaning of the war and the loss of their promising young men, Allen's touching vigil provided a powerful symbol. After Spurr's funeral service, several Worcesterites, including Henry W. Miller, Albert Tolman, and John H. Brooks, approached George Frisbie Hoar "to ascertain the ability of Allen" for employment, according to an account left by Brooks's son. The fact that all three men engaged in iron-working suggests that Allen already had some expertise in this field. Brooks, a local farmer and blacksmith, "took him in his shop," recalled his son, where "he proved to be a good horse shoer and iron worker." The Brooks family took a deep interest in Allen. Daughter Alice taught him to read and write, and he continued to work for the Brooks family until 1863.[34]

Inspired by the enlistment of Brooks's son, Lewis, in the 36th Massachusetts Infantry, Allen joined the Union army in 1863, as soon as the Federal government allowed blacks to enlist. The former slave explained to the family that "as the white men were fighting for his race, he must go too and do his part." Allen enlisted in the 2nd North Carolina Colored Infantry (later renamed the 36th U.S. Colored Troops) in New Bern. The 1st and 2nd North Carolina were part of Colonel E. A. Wild's "African Brigade," raised by the Bostonian in the summer of 1863 — and supported by numerous Massachusetts abolitionists, including Governor John Andrew — and they represented one of the first attempts authorized by the Federal government to enlist former slaves into the Union army. Although the regiments drew most of their recruits from New Bern and other towns and counties under Union control, nearly half of the 2nd consisted of former slaves from Virginia. Allen's decision to join a North Carolina unit reflected the strong ties between his adopted city of Worcester and eastern North Carolina, established by Horace James and the 25th Massachusetts. The Massachusetts and Worcester connections to the New Bern area likely played a part in influencing Allen to join this regiment.[35]

After serving a full three years as a blacksmith in the Union army, Allen returned to New Bern, North Carolina, the city still swarming with Worces-

Isaiah Allen in 1900, when veterans of the 15th Massachusetts regiment visited him in Leesburg, Virginia. This photo appeared in a commemorative booklet about the veterans' excursion. Courtesy of the Worcester Historical Museum.

terites. Writing to George Frisbie Hoar and his family in Worcester in January 1868, Allen appealed for money to start a shingle business with black compatriots. Self-employment, he explained, was a necessity, for "if we work we cant get our pay," as white employers simply refused to pay their black employees. A month later, writing from the Trent River Camp, originally founded by Horace James, Allen explained that he planned on returning to Worcester, "but there is so much suffering here that I feel it [my] duty to try to help them what I can."[36]

Allen soon returned to Worcester, where he resumed employment with the Brooks family, even nursing family members during a typhoid fever outbreak in 1871. That same year, veterans of the 15th Massachusetts honored Allen by inviting him to their annual reunion. The *Spy* noted that "Isaiah, the faithful friend of Lieutenant Spurr, was providentially present" and "added not a little to the meeting by his quaint account of escape from slavery from Leesburg to Poolesville, and subsequent service as a soldier in Texas."[37]

In addition to the North Carolinians and Virginians who dominated the first wave of Civil War–era migrants who came through military connections, ten young Louisianans appeared in Worcester County in the immediate aftermath of the war. Adopted by members of the 53rd Massachusetts, a nine-month unit organized in mid-1862 and largely made up of men from northern Worcester County, these contrabands connected with members of the 53rd during the Teche and Port Hudson expeditions in the spring and summer of 1863. As Union troops traversed southeastern Louisiana, slaves flocked to them, many offering their aid to the expedition. Henry Willis of the 53rd remembered "friendly negroes" who "swarmed out from every plantation," offering fresh food and delicacies from their abandoned plantations to the Massachusetts soldiers. The 53rd soon "accumulated a motley array of camp followers," contrabands who "were only too ready to go with us." Aiding the Yankees by carrying belongings, cooking and doing laundry, and even confiscating cotton bales from local plantations, an estimated 8,000 runaway slaves accompanied the "Army of the Teche," which extended over five miles. In the words of historian C. Peter Ripley, the runaways "comprised an army of liberation by their example."[38]

One contraband, known as "Opelousas Tommy," likely joined up with the 53rd Massachusetts in Opelousas, Louisiana, which Yankees raided in the spring of 1863. Tommy worked as "the surgeon's boy," the personal servant of Dr. William Barrett of Fitchburg. A camp favorite, fourteen-year-old Tommy accompanied Barrett back to Fitchburg after the 53rd mustered out of service in August 1863. According to the regimental history, Tommy "lived in Fitchburg and Princeton." The 1865 Massachusetts census lists a Thomas E. Littler, aged fourteen, born in Louisiana, living in Westminster, a town adjacent to Fitchburg, and residing in the household of Amos Miller and his wife. According to Henry Willis, Tommy "was afterwards a servant in Young's Hotel, Boston, and the last the writer knew of him he was ministering to the comfort of Harvard students at Memorial Hall, Cambridge."[39]

In the late summer of 1863, Colonel John W. Kimball of Fitchburg, who headed the 53rd regiment, "brought home a tall, full grown, athletic negro named John Lewis," age twenty-five, who, the regimental historian noted, had "come to us on the march." By 1865, Lewis lived in the city of Worcester, where he worked as a laborer. By 1880, he resided in North Brookfield with a small group of black Virginians; he worked as a barber and lived with his Irish immigrant wife.[40]

A twelve-year-old Louisianan, with the unlikely name of Spencer Contraband, also returned to Worcester County with a Civil War surgeon, Dr. Samuel C. Hartwell of Southbridge. Hartwell served in the 38th Massachusetts, which, with the 53rd Massachusetts, participated in the Louisiana expeditions of 1862 and 1863. The boy resided in Hartwell's home in 1865. Several other young Louisianans appeared in Worcester County by 1865, all in northern towns with large representations in the 53rd Massachusetts. The towns of Phillipston, Lunenberg, and Sterling each quartered a single young man, and Athol claimed two.[41]

The stories of "Opelousas Tommy," Spencer Contraband, and their many compatriots all point to the fact that the pioneer generation of wartime migrants to Massachusetts was overwhelmingly young, male, and unmarried. In sharp contrast to midwestern migrants in the same period, the majority of whom were women and children, approximately 80 percent of southern-born residents in Worcester and Worcester County in 1865 were in their teens and twenties and nearly all were single and childless. These war migrants to New England had been touched directly by the war at a stage in their lives when, without family obligations, migration was less complicated and offered a chance to gain security in an extremely uncertain time. Many were probably either orphans or "displaced persons," that is, separated from their families by the war or slavery. While soldiers also hired contraband women as servants in the field, returning to Worcester County accompanied by a black female would have been considered scandalous. Young black males who accompanied soldiers back to Worcester County were far more acceptable to spouses and families of soldiers. As many initially lived in the households of their military benefactors, black males did not complicate domestic relations as females might have. One of the few females who migrated through military connections, Jane Waples, provides insight into the dynamic of gender and migration. Waples accompanied General and Mrs. Sprague back to Worcester after the war. Having the approval of Mrs. Sprague, her move to the city would not have elicited scandal or shock in the community.[42]

That most wartime migrants were young men, rather than women and children, likely shaped a more positive public response in another important way. As able-bodied young men, they would have been viewed as valuable contributors to the local economy still suffering from wartime labor shortages. By contrast, despite the fact that many black female migrants to the Midwest ended up working in the fields due to the absence of white laborers, the mass relocation of women and children likely raised fears that they would become dependent wards of the state.

Migration through military connections sometimes occurred a decade after the end of the war and, unlike the first phase of migration, included married couples. Joseph and Nellie Fowle's move to Worcester, around 1875, attests to the enduring nature of these military networks and the longevity of wartime relationships. Originally a slave from Plymouth, North Carolina, Fowle got to know many members of the 25th Massachusetts regiment when he operated a hotel in Washington, North Carolina, a "junior Parker House," in the words of J. Waldo Denny of Worcester, an officer in the unit. In addition to offering refreshment for Massachusetts soldiers, Fowle played a much more serious role in the war, serving as a spy for the Union army. According to Denny, Fowle "was highly esteemed by General Foster." After the war, Fowle aided Worcester's missionary teachers in their efforts to educate freedpeople. A letter to the *Freedmen's Record* in April 1866 reported that "one of our good colored friends, Joseph Fowle, . . . has built a nice little house" for four teachers, including Worcester's Anne Merriam. The house contained "four rooms, that are tight and warm, — quite an uncommon thing in this country." Another teacher reported additional support from Fowle to the *National Freedman*, noting that the donation "is a very large one for his income."[43]

The Fowles lived in New Bern for approximately ten years after the war, with Joseph working as a "huckster" and his wife, Nellie, employed as a schoolteacher and seamstress. But by 1875, they moved north to Worcester, where Joseph first worked as a laborer and then ran a fruit stand on Front Street. The couple separated in 1879, and Joseph moved to Boston, where he worked as a servant. Nellie remained in Worcester and labored as a laundress.[44]

The Fowles's story demonstrates how military and missionary networks reinforced each other. By 1870, Worcester County missionary teachers to the South broadened and deepened military networks of migration. Following in the wake of local units, some of the young men and women who taught freedpeople in the South, like the soldiers before them, developed personal relationships with their black students as they shared similar goals and common hardships. And, like the soldiers, missionary teachers came to symbolize Massachusetts in the eyes of freedpeople, serving as ambassadors for the Bay State. "Free Massachusetts" loomed large in their imaginations as a destination offering freedom and sympathetic support. Seeking the promise of Massachusetts, some freedpeople accompanied their teachers back to Worcester County at the end of their service in the South. Like their military counterparts, teachers fostered sponsorship of former slaves in New England.

Veteran Yankee missionary teacher Sarah Chase became a patron to several black Virginia couples who migrated to Worcester with her when she completed her service. With her sister Lucy, Chase taught for three years in the Norfolk area during the war and served schools in Georgia and South Carolina afterward. Stirred by the plight of freedpeople, who asked only for the opportunity to earn a living, the Chase sisters became outspoken ad-

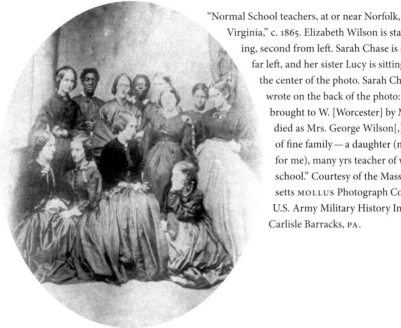

"Normal School teachers, at or near Norfolk, Virginia," c. 1865. Elizabeth Wilson is standing, second from left. Sarah Chase is sitting, far left, and her sister Lucy is sitting in the center of the photo. Sarah Chase wrote on the back of the photo: "Betty brought to W. [Worcester] by Me — died as Mrs. George Wilson[,] head of fine family — a daughter (named for me), many yrs teacher of white school." Courtesy of the Massachusetts MOLLUS Photograph Collection, U.S. Army Military History Institute, Carlisle Barracks, PA.

vocates for their employment and implored freedmen's aid societies to help find them work. In May 1865, Sarah Chase, writing to the *Freedmen's Record* from Richmond, wrote of "a large number of young women, and women with families, whose husbands are 'de Lord only knows where.'" These women "*will* not beg," Chase wrote, and wished only to support themselves: "I continually hear from those imploring 'for something, missus, — any thing, to be earning a little something,' and I find very many of them are living *miserably*." She pleaded, "Cannot your society furnish work to these?"[45]

In 1866, suffering from ill health, Sarah Chase returned to Worcester with several black Virginians. George and Elizabeth Wilson of Norfolk were one of several couples who accompanied Chase back to Worcester. Several other Norfolk migrants appeared in Worcester after the Civil War, including Daniel Edwards and Alex Wilkinson.[46]

National freedmen's aid associations also facilitated local migration through missionary networks. In 1864, Daniel Tainter, a machinery manufacturer in Worcester, opened his home to two freedpeople, Joseph Perkins, a native of New Bern, and Jane Watts. Tainter's sister-in-law, Helen A. Simmons, a volunteer teacher awaiting assignment in the South, wrote to her Sunday school class about her stay in Tainter's household. Her brother-in-law, she wrote, played an active part in aiding the National Freedman's Relief Association, which was "doing all in their power to touch the emancipated slaves . . . by finding good homes for them in families."[47]

In Worcester, additional white abolitionists served as patrons to former slaves seeking a new start in the North. Abolitionism and freedmen's relief went hand in hand, and when abolitionists finally witnessed the end of slavery, many came to the aid of freedpeople. Abby Kelley and Stephen Foster, nationally known white abolitionists, employed and housed George Hollister Wiggins, a young migrant from New Bern. Wiggins worked as a farm laborer on the Foster farm and ultimately settled in Worcester, where he married a fellow southern migrant and raised a family. Once a stop on the Underground Railroad, the Foster farm continued to serve as a passage to a new life in the North after emancipation.[48]

The city's black abolitionists, like their white counterparts, served as benefactors, demonstrating an ongoing commitment to southern blacks that went beyond emancipation. As it had done for the Bryants, the first North Carolina contrabands to settle in Worcester, Worcester's black community embraced subsequent wartime migrants and in many cases found them employment. Isaac and Anna Mason continued to aid former slaves as they had aided the Bryants, finding room in their large, extended household for several migrants. Black activist and barber Gilbert Walker and his wife, Sarah, opened their home to numerous southern newcomers, including Laura Edwards of New Bern, Thomas Barber of North Carolina, and Edward Stokes of Virginia. Barber and Stokes, a barber and barber's apprentice, respectively, probably worked in Walker's shop. Similarly, J. G. and Elizabeth Mowbray hosted seven southern migrants in 1865. Long involved in antislavery activities in Worcester, Elizabeth Mowbray served as president of the Colored Freedmen's Aid Society, formed in Worcester in 1864. The Mowbrays' daughter, Eliza, married Jacob Gaylord, a migrant from New Bern, soon after the war. Listing his occupation as "whitewasher" in 1865, Gaylord likely worked for Mowbray. Overall, in 1865, roughly one of every four southern migrants resided with an established black family in the city and county, a number that dropped to roughly one in five by 1870.[49]

"I have imagined myself . . . getting a little home with a garden"

The residential patterns of migrants attest to Worcester's distinctive migration dynamic, especially when compared to migration to the Midwest occurring at the same time. Compared to black migration to Iowa and Kansas, many more migrants to Worcester and Worcester County resided in white households, a significant number with either military, missionary, or antislavery connections. In both 1865 and 1870, nearly 40 percent of black southern migrants resided in white households. By contrast, historian Michael Johnson found that in the less sympathetic atmosphere of the Midwest, only one in ten migrants to Iowa and Kansas resided in a white household in 1870.[50]

The fact that many of the first generation of migrants worked in domestic service suggests that their white benefactors had mixed motives in bringing them north. White military patrons may have merely wanted to continue the personal service that they had become used to in wartime, and other patrons may simply have been seeking cheap household help. That many migrants, such as David Porter Allen and Jane Waples, continued working as servants after their arrival in Worcester County may also reflect the racialist notions of some of their white benefactors, who may have believed that personal service fit supposed black characteristics of devotion and humility.[51]

Although motivations for sponsorship and employment may have been complex and even ambiguous, it is clear that at least some of the pioneer migrants did not continue in subservient positions for very long. And those who did remain as servants or unskilled laborers nevertheless managed to establish a separate household and a life independent of white patrons. Whenever possible, wartime migrants seized opportunities available in the North to assert their independence.

Just as emancipated slaves in the South sought landownership as a means of achieving independence, former slaves who migrated north sought a home of their own — and property ownership, if possible — to secure the autonomy denied them in slavery. Virginia migrant Bethany Veney explained the depth of that dream: "I have imagined myself . . . working hard and carefully saving my earnings, then getting a little home with a garden." While that dream would be delayed by "far deeper sorrows" that she endured in bondage, she, like many of her counterparts, nevertheless fulfilled her dream in Worcester after the Civil War. By 1870, nearly half of the migrants to the city and county lived in independent households. This number represented an increase of over 10 percent from 1865.[52]

Patronage networks often proved to be critical for migrants' ability to establish themselves on their own. David Porter Allen translated his connections with the Walker family and his position as an in-house servant in North Brookfield into a professional career. While working as a servant for S. S. Edmands, Allen "made very rapid progress in his studies" in the local public schools. Through "his own exertion," in the words of one observer, Allen convinced his patrons that he was capable of advanced education. With the encouragement of Edmands and the Walkers, Allen entered Westfield Normal School in western Massachusetts in 1869 and pursued advanced studies in languages and science. With his teaching certificate in hand, Allen decided to go to North Carolina in 1872 to educate freedpeople and their children. Before his departure, the community of North Brookfield feted him with a small celebration "to offer him words of cheer and Godspeed to his new field of labor," presenting him with a "purse" to pay his expenses and begin his work. By 1880, Allen's brother Albert had migrated from Virginia to work for the Edmands family. Unlike his brother, Albert remained in North Brookfield, where he worked as a shoe finisher.[53]

Allen's fellow contraband in North Brookfield, Robert Morse, also managed to establish an independent life for himself after his initial years of service in the household of Dr. Warren Tyler. Like Allen and William Bryant before him, Morse used his Civil War service and connections as a springboard to his position in his adopted town. What is most notable about Morse is that he rose to distinction in a nearly all-white town with no separate black community or organizations; yet he played an active role — even rising to positions of leadership — in North Brookfield's most important community institutions. Leaving Tyler's household in the late 1860s, Morse found work as a fireman in one of the town's many shoe factories. He purchased a home in North Brookfield after his marriage to fellow Virginian Frances Williams, and they raised three children there. Their daughter Elizabeth married Virginian James Saunders around the turn of the century. Morse, according to the local newspaper at the time of his death, "was respected by everyone." He served as a deacon in the Union Congregational Church; after the church became an Episcopal parish at the turn of the century, Morse was elected to the vestry. And although he had never served in a Union army uniform, North Brookfield honored his Civil War service as Dr. Tyler's servant by making him an honorary member of Ezra Batchelder Post 51 of the Grand Army of the Republic. The Morses' daughter Isabel regularly participated in joint meetings of the post and the Women's Relief Corps, the organization's women's auxiliary, and occasionally provided dramatic readings. The 36th Massachusetts regiment also invited Morse to attend its reunions as an honored guest. The announcement of Morse's death in the *North Brookfield Journal* in 1912 stressed his Civil War connection to the town, as well as his participation in the conflict. Morse, according to the newspaper, "often told the story of how he was assigned to the duty of firing the bridge over Acquia [*sic*] Creek, after the Union forces had passed over it, to hold back the Confederates." His funeral

The Robert Morse family, North Brookfield, Massachusetts, 1901. Standing: Robert Morse, Frances Morse, and daughter Elizabeth Morse; sitting: son-in-law James Saunders and daughter Clara Isabel Morse. Courtesy of the Worcester Historical Museum.

drew over 200 mourners, including members of the GAR, the Women's Relief Corps, and the Sons of Veterans, who "attended the service in a body."[54]

Similarly, Virginia-born William Waters benefited from the patronage of Dr. Tyler. Initially employed as a servant in the Tyler home in 1880, Waters secured employment a few years later in a North Brookfield shoe factory, where he worked first as a "shoe mechanic" and later as a shoecutter. Like Morse, Waters also purchased his own home in North Brookfield, where he and his wife, Jennie, raised their son, Oswell. Albert Allen, David Allen's brother, boarded with the family.[55]

While Jane Waples remained a servant in Worcester, she nevertheless eventually used that position to purchase a home for herself and an extended New Bern family in the North. In 1867 Waples married Andrew Mero, a native of Vermont and veteran of the renowned 54th Massachusetts Volunteer Colored Infantry. The next year, Jane gave birth to a son, Charles Sumner, whose name reflected the couple's reverence for the fiery abolitionist senator from Massachusetts. She and Andrew also had a daughter, Susan. In 1870, Andrew Mero died from a war-related illness. Left with only a meager $10 per month pension from the U.S. government, Jane, as her obituary explained, "was thrown out on the world to fight it out as best she could." Desperate to support herself and her children, she used her connections with the Spragues to find work as a servant for some of Worcester's most elite families. According to her obituary, she was "connected more or less with nearly every family of any prominence or distinction in this city."[56]

Sprague proved to be a long-term and valuable ally to Jane Waples Mero. He returned to the city after four years of military service and became a successful businessman, heading both the Worcester Electric Light Company and the Mechanics Bank. Moreover, he held a number of prominent positions in local government, including sheriff of Worcester County and mayor of Worcester.[57]

Jane Waples Mero's ties to the Sprague family provided important employment networks. Being the widow of a Civil War soldier likely enhanced her status. In addition to all of his civic duties, Colonel Sprague served as commander of the Grand Army of the Republic for Massachusetts and even had a local GAR post in nearby Grafton named in his honor. At the time of his death, a local writer noted that while he "endeavored to conceal his charities, hundreds of his old comrades-in-arms" benefited from his generosity. "Many are the stories told of the big-heartedness of the man." That Mero appointed Sprague as executor of her will in 1885 is testament to their long-term association.[58]

In 1874, Mero managed to purchase a house for her growing family, which included not only her children but also family members she brought from New Bern: her elderly mother, Sarah, and Mero's daughter, Susan, and her son-in-law, George Shannon, a native of Elizabeth City, North Carolina. Her brother, Thomas Waples, and sister-in-law, Eveline, also from New Bern, moved nearby.[59]

Waples played an active role in the Worcester black community's organizational life, first as a member of the Mission Chapel and then as a member of the city's AME Zion Church. Her funeral service reflected her prominence in the community. Led by Rev. E. George Biddle, the presiding elder of the New England district of the AME Zion Church, her funeral featured "floral tributes," both "many and beautiful," as well as a plaque from her original patron, A. B. R. Sprague.[60]

Similarly, former slave Bethany Veney drew on Worcester's support net-

Bethany Veney, c. 1910. Courtesy of the Worcester Historical Museum.

works and played an active role in aiding the migration of her extended Virginia family, purchasing homes not only for herself but also for her family members. Veney, who published a narrative of her life in 1889, was born a slave in Luray, Virginia, and gained her freedom when two residents of Providence, Rhode Island, purchased her and brought her to that northern city in 1858. Veney worked in the household of the George Adams family and moved with them to Worcester during the Civil War. At the mostly white Park Street Methodist Church, she explained, "[I] was treated with such kind consideration by the brothers and sisters there that I was at home with them." In Worcester she found such a supportive community of friends that, as she put it, "I decided to cast my lot with them." Veney noted that she was also able to "find all the work [she] was able to do" and "was comfortable in many ways."[61]

Managing to save money from her toil as a domestic during the war, Veney returned to Virginia when the war ended, seeking her daughter, Charlotte, whom she had left behind. To her great joy, she "found Charlotte grown to womanhood and married" with a child. The reunited family returned to

Worcester, where Charlotte, her husband, Aaron Jackson, and their child resided with Veney. Veney traveled to Virginia three additional times on "the same journey," as she explained, "bringing back with me, from time to time, in all sixteen relatives," most of whom resided with or near her. By the 1880s, Veney, like Jane Waples Mero before her, had managed to purchase her own home, at 21 Tufts Street (now Winfield Street) on the west side of the city. In addition, she also housed her daughter and her family "near me, in an adjacent house, also owned by me."[62]

Bethany Veney and Jane Waples Mero successfully navigated between two communities: that of sympathetic white patrons and the city's black community. While they continued to work in the homes of prominent whites, they were able to establish their own independent households not only for themselves but also for their extended families.

"It was not easy . . . to accommodate myself to the new surroundings"

The adjustment from the South to the North, slave to free, was far from easy, even with networks of support. Bethany Veney likely spoke for scores of southern migrants when she stated simply, "It was not easy at first to accommodate myself to the new surroundings." She expressed complicated emotions about her life in the North, relating deep feelings of both elation and loss: "A new life had come to me. . . . No jailer could take me to prison, and sell me at auction to the highest bidder." But at the same time, "I had left behind every one I had ever known. . . . I was a stranger in a strange land." Often overcome with "a dreadful loneliness and homesickness," Veney "very, very often longed to see the old familiar faces and hear the old sounds," and even momentarily "wished myself back in 'old Virginny,' with my own people." Veney also found working in northern households confusing, with "all sorts of Yankee inventions and improvements" with which she was unfamiliar: "dishes and pans of every description, clean and distinct cloths for all purposes, brushes and brooms for different uses." She "couldn't help feeling bewildered sometimes at the difference in so many ways."[63]

Reconstructing family life by aiding the migration of family and friends from the South helped take the sting out of relocation. Replicating the culture and institutions of their homeland also helped southern migrants to the North adjust to their new surroundings, as it did their ethnic European immigrant counterparts. Despite the horrors of slavery, many emancipated slaves retained powerful emotional bonds with the South, as Veney explained.

Southerners were "her people"; the South was her home. Those attachments, and the shared experiences of slavery and emancipation, would provide the foundation for black southern community life in Worcester.

"So that the children could go onward and upward"

Initial patronage networks conferred advantages to the children of some of Worcester's first generation of wartime migrants. Jane Waples Mero's grandson, Alonzo Shannon, managed to attend the Massachusetts Agricultural College at Amherst. Missionary teacher Sarah Chase cultivated a lifelong relationship with George and Elizabeth Wilson, the couple who accompanied her back to Worcester after her teaching service in Virginia. The Wilsons named their first-born daughter, Sarah Ella, after Sarah Chase. Chase "took immediate pride in her namesake," according to Sarah Ella's niece, and became her mentor. She enthusiastically tutored her in the graces of middle-class womanhood. Chase taught Sarah Ella how to play the piano, "took her sightseeing all over New England, especially to all types of artistic and cultural places," and gave her religious instruction. They spent leisurely hours in Chase's rooms, reading books and looking "at art treasures from different countries." Polishing and preparing her young charge for a professional life, "Miss Chase would correct her speech and mannerisms."[64]

Sarah Chase's careful grooming of her charge combined with the inspirational influence of her own migrant parents led to a brilliant career for Sarah Ella Wilson. Graduating from Classical High School in Worcester, the city's premier public high school, Sarah Ella Wilson entered Worcester Normal School and graduated in 1894. She subsequently became a beloved teacher in the city's public schools and taught first grade for forty-nine years at the Belmont Street Elementary School. One of the first African Americans hired in the Worcester school system, Wilson was a pioneer, mentor, and role model to countless children, regardless of race or ethnicity.[65]

As an educated, middle-class black woman, Wilson joined the ranks of her activist sisters and emerged as both a local and a national leader in the women's club movement. Founding a plethora of clubs across the country, black middle-class women dedicated themselves to the collective "uplift" of their race. Believing that "a race could rise no higher than its women," black club-women organized the National Association of Colored Women (NACW) in 1896 as a vehicle to unite local clubs in their efforts to improve the condition of the nation's blacks. Bound together by their faith in racial uplift through self-help, and their motto, "For God and Humanity," the NACW focused on

Teacher Sarah Ella Wilson and her class at the Belmont Street School, Worcester, 1907–8 school year. Courtesy of the Worcester Historical Museum.

improving social services for the race, especially improving home life and aiding poor mothers and children.[66]

In Worcester, black clubwomen, led by Sarah Ella Wilson, focused on the care of both young children and the elderly. Worcester's Women's Progressive Club was one of hundreds of clubs organized in the years surrounding the NACW formation. As a member of the Woman's Progressive Club, Wilson helped found the Home for Aged Colored People, an institution established when local homes for the aged refused to admit blacks (see Chapter 5). Wilson served as both vice president and auditor of the Home for Aged Colored People. In addition, she was a charter member of the Negro Woman's Club at the YWCA and founder and chair of its scholarship committee.[67]

As a result of her activism locally, Sarah Ella Wilson soon rose to leadership in the national black clubwoman's movement. She served as treasurer of the Northeastern Federation of Women's Clubs, the regional organization of the NACW. Wilson held that position for twenty-five years, rubbing shoulders with prominent clubwomen such as Mary McLeod Bethune and Elizabeth Carter Brooks. In addition, she served as the head of the scholarship committee of the NACW.[68]

Wilson's social activism extended far beyond the boundaries of women's organizations. She served as a member of the Worcester Inter-Racial Council and belonged to the local chapter of the NAACP. Wilson was so well-known and respected that the local newspaper, the *Worcester Telegram*, announced her death on the front page, an unusual honor, especially for a black woman.[69]

Sarah Ella Wilson clearly fulfilled her mother's dream; she and her husband had migrated north "so that the children could go onward and upward." Notably, the whitewashing and paperhanging business established by Wilson's father, George, after he and his wife, Elizabeth, came to Worcester after the Civil War thrived for several generations, and passed successfully from father to son to grandson. The outstanding accomplishments of the Wilson children, only one generation removed from slavery, epitomized the promise of life in the North that drew so many former slaves to Worcester.[70]

Similarly, patronage networks established with elite whites provided social capital for the next generation in the case of the Wiggins family. For George Hollister Wiggins of New Bern, who originally resided with and worked for abolitionists Abby Kelley and Stephen Foster at their Tatnuck farm, connections with the Whitcomb family and their well-to-do neighbors in Worcester resulted in long-term employment for Wiggins and unusual opportunities for his only child, Florida. After his initial stay in Worcester, Wiggins took employment with a member of the Whitcomb family in New Hampshire. According to family lore, as explained by Wiggins's grandson, Stanley Gutridge, Whitcomb "was pleased with [Wiggins's] work. And when his brother, David, here in Worcester, needed a coachman, he came to Worcester." A native of Hancock, New Hampshire, David Whitcomb started out in the tinsmith and peddling business, then made his fortune as a hardware dealer, and, with his son G. Henry Whitcomb, established Whitcomb Envelope Company. Due to its many ingenious technological innovations, Whitcomb Envelope emerged as one of the largest envelope companies in the nation by the 1890s. After David Whitcomb's death in 1887, G. Henry Whitcomb succeeded his father as president. He subsequently sold the company to U.S. Envelope in 1898. G. Henry's son, Henry E. Whitcomb, managed the Whitcomb Envelope Company Division of U.S. Envelope in Worcester.[71]

As a coachman, George Hollister Wiggins worked for several generations of the Whitcomb family on Harvard Street. Wiggins and his wife, Susie Holmes, a migrant to Worcester from Farmville, Virginia, via Washington, lived in the small mansard-roofed carriage house behind an elegant and substantial home at 6 Harvard Street, owned by David Whitcomb and inhabited for many years by his widowed daughter, Abby Smith, and later by his grandson, Henry E. Whitcomb. The Wigginses' daughter, Florida, was born there in

1884 and grew up in the carriage house on Harvard Street, with George employed by the Whitcomb family, from the mid-1870s until around 1918.[72]

Wiggins's employment as a coachman provided financial security as well as vital connections for his young family. Not only did he escape the dirty jobs and back-breaking labor typically reserved for Worcester blacks, but his occupation also provided a lovely home on one of Worcester's most prominent residential streets. On Harvard Street, home to some of the city's leading citizens, including the A. B. R. Sprague family, the Wiggins family became acquainted with some of the city's most influential citizens, including Alfred S. Roe. A native of New York, Roe enlisted with the 9th New York Heavy Artillery in the Civil War in 1863 and suffered in a Confederate prison for seven months. After the war, he attended Wesleyan University and in 1875 moved to Worcester, where he taught at Classical High and served as principal from 1880 to 1890. In addition, he served in the Massachusetts House of Representatives from 1892 to 1895 and was a state senator from 1896 to 1898. Prominent in numerous local organizations, such as the YMCA, Roe was a member and a commander of Post 10, Grand Army of the Republic. As he noted in his historical essay on Harvard Street, Roe resided on Dix Street, "very near to the Harvard border." In order to "reach the scene of [his] daily labors" at Worcester Classical High School, "it was necessary to pass and repass many of the buildings on Harvard Street"; thusly, he established "passing acquaintance with most of the dwellers of the street."[73]

For veteran Roe, the Wiggins family's presence on Harvard Street provided a daily reminder of the meaning of the Civil War. And in young Florida he saw the future hope of the black race. In his Harvard Street essay, which he penned in 1896, Roe described the young girl, "having the happy appellation of Florida Wiggins," whom he regularly observed emerging "from the rear abode" of 6 Harvard Street on her daily trip to school. Roe mused that her name, Florida, bore "a suggestion of the War and of the people whom the liberation of the slaves sent into our midst. She is doing her best to make a juvenile showing for Harvard Street."[74]

Roe may have been a guiding force in Florida Wiggins's education. As principal of the prestigious Classical High School in Worcester, he may have encouraged her to attend the school, whose rigorous curriculum included Latin and five years of classical Greek, along with a large dose of history and mathematics. In addition, her parents set very high standards for their daughter. Active in the AME Zion Church, George and Susie Wiggins were "both very strict," according to Stanley Gutridge. They imbued their daughter with values of "honesty and truth." "Work hard for a living and everything

The George Wiggins family, Sarah, Florida, and George, resided in the carriage house (right) when George was employed as a coachman by the Whitcombs. The Whitcomb house, 6 Harvard Street, is on the left. Courtesy of Stanley Gutridge.

that you have," they advised. "Believe in God and have faith that things are for the best."[75]

In addition to her parents, both former slaves, Florida had the examples of other family members, an extended network of George's New Bern family who followed him north to Worcester. Florida's aunt (George's sister), Louise, and Louise's husband, Martin Smith, migrated from New Bern to Worcester in the 1870s, with Martin first working as a waiter. By 1884, he was working as a coachman for businessman Jerome Marble and his family at 23 Harvard Street. Roe described Smith as a "faithful colored man" who for years "was as clock-work in the performance of his duties; his long retention is alike creditable to employer and employee." George likely used his connections to secure the job for Martin. A few years later, around the time Florida was born, Matilda Wiggins, George's mother, migrated to Worcester from New Bern. A bonnet maker in New Bern, Matilda found work as a washerwoman in Worcester, residing near the Wigginses on John Street, which, in the 1880s, was fast becoming the nucleus of a neighborhood of southern black migrants, mostly from Virginia and North Carolina, who would soon establish their own Baptist church there.[76]

The examples and values of her hardworking family members, all emancipated from slavery, coupled with the influence of neighbor Roe, helped propel Florida to several professional careers. In 1906, after graduating from Classical High, Florida left Worcester to teach in a one-room school in Maysville, South Carolina. Like her contemporary Sarah Ella Wilson, Florida Wiggins maintained a connection to the South; in her particular case, she chose to aid African Americans who did not have the same opportunities she did in Worcester.[77]

After several years, Florida returned home to Worcester, married, and had three sons. As her marriage collapsed, and she was left to raise her children alone, she scrambled to make ends meet, and for several years, operated her own massage business in Oak Bluffs, on Martha's Vineyard. During the Depression, amidst housekeeping jobs, she managed to take a clerical course at night. She eventually secured a job with the Worcester Mailing Company, owned by Grace Swan. According to her son Stanley, "the Swans were nice, old New England people," open to hiring a black woman as a clerk. Florida and Grace Swan "became good friends, and she worked there for years." The Swans, like Alfred Roe, encouraged Florida to aim higher and take the civil service exam for social work. She scored well, placing eighteenth on the list. With the state hiring thirty-five new social workers, a position seemed assured. But she soon faced the hard reality of racial politics — civil service or not. Her son recalls, "So they appointed the first, the top seventeen, skipped my mother, and appointed the rest. Those were the days when they didn't have black social workers." But Florida Wiggins refused to accept the snub. Instead, "there was quite a political battle." Using the connections she and her family had established over the years, Florida appealed to city councilman George Wells, who agreed to take up her cause. Stanley Gutridge recalls: "And finally she got an appointment — a temporary appointment as a social worker — in Boston!" — over forty miles away. Enduring a brutal commute by train for several years, she finally received an appointment in Worcester, but only after "the politicians took it up again." Florida Wiggins Gutridge worked as a social worker in Worcester until her retirement in the 1950s.[78]

For black migrants with influential white patrons who provided employment and, in some cases, access to education, Worcester and Worcester County, while far from perfect, fulfilled its promise as a land of opportunity, especially for the second generation. Due to the inaccuracies of the census, with its perennial problem of undercounting people of color — perhaps by as much as one-third of their total population — it is difficult to measure with any certainty the persistence of the first generation of southern migrants. Moreover, as Elizabeth Pleck found in her study of southern black migration to Boston, migrants "moved between friends and kin spread across the North," and some moved seasonally, making it difficult to keep track of them. Despite problems measuring persistence with any sense of accuracy, it seems clear that migrants with patrons who aided their transition more often established themselves permanently in the North. For migrants who came through less personalized connections, Worcester proved to be less of a promised land.[79]

"First-class colored help"

In September 1867, the *Worcester Daily Spy* announced a new "movement" focused on the employment of freedpeople. A "number of citizens" had organized "to establish in this city a freedman's home and intelligence office, where colored help can be furnished." By April 1868, the Freedman's Home and Intelligence Office had been established on Boyden Street, near the College of the Holy Cross. An ad in the *Spy* appealed to readers to employ three freedmen, "first-class men," seeking jobs in the city "attending to horses, taking charge of a gentleman's place, or to act as a Porter in a Wholesale Store, delivering goods, &tc." No further mention of this office can be found in the *Spy* or other local records. But, simultaneously, privately owned employment agencies also began publicizing the availability of "colored help."[80]

Beginning around 1867, Worcester's white middle class — like their counterparts in other northern towns and cities — seemed to have an insatiable appetite for employing blacks in domestic service. As an agent of the Freedmen's Bureau in Washington discovered during a fund-raising trip to New England, "There is a great demand for laborers (particularly women) in Rhode Island, Connecticut, and so far as I have been, in Massachusetts." Ads appeared regularly in the local press from those seeking "colored help" as well as from employment agents specializing in "colored help." An Elm Street matron placed an ad seeking "a colored cook." Another city matron advertised with much more specificity: "A Colored Woman Wanted — To do housework. She must be neat, a good cook, washer and ironer, and between twenty-five and fifty-five years old." Mrs. E. J. Browne, who ran an employment agency on Main Street, began to specialize in black domestic workers, advertising "Situations wanted for colored help." She announced in March 1869 that she was "now prepared to furnish at short notice coachmen, cooks, second girls, and for general housework." She followed up with numerous ads offering "colored men, as private coachmen, gardeners, and porters." A rival employment agency played on the fears of ladies who might risk their health in the pursuit of slovenly Irish servants: "Ladies! Why will you visit the slums of the city in search of servants? Why dive into dark and muddy alleys, grope up rickety stairs, and enter reeking rooms, inquiring for Marys or Biddys, at the risk of carrying away parasites, and perhaps disease, when you can get a smart, neat servant by stepping into the clean, cheerful, carpeted room known as Irwin's Employ Office, opp. Mechanics Hall?" Along with "hardy daughters of Nova Scotia" and "frugal Germans," Irwin's emphasized that it offered "the olive-cheeked daughters of our own sunny South."[81]

As with the case of Civil War soldier-sponsors of migrants, the degree to which selfish or racialist sentiments figured prominently in decisions to employ southern black migrants remains unclear. White middle-class families seeking "colored help" may simply have been seeking cheap domestic labor. Yet, as the employment agency ads noted, other ethnic groups flooding into industrial Worcester after the Civil War also supplied inexpensive household help. Employing black servants may have seemed more exotic and perhaps represented more prestige than hiring an Irish maid. Hiring preferences may have merely been a fad, black servants a novelty. In addition, as Anna Lowell, who facilitated the relocation of hundreds of contraband women to New England through the Freedmen's Bureau, noted, some simply "look[ed] out for colored women as more easily imposed upon." At the same time, given Worcester's abolitionist tradition and its long-term involvement in the plight of freedpeople through its soldiers and teachers — coupled with the increasingly troubled climate of southern Reconstruction — liberal white Worcesterites may also have viewed black migrants as refugees of a despotic regime who deserved their help. Like the many Americans who felt a moral responsibility to resettle refugees in the aftermath of World War II and the Vietnam War, white Worcesterites may have acted from a deep-seated sense of obligation. As living symbols of the South's repression, southern blacks who were granted a fresh start in Worcester may have represented the commitment of the city's citizenry to the concurrent battle for equal rights and opportunity.[82]

It is likely that when "interested" local citizens established the Freedman's Home and Intelligence Office in 1867, they worked directly with the Freedmen's Intelligence and Employment Agency in Washington. The employment of former slaves emerged as an immediate problem after emancipation. Following her sister Sarah's entreaties to freedmen's aid societies to help find former slaves work in the *Freedmen's Record*, Lucy Chase, writing from Norfolk, encouraged Mrs. Samuel May of Leicester, Worcester County, to pursue this course: "Shan't you band together for the elevation of the Negro? An Employment Society or something of that nature?" she suggested. Pioneered by the New England Freedmen's Aid Society — in cooperation with the Pennsylvania Freedmen's Relief Association; the Baltimore Association for the Moral and Educational Improvement of the Colored People; the Friends' Association in Aid of Freedmen, Baltimore; and the National Freedman's Relief Association, Washington — the Union Freedmen's Aid and Intelligence and Employment Agency opened in May 1865 on Eleventh Street, near K, in Washington. Two months later, in July 1865, the aid society transferred the agency to the Freedmen's Bureau.[83]

The nation's capital became a magnet for African Americans freed during and after the Civil War. An estimated 30,000–40,000 freedpeople flocked to the city, and the District's black population exploded by over 200 percent between 1860 and 1870, creating a severe refugee crisis as former slaves desperately sought food, clothing, and adequate shelter. As early as February 1865, reports from Washington noted that conditions were so harsh that they were "likely to suggest . . . the question, 'Are these people really better off now than they were in slavery?'" One observer found refugees generally "ragged; stripped of everything; many of them sick; few accustomed to any other than agricultural labor; at the mercy of speculators — the condition of newcomers, especially, is abject and miserable in the extreme."[84]

To alleviate this crisis, in May 1865, the New England Freedmen's Aid Society's Intelligence and Employment Agency invited "applications for help of any description which these people can render, both from residents of this vicinity, and from any quarter where labor is required, or homes can be furnished." Applications were to include specific offers of compensation and "a guarantee of just and kindly treatment." The agency warned potential employers "that few able-bodied men can be had, at present, and not many first-class, well-instructed house servants." Instead, "there are many mothers with children . . . and many young women, girls, and boys, who, with proper and kindly training, will become most valuable domestics, farm-laborers, &tc."[85]

By the winter of 1865–66, Washington's refugee crisis worsened and had become an embarrassment to the Freedmen's Bureau, which was struggling to aid suffering former slaves. That year, Charles Howard, assistant Freedmen's Bureau commissioner for the District of Columbia, established an aggressive, systematic program to transport willing freedpeople to jobs in the North, the West, and even the South. While freedpeople had been moved north under the bureau's auspices since 1865, Howard's program greatly broadened the scope of its efforts. He established several employment offices in Washington that worked with bureau-funded employment offices in New Jersey; Providence, Rhode Island; Hartford, Connecticut; and Boston to place ex-slaves in jobs. While not funded directly by the Freedmen's Bureau, Worcester's Freedman's Home and Intelligence Office, established in 1867 in the midst of the bureau's massive refugee employment program, was probably an offshoot of these efforts.[86]

The Freedmen's Bureau promised refugees transportation to jobs with "fair wages" and "kind treatment." Minors needed the consent of a parent or guardian, if possible. But for those just freed from the chains of slavery, the decision to be transported to work in a distant, strange place, far from family and friends, was fraught with tension. Many had just begun the process of reuniting with family members, and many could not bear the thought of once again separating from loved ones. One mother's written approval reflected that concern: "I am willing for my son Thomas Johnson to go a way to heartford Ct," she wrote, but "I should like to hear from him as often as posable." In addition, some feared that leaving Washington meant abandoning their newly won freedom. Harriette Carter, who visited the employment agency in August 1866, reported, "It is difficult to persuade the most ignorant and the most degraded that it is perfectly safe for them to leave the city, where, whatever may be their trials, they know that they are free." Furthermore, freedpeople faced the possibility of being returned once again to plantation labor, since southern planters themselves applied to the bureau for large numbers of laborers to work their fields. Those who left Washington also faced the loss of protection from the federal government. Finally, harsh northern and midwestern climates had little appeal. To counter these concerns, the Freedmen's Bureau refused applicants any additional requests for government aid of food, clothing, or fuel unless they agreed to accept a job with the bureau employment agency.[87]

The program faced harsh criticism from both ends of the political spectrum, as well as from some freedpeople themselves. President Andrew Johnson, an outspoken enemy of the Freedmen's Bureau, called it "traffic in negroes." Similarly, some abolitionists compared the program to the slave trade.

Freedpeople complained about mistreatment and claimed that bureau employment agents callously separated families, shipping their children north without their permission. In addition, some northern communities reacted with hostility to the arrival of migrants.[88]

Despite criticism and the hesitancy of many freedpeople to leave the safety of Washington, the Freedmen's Bureau managed to relocate roughly 11,000 former slaves between 1865 and 1868, when the bureau ended its employment program. Approximately 30 percent ended up in New England, and another 30 percent moved to the mid-Atlantic states, their journeys for gainful employment a crucial "aid . . . in self-support" and a critical factor in "distinguishing freemen from slaves." Female employment agents and abolitionist allies, historian Carol Faulkner notes, played a special role by guiding migrants to the North rather than to plantation districts, believing that the North offered not only better job opportunities but also educational opportunities and protection under the law.[89]

Freedmen's Bureau records indicate that requests for "colored servants," especially women, inundated the employment agency. A Philadelphia agent asked the bureau "to send me a number of women and girls (freedwomen), as I have constant demand for them." Similarly, an agent in Brooklyn wrote the bureau, "There is not a week which passes during which we do not have application for Servants, especially females. . . . There are so many ladies and gentlemen wanting coloured help, that I think it would be well to keep the matter constantly before the public." At least some of those who hired freedpeople and brought them north felt an obligation to educate them and prepare them as well as possible for life after slavery. Bureau employment agent Josephine Griffey noted, "Inducements for these people to learn are also great," pointing out that "most of those who went to the North, one year ago, are now able to read and write." According to Griffey, the chance for honest labor created "improvement in Industry, economy, and thrift" as well as in "personal appearance." Griffey also reported that some refugees "who were in extreme debilitation when they left this District are now in houses they have bought and paid for." Employment agent H. G. Stewart of Providence's Rhode Island Association of Freedmen even managed to start an evening school, with public funds, for those who came to the city under bureau auspices to work.[90]

Estimating the number of freedpeople who came to Worcester under the bureau's auspices remains problematic for several reasons. Freedmen's Bureau transportation and employment records are incomplete. Rich and detailed for some months, records are missing entirely for others. In addition, it is impossible to know how many freedpeople who were sent to official Freedmen's Bureau employment agencies in Boston, Hartford, and Providence eventually found employment in Worcester County. Elizabeth Pleck estimates that the bureau sent at least around 1,100 ex-slaves to Boston and Cambridge between 1866 and 1868. In that same time period, bureau agent Anna Lowell sponsored approximately 818 migrants herself and established the Howard Industrial School in Cambridgeport in 1866 "for the purpose of giving shelter and help in obtaining employment for Freedwomen and children coming from Washington and Hampton." Modeled on General Samuel Armstrong's Hampton Institute, the Howard School aimed at "elevating [freedwomen and children] and improving their condition" by teaching them useful skills, such as housekeeping. In addition, Rev. H. G. Stewart's Rhode Island Association for Freedmen in Providence also sponsored at least a thousand freedpeople, with Stewart reporting 968 brought to Providence from January through September 1867 alone.[91]

Worcester's Freedman's Intelligence Office, as well as independent employment agents in Worcester, probably worked directly with Lowell in Cambridge and Stewart in Providence, as well as the Hartford office, to bring freedpeople to Worcester for employment. Fragmentary bureau records reveal that thirty-nine people were sent directly to Worcester County between 1866 and 1868 under federal auspices. Another sixty people listed in the 1870 census for Worcester County fit the profile of those the bureau typically transported north for employment in terms of age, birthplace, and occupation. That is, they were born in the District of Columbia, Virginia, or Maryland, the birthplaces of most of the Washington-area refugees; they worked as domestic servants or farmhands, the typical occupations of the transported refugees; and they were overwhelmingly in their teens and early twenties, the typical age group of those transported north.[92]

This identified group of ninety-nine suggests the distinctive composition of bureau migrants. Unlike the military and missionary migration, which was overwhelmingly male, women made up the majority — roughly 60 percent — of the bureau migration. Nearly all of the women worked as domestic servants, and some may have been trained at Anna Lowell's Howard Industrial School in Cambridgeport. A few worked in factory settings; Josephine Peters and Letitia Waller, for example sewed hats in a straw factory in Milford. With only a few exceptions, the men worked as farm laborers in the county and as servants and waiters in towns and cities. The bureau often responded to requests from local citizens for specific kinds of laborers: George Gibbs of Whitinsville sought "a young woman for general housework," while J. L. Libbey of Worcester requested "a man and wife — man for farm & woman for kitchen; good wages." Proprietor A. Brown of the Warren House in Warren requested and received three young men whom he employed as waiters. The majority of bureau migrants clustered in the city of Worcester with the remainder scattered throughout the county.[93]

Like those who came to Worcester through military and missionary networks, most bureau migrants were in their late teens and early twenties. And similar to the military/missionary migration, the Freedmen's Bureau migration also included a handful of children, most of whom were probably orphans. These included ten-year-old Bird Taplet, who was sent to Milford, and eleven-year-old Daniel Grey, who ended up in Gardner. Six young girls, ranging in age from eleven to seventeen, resided at the State Industrial School in Lancaster, to learn a skill for their self-support.[94]

At least one Worcester family who arranged for an employee from the Freedmen's Bureau had deep abolitionist roots. Prominent Worcester businessman Edward Earle wrote to the Freedmen's Bureau in October 1867 requesting "a young girl" whom he and his wife, Ann, a founder of Worcester's freedpeople's relief organization in 1861, could employ as a nurse. Earle, a prominent industrialist and proprietor of a card clothing manufactory, and his wife were active Quakers engaged in a variety of social reforms, including antislavery; upon his death, Edward Earle was remembered as a man who was a friend to "the poor and needy" who "strove with an untiring energy to make the world and those around him better and happier." In the last year of the Civil War, Edward and Ann Earle served on a committee of the New England Yearly Meeting of Friends devoted to "aiding and promoting the welfare of the Freedmen in Washington." To implement their plan "to educate and so to assist them as to render them as soon as possible, self-sustaining," the committee established the New England Friends Freedmen's Mission on 13th Street, which offered clean, reasonably priced rooms for freedpeople as an alternative to the miserable, crowded, and disease-ridden housing available to them.[95]

Familiar with the plight of Washington-area freedpeople, the Earles employed two Washington contrabands under the auspices of the Freedmen's Bureau Employment Office: Annie Brooks, who arrived in Worcester with three other women in the spring of 1867, and fourteen-year-old Maria Lewis, who arrived in October of that year. Lewis had been a slave owned by Elias Green in Caroline County, Virginia, and had made her way to Washington after the war. Without surviving parents, Lewis had her guardian, Henry Hopkins, make "his mark" on a letter giving approval for her transportation to the Earle family. Typical of many bureau-facilitated transplants to the North, Hopkins soon followed his charge to Worcester. Freedmen's Bureau records indicate that not long after Lewis made her way north, "Henry Hopkins and 2 others" also received transportation from the bureau to Worcester for employment.[96]

But neither Maria Lewis, Henry Hopkins, nor Annie Brooks can be found in local records. In contrast to the first wave of Civil War migrants to Worcester County, many of whom stayed in the area, fewer Freedmen's Bureau migrants remained in Worcester County, reflecting the overall experience of bureau-relocated contrabands in general. Historian William Cohen concluded from census data that many who went north under the bureau's auspices did not remain there and thus did not help initiate a chain migration from the South to the North. Approximately 60 percent of those listed in the 1865 Massachusetts census (38 of 65) — who most likely came through military and missionary networks — can be found in the 1870 census; another roughly 20 percent of migrants present in 1870 can be found in later records. But only 1 of the 39 people named in Freedmen's Bureau records as relocated to Worcester County can be found in subsequent records: Jennie Brown, who died in Worcester in 1875. Even accounting for the census's underreporting of people of color and the fact that some women married and changed their names, making it nearly impossible to trace them, few southern migrants who came through bureau or employment office auspices established roots in Worcester. Cohen argues that low wages and lack of job opportunities contributed to the low persistence rate among the bureau migrants. Since employers sought out "big bargains" in contraband labor, wages offered to freedpeople transported north were "pitiably low." Yet Worcester Countians appear to have offered fair and sometimes even generous wages. According to Freedmen's Bureau records, contraband laborers received anywhere from $16 to $26 per month in Worcester County. The average wage for farm laborers in New England in 1860 was $14.73, and by 1870, $19.84. Paxton farmer J. F. Damon promised his farm laborer Jacob Holland a generous $26 per month, plus "a handsome present after harvest." Female domestics earned from $7 to $10 per month in Worcester County, and waiters earned $16 per month. While low wages did not seem to be an issue in Worcester County, without the strong personal patronage networks enjoyed by the military and missionary migrants, bureau migrants appear to have found the area a less attractive place to settle.[97]

The hostility of whites, many of whom resented migrants' presence and feared competing with them for jobs, likely contributed to the migrants' decision not to make Worcester home. Racial confrontations seem to have increased in 1868 and 1869, in the wake of the Freedmen's Bureau employment program. In March 1868, for example, the *Daily Spy* reported an altercation at a Mechanics Hall concert when a white man refused to move from a seat for which a black man had purchased a ticket. "When the colored man first appeared," noted the *Spy*, "several hisses were heard," but when he rightfully took his seat, after the police "ejected the intruder," concert goers responded with "a burst of applause . . . which lasted long enough to drown the quartette and compel the singers to retire." Alluding to the *Dred Scott* decision, the *Spy* concluded, "The intruder evidently got a lesson that a black man has rights which he was bound to respect."[98]

Another incident, in May 1869, involved a white man kicking the dog of barber Henry Walker, a twenty-year-old black Virginian who had recently migrated to the city. When Walker refused the challenge of the white perpetrator to fight him, the man aimed a pistol at Walker. Fortunately for the young barber, the local press reported, a police officer intervened "before he had a chance to discharge his weapon."[99]

Like their compatriots in other northern cities, Irish workers in Worcester County felt especially vulnerable in the wake of black migration, fearing that the new arrivals would take their jobs for lower wages. In September 1869, the *Spy* reported that an "Irishman with more whiskey than reverence in him" disturbed a service at the black Bethel Church. When he refused to leave, "quite a tumult ensued," including "a lively tussle" on the street that "drew quite a large crowd."[100]

A more serious incident that year involved two bureau migrants and resentful Irish workers. James H. Washington and George Williams, two young black men who were hired to work for J. L. Libbey in Worcester through the Freedmen's Bureau, "encountered a group of Irishmen" on Grove Street as they walked home from work. "The colored men," the *Worcester Daily Spy* reported, "were somewhat afraid of trouble," so Williams fell back and Washington went ahead alone. As Washington passed the group, "they made some fun of him." In response, Washington "turned and addressed an offensive remark to one of them," prompting one of the Irish workmen, Patrick Kennary, to run after him. When Kennary attempted to strike Washington, Washington "stabbed him in the abdomen with a common large pocket knife, cutting through his clothing and inflicting a perpendicular gash two or three inches in length." Kennary, the father of three, died two months later. Washington was arrested and put on trial, but a jury, displaying unusual sympathy to Washington, exonerated him, as they were convinced that the fatal wound was "made in self-defense, from an unprovoked assault by Kennary."[101]

In addition to a growing atmosphere of hostility, many bureau migrants faced isolation. For young male farm workers and female domestics, scattered across the county in towns such as Harvard, Sutton, Millbury, and Princeton — and often the only African Americans in those communities — employment in rural households must have been an especially lonely experience. As Bethany Veney noted, the adjustment from the South to the North was difficult, even with networks of support; for those arriving alone and with no black community in remote Worcester County farms and villages, the transition would have been even harder. Moreover, the Freedmen's Bureau jobs did not allow the independence and autonomy from white oversight that many former slaves deeply desired. For black women, working as live-in domestic servants apart from their families may have too closely replicated the dynamic of the plantation household. Also, many farmers employed bureau workers only seasonally, so laborers moved frequently from job to job. For example, William Gibson, a native of Rappahannock County, Virginia, first worked odd jobs in Boston, then relocated to Paxton, Worcester County, where he labored for three farmers, and then returned to Boston. Farmer J. F. Damon's promise to his bureau worker of "a handsome present after harvest" indicates that he planned to employ his farm laborer only until the fall.[102]

Census records suggest that those who worked in cities, such as Worcester or Fitchburg, had a higher tendency to stay. Marriage partners could be found in the city, African American community life enjoyed, and educational opportunities taken advantage of. In 1869, for example, the city of Worcester, "in answer to a growing want," opened several evening schools, two for girls and one for boys and young men. The *Daily Spy* noted, "There would appear to be no 'prejudice of race,' for among the pupils are Americans, Irish, English, negroes, Canadian French, Germans, and Swedes, and all appear to work harmoniously together."[103]

WHETHER THEY ARRIVED through military, missionary, or Freedmen's Bureau networks, the mostly young and vital southern black migrants who planted roots in Worcester and Worcester County in the aftermath of the Civil War had a transformative impact on black community life. Those who came with the advantages of personal patronage almost immediately defined their freedom by purchasing homes, establishing households, and bringing family members north, as Bethany Veney explained, "to share . . . these blessings of freedom."[104] In doing so, they perpetuated migration networks that were established in wartime and created a long-standing migration tradition. Once established in Worcester, southern families not only participated in the black community but also soon imbued their community with a distinctive southern flavor as they transplanted their culture in northern soil.

Chapter

5

A COMMUNITY

WITHIN A COMMUNITY

On the afternoon of 22 June 1891, members of the Mount Olive Baptist Church gathered to lay the cornerstone for their new church on John Street in Worcester. Joined by representatives from the city's two other black churches as well as white Baptist congregations, church members and their supporters reflected on the long journey from the South to the North, from slavery to freedom, that many of them had made.

Amidst prayers, invocations, and joyful hymn singing, George C. Whitney, a member of the First Baptist Church, presented a historical address. As a teenager in 1862, Whitney had joined the 51st Massachusetts regiment and served in New Bern, North Carolina. He was one of many white Worcesterites who helped liberate slaves there. He began his address by providing a brief overview of the black congregation's beginnings, of the "faithful brethren" who made their new church a reality. He praised the Mount Olive congregation for its self-reliance, noting that "it was a pleasure to assist those who are zealously striving to help themselves."[1]

Whitney then focused on what he called the "unwritten history of some of those present." Pointing out that the full story of the South's liberated slaves remained unknown to many, the aging veteran took the opportunity to highlight that saga and to draw connections between slavery and the Civil War and the cornerstone-laying. The "unwritten history," Whitney explained, prompted "reason for great rejoicing over the improvement of [former slaves'] condition during their lives." He continued, "History would lead one to say that if anything could be done to aid this race it should be done." Whitney then pointed out the "little bronze buttons" that graced the lapels of several persons around him. Several members of the church, including Charles Clark and Andrew Jackson, were black Civil War veterans and belonged — with Whitney — to Worcester's George H. Ward Post No. 10 of the Grand Army of the Republic; they proudly wore the button that designated their Civil War service. While "a simple thing," Whitney explained, "that little button is a reminder of a great contest for freedom. It reminds all that the colored race was once enslaved, even in this boasted land of liberty, which called itself a Christian nation. But the button reminds all, also, that the shackles of the slave were broken by war, and that the oppressed were set free."[2]

Whitney's comments attested to the bonds that remained between some Union veterans and the people they helped liberate, even as the cause of black civil rights foundered nationally and locally. With Reconstruction and its promises of black equality a distant, unfulfilled dream, and with white supremacy once again surging in the American South, the slaves' past and the war that liberated them was never far from the minds of the small congregation and the white benefactors who continued to aid them, nearly thirty years after the first "contrabands of war" arrived in Worcester.

The founding of the Mount Olive, later renamed John Street, Baptist Church symbolized the coming-of-age of the southern migrant community that took root in Worcester beginning in the era of the Civil War. The church, built in the heart of the city's southern black residential enclave, embodied long-standing patronage networks as well as the independence and pride of the southern blacks who founded the church. Self-consciously southern in its membership and worship style, the church signified the migrants' long-term commitment to the city of Worcester and served to maintain southern culture and tradition in the North.

As Whitney's speech suggested, historical memory provided the foundation for building black southern community in Worcester. Southern identity centered on history — the historical experience and memory of slavery and the Civil War. Southern migrants and their children, sometimes aided by older white patrons like Whitney, fought to keep that memory, and the nation's promises of full-fledged freedom, alive. They did so by establishing community institutions and celebrations and engaging in political activism. In addition, several of the city's former slaves published narratives in which they recounted their personal journeys from slavery to freedom.

In engaging in these activities, former slaves embraced what historian David W. Blight termed "African American patriotic memory," part of an

John Street Baptist Church, c. 1920. Courtesy of the Worcester Historical Museum.

"emancipationist vision" of the Civil War. As many white Americans conveniently erased slavery and emancipation and its radical vision of equality from their historical memory, replacing it with romantic reconciliation and white supremacy, black Worcesterites, like many of their brothers and sisters across the nation, insisted "that the black soldier, the Civil War Constitutional Amendments, and the story of emancipation ought to be at the center of the nation's remembrance." Like Frederick Douglass, they believed "that black memory was a weapon" against injustice, and they wielded it in their attempt to defend and to secure what was rightfully theirs, in both Worcester and the South.[3]

While the Mount Olive Church embodied the growing strength and vitality of Worcester's southern migrant community, it also reflected some of the problems the black community faced. Many struggled economically in the 1880s and 1890s. By the 1890s, as Whitney's speech suggested, the city's Civil War generation of white "benevolent sympathizers" was passing from the scene, replaced by a rising generation of Gilded Age go-getters, unmindful of Worcester's abolitionist heritage and its role in emancipating and settling former slaves. Buffeted by the vertiginous late-nineteenth-century economy, blacks in Worcester found themselves victimized by a color bar that limited their opportunity to work in Worcester's many and varied industries. Unlike white European and Canadian immigrants, who managed to gain a foothold in industry, paving the way for the advancement of their sons and daughters, black Worcesterites found themselves excluded from jobs that provided a modicum of security for their children, leaving them, in many respects, a poor and isolated group by the turn of the twentieth century.

Small in number and resource-poor, the city's black community often depended on white financial support to maintain its institutions. But while white patronage enabled the establishment of vital institutions, such as the Mount Olive (John Street) Baptist Church, at the same time, it also, in the view of some community members, sapped their autonomy and frustrated the self-sufficiency they so deeply desired.

The city's black community did not react passively to the challenges it faced. In the 1890s, its members implemented new political strategies in an attempt to better their lot. As in the upper Midwest, struggles over civil rights initiated a new era of activism. Headed largely by a cadre of new political leaders — most of whom were Civil War–era southern migrants and their children — they employed new approaches that marked a shift to more radical political activism than that of the 1870s and 1880s. Spurred in part by the lynchings, disfranchisement, and Jim Crow laws crushing African Americans in the South, blacks demanded respect from white residents and representation in local government. They also insisted that black citizens get their share of city jobs, which were dispensed as patronage by local officials, in return for their votes. But they made little headway, hampered by size, internal divisions, and unresponsive white politicians.[4]

Black women, like their white counterparts, while interested observers of the local political scene, were barred from casting ballots. Nevertheless, they, too, challenged the second-class treatment of blacks in the city, channeling their energies into establishing clubs and self-help organizations and resisting unofficial Jim Crow. Like their sisters in other parts of the country, they "lifted as they climbed." Notably, they, too, like their male counterparts, divided internally over the issue of white patronage and found themselves in the same predicament. As the community split over the issue of dependence, the overall racial atmosphere in the city — as in much of the rest of the country — deteriorated. In many ways, black Worcesterites found themselves much more marginalized at the turn of the century than they were at the time of the Civil War.

In the midst of challenging conditions, southern migrants put their stamp on the community. In the new political activism they implemented, in the community institutions they built, in the community celebrations they inspired, and in the narratives they wrote, southern migrants and their children shaped the city's black community into a "southern village," in the words of one of its twentieth-century members. They gave it a distinctive flavor that would endure for years. The memory of slavery and Civil War bonded Worcester's southern migrant community, providing a common identity as well as inspiration and strength to continue to fight for justice.[5]

"A 'little flock'... precious in the sight of the Great Shepherd"

Southern black migration to Worcester and Worcester County continued through the turn of the century. While it slowed between 1870 and 1880, it increased noticeably between 1880 and 1900, just as segregation laws and disfranchisement went into effect. Nearly 300 southern migrants can be documented living in Worcester and Worcester County by 1880. Between 1880 and 1900, approximately 320 lived in the city of Worcester, with over 100 more living in the county. In the last three decades of the nineteenth century, North Carolinians and Virginians continued to dominate, making up 66 percent of the total number of migrants to Worcester between 1880 and 1900. While most of this group hailed from Virginia between 1865 and 1880, by 1900, North Carolinians represented the largest single southern-born group in the city. In 1880, southern migrants made up roughly one-third of the adult black population in the city of Worcester. By 1900, they made up almost half.[6] (See Table A.3.)

Birthplaces for migrants in the late nineteenth century that are listed in city vital statistics records confirm that migrants hailed from the same places as Civil War–era migrants. New Bern natives dominated among North Carolinians, whereas migrants born in Norfolk, Culpeper, and Petersburg prevailed among Virginians. Several New Bern families who would establish deep roots in Worcester, such as the Cullys, Gilliams, and Wards, appeared in the census by 1900. Virginians also continued to migrate, although, for the first time, in smaller numbers than their Tar Heel compatriots. Through ongoing migration, based on the highly localized networks established in the era of the Civil War, southerners consistently made up nearly half of Worcester's adult black population from 1870 to 1900. Notably, migrant Mary Cutler, who first appeared in Worcester in 1892, cited her birthplace as James City, originally the site of a model contraband village established by Worcesterite Horace James in 1863, a reflection of the bonds that continued to connect the two cities almost thirty years after the Civil War.[7]

Several developments as early as the 1870s indicate the establishment of a permanent southern migrant community in the city of Worcester and the ways that southerners shaped local culture. Beginning in the 1870s, Virginians and North Carolinians created their own residential pocket off of Highland Street, on the city's west side. Previously, Worcester's small black population had clustered in two areas, both on the city's east side: around Pine Street and on the south side of Belmont Street, roughly bounded by Liberty and Laurel streets. While never exclusive to the southern-born alone, the new residential pocket on the west side suggests that southerners made a conscious effort to live together.[8]

By 1880, the Highland Street enclave, which included North Ashland, John, and Lilly streets, surpassed both of the older east-side residential pockets in size. Moreover, it contained the highest number of southern-born blacks, mostly from Virginia and North Carolina. Nearly half of its residents either were born in the South or had one southern-born parent.[9]

Whether southern migrants voluntarily chose to live in close proximity or were unwelcome in older African American residential clusters is not entirely clear. The black community's embrace of the early contrabands and the presence of early migrants, such as the Bryants, in the Belmont Street area suggest that newcomers in the Civil War years did not experience animosity from older residents. But by 1870, so many southern blacks had come to Worcester that they made up well over a third of the city's black population. Established black Yankee families may have, by that point, resented the arrival of large numbers of the poorer, less-educated southern cousins. E. Franklin Frazier noted that during the Great Migration, "the Negroes who had been North for quite some time met their fellowmen with disgust and aloofness." Similarly, in the late nineteenth century, in cities like New York, well-established German Jews resented the massive influx of impoverished, less sophisticated Russian Jews.[10]

But marriage statistics suggest a lack of outright animosity between the two groups. Southern migrants tended to marry northern-born people of color in Worcester, quickly integrating themselves into the city's small black community while putting their imprint upon it. Of all southern-born migrants who married between 1862 and 1880, 60 percent chose a northern-born spouse while 40 percent chose a southern-born partner, a lower percentage than Elizabeth Pleck found among black southerners in Boston, where southern migrants married each other over 80 percent of the time. Between 1880 and 1890, the number of "mixed" marriages increased to approximately 70 percent.[11]

The prevalence of marriages between southern- and northern-born blacks suggests that the creation of residential enclaves of southern-born migrants was more likely a result of insufficient housing stock in older residential areas to contain the southern influx than a result of the animosity on the part of black Yankees. It is also likely that the Virginians and North Carolinians simply felt more comfortable living near each other — like the Irish, French Canadians, and Swedes who immigrated to Worcester in the same period and created their own ethnic enclaves. Given the fact that many migrants came from the same parts of the South and often shared family ties and a common culture, they would have voluntarily gravitated toward one another.

By the mid-1880s, some southern migrants cemented a separate identity when they established their own church in the Highland Street residential enclave. Just as the immigrant church served as the cornerstone for ethnic community life in the nineteenth century, the Mount Olive (John Street) Baptist Church represented a sense of common identity and purpose in sustaining the culture of the migrant's "homeland." Self-consciously southern in its membership, leadership, and worship style, the church served as the focal point for many members of Worcester's southern black community. As one contemporary observer noted, black churches in New England "have done much in the past to perpetuate race feeling, and have furnished a church home to many a weary pilgrim in a strange land." As George Whitney's historical address at the cornerstone-laying highlighted, the war continued to inform relations between southern blacks and white patrons, some of whom, like Whitney, served in the Civil War and insisted — long after the rest of the nation had given up on black rights — that the nation owed a debt of obligation to those it had enslaved.[12]

Mount Olive (John Street) Baptist Church began as a prayer meeting in 1878, led by James Mason, a native of Petersburg, Virginia. Described as "a little band of Southern Negroes," all of its original members, according to the local press, had once been slaves. In a letter to the Worcester Baptist Association in 1885 seeking admission to the association, a member described the group as "a 'little flock,' lightly esteemed by men, but precious in the sight of the Great Shepherd; poor and little burdened by worldly effects, yet rich as to privileges, and abounding in promises concerning the life that now is, and the Life to come." Pointing out the limited literacy of some members of the group, he wrote that they were "not all readers of God's word but hearers." He then affirmed the group's commitment to Baptist orthodoxy: "God's love for the world, and his great Gift, — the sinner's Friend, — the Cross, — the tomb, — the going on high, — intercession and the sending of the Holy Spirit, — has been the story we have heard since childhood. The new birth we know by experience. The Bible is our guide, and has confirmed us in the great fact — 'One Lord, one Faith, one Baptism.' We desire to unite with you in the Master's work."[13]

Similar to many black churches that would be founded by southerners in the urban North in the period of the Great Migration, the small band of southerners first held prayer meetings in homes and halls as a mission church under the auspices of an established church. The predominantly white Pleasant Street Baptist Church in Worcester welcomed southern migrants as members in the late 1860s and 1870s. Chowan County, North Carolina, native Allen Parker belonged to the church after he first came to Worcester in 1869 and later rejoined upon his return in the 1880s. George W. Lee and his wife, Ann, natives of Maryland and Washington, respectively, also joined the church in 1871. In February 1885, as the prayer meeting grew into a congregation, a Baptist ecclesiastical council, made up of pastors and representatives of all of the city's Baptist churches, as well as the Union Church of Cambridgeport and the Joy Street Church, Boston, convened in Worcester to officially recognize the "Mount Olive (colored) Baptist Church." The church, the local press reported, "consists of 22 members, all originally from the South." While this statement was not entirely accurate (one founder, Alexander Hemenway, was a northern-born Civil War veteran married to a southern woman), church founders and subsequent members were overwhelmingly southern-born, and the church rooted its identity in southern culture.[14]

A list of church members from the 1880s and 1890s confirms the southern origins of the Mount Olive (John Street) Baptist Church. Of 51 names generated through church records and newspaper accounts, 26 could be found in the manuscript census or birth, marriage, and death records for the city of Worcester. Of the 26 members identified, either specifically or through family surname, all but four were southern-born, with nearly all hailing from Virginia and North Carolina. Two northern-born members, Alexander Hemenway, born in Massachusetts, and John J. Wilson, a native of Connecticut, had southern-born wives. Members John and Sarah Clark, a married couple, were both Massachusetts natives.[15]

Several other common characteristics emerge from the church membership list. Membership often encompassed extended families. Two generations of New Bern Colemans and Virginia Johnsons, for example, belonged to the church. Moreover, although the generated list is skewed toward those who held leadership positions, most members tended to be in their twenties and thirties. They created a dynamic and energetic congregation with a strong sense of identity. While a few, such as barber Alexander Hemenway and machinist Charlie Clark, held skilled positions in the workforce, most toiled in unskilled jobs, as washerwomen, laborers, or servants. Developing and sustaining a new church would take immense dedication from such a resource-poor congregation.[16]

In many ways, the Mount Olive/John Street congregation's economic status reflected that of Worcester's black community at large. Like their counterparts in the Midwest, black Worcesterites, men and women, found themselves mired at the bottom of the occupational ladder, with only a handful in the professions. Moreover, few found jobs in manufacturing; they were victims of a color bar established in northern industry that would have long-term consequences for black residents. According to the 1880 census, approximately 62 percent of the 340 individuals in the labor force worked in unskilled positions, mostly as common laborers, with well over one-third of that number in domestic service. Women in particular found themselves relegated to unskilled work. Three of every four black women reporting paid employment in 1880 worked as either a laundress or a household servant. Roughly 18.5 percent of black workers — nearly all men — held skilled positions, with male barbers and a few female hairdressers making up the majority of this group. Another 9 percent worked in semiskilled positions, with female seamstresses the single largest group. Professionals accounted for roughly 4 percent of the total black workforce. This group consisted of three male preachers, three male clerical workers, two teachers, one of whom was a woman, two business proprietors, one male and one female, and a woman who defined herself as an "Indian doctress." A total of twenty-one people (6 percent) reported that they were unemployed.[17]

The socioeconomic profile of Worcester's southern-born population differed only slightly. Of 108 southern-born black Worcesterites reporting paid employment, 69 percent worked in unskilled positions, with 42 percent, mostly women, in domestic service. Like the city's black population at large, approximately 9 percent worked in semiskilled positions and 18.5 percent worked in skilled jobs, mostly as barbers. One southern-born preacher and a clothier made up the professional category. Only two southern-born Worcesterites reported that they were unemployed.[18]

Because of the community's lack of resources, southern-born black Baptists' decision to create their own church generated controversy in Worcester. According to a white Baptist leader, "Some of their friends in the other churches considered the movement rather questionable." Indeed, Worcester already had two black churches at this time: the AME Zion Church, located on Exchange Street, and the Bethel AME Church on Hanover Street, in the two east-side residential enclaves. Each church had drawn southern migrants to membership after the Civil War. For example, the AME Zion Church, the city's "black Yankee" church founded before the Civil War, counted as members Jane Waples Mero, who migrated to Worcester from New Bern with Colonel A. B. R. Sprague, and her extended family.[19]

The Bethel AME Church, founded in 1867, appears to have had a more southern flavor than the AME Zion Church. The church was founded by a mix of old and new southerners: J. G. Mowbray and Isaac Mason, both Maryland-born pre–Civil War migrants, and Civil War–era migrants Henry Johnson of Mississippi, his wife, Julia Bryant, sister of the original Worcester contraband, and Henry Cooper, also of Maryland. (Johnson and his wife later joined the Mount Olive/John Street Church.) In 1878, the church laid the cornerstone of a new house of worship at the corner of Hanover and Laurel Streets.[20]

But the small band of southern black Baptists refused to let practical considerations trump their desire for their own church. Coming from a non-liturgical tradition, they would not have felt comfortable in the more formal, ritualistic worship of the AME and AME Zion Churches, especially since, as the church member in 1885 noted, some of them could not read. They also likely sought denominational continuity, preferring to worship as Baptists rather than as African Methodists. At the same time, they wished to be in charge of their own congregation and to worship separately from the city's white Baptist churches and missions, a reflection of the autonomy central to former slaves' definition of freedom. By establishing their own church, the southern migrants could perpetuate their own style of worship and sustain a key element of southern black culture in the North. In his study of Chicago during the Great Migration, historian James Grossman notes that many of the "Old Settlers" in that city found the southern-style worship of their recently settled compatriots "outdated, unrefined, and embarrassing." But having their own church allowed southern migrants to exercise self-determination as well as bolstering a sense of community.[21]

Joining established churches and then spinning off a separate congregation reflected southern migrants' growing sense of confidence and optimism. As Grossman found in his study, established churches provided a support system for migrants, aiding them in finding jobs and housing and in meeting other southern migrants. As they gained a foothold in the North, some migrants chose to leave established churches and replicate and sustain southern culture through organizing southern churches. The urban North, as Grossman notes, "increased the number of available options," one of which was "to adjust to the urban North while still retaining aspects of one's southern cultural heritage." He argues, in addition, that southern migrants could "realistically look forward to 'bettering their condition' either by joining a more prestigious church or by organizing and leading a new congregation." In the end, newly formed southern churches, such as Mount Olive/John Street, provided migrants a way to adjust to living in the North while maintaining a vital link to their southern heritage.[22]

Despite the doubts and concerns of others, the black southern Baptists moved forward and, in 1887, two years after their official recognition, called one of their own as their pastor: a young fellow southern migrant. A charismatic evangelist, the Reverend Hiram Conway pastored the church for the next thirty-four years. He shepherded the congregation from its humble beginnings to a burgeoning congregation of well over 100 members by the early 1890s. Conway was born a slave in Northumberland County, Virginia, in 1850, and managed to migrate to North Bridgewater, Massachusetts, with his parents before the Civil War. He came to the attention of minister Charles H. Corey, who introduced him to the Pleasant Street Baptist Church in Worcester. Conway impressed the congregation "as a young man of substantial character, and of promise for future usefulness," so the church decided to finance his theological education, paying for his room and board "so that he was enabled to do his work unhampered by financial anxieties." Conway "improved his opportunities to the fullest extent," first attending Newton Theological Seminary and then completing a five-year course at Richmond Theological Seminary in Virginia.[23]

In 1886, members of the Mount Olive Church "sent to him the Macedonian cry," and the "Boy Preacher," as the local press dubbed him, accepted the church's pastorate, which he would occupy until his death in 1920. Described as "quiet by nature and self-controlled in his manners," Conway provided dynamic leadership for his tiny flock as well as the black community as a whole. The young minister admitted later that he was surprised to find his field of labor in a northern city: "I felt that I could do better work in my own state" or "across the sea" in Africa. But, he concluded, the work "was seemingly laid out for me, and I have tried to do what through the Lord was appointed for me to do."[24]

Upon his arrival in the city, he remembered, "everything looked cold and dark and indifferent." He added, "It was said that there was no place for me here; that there were too few people to make the work a success." Conway recounted "times of discouragement, times of coldness, and times when the work would lag." "For the first three months after I came here," he admitted, "I felt every Sunday that I was preaching my farewell sermon." But the "little handful of people," about two dozen members, doubled in size in his first four years, and the church, although "a feeble band financially," had branched out beyond 32 Front Street, where the group first met in a meeting hall, and managed in 1891 to purchase a plot of land on John Street. Mount Olive soon changed its name to the John Street Baptist Church to reflect its new location. By the time the members laid the cornerstone for their new church, the congregation numbered nearly 100.[25]

That historical memory of the journey from slavery to freedom remained a central part of the Mount Olive/John Street Church's identity is evident beyond George Whitney's speech given at the church's cornerstone-laying. An early annual report from the church to the Worcester Baptist Association noted, "It is because of Infinite mercy we have our freedom and the right to enjoy the worship of God in our church home, to gather ourselves for praise and prayer, and maintain the observance of that cherished rite which shows our appreciation of the Great Sacrifice."[26]

Four months after they laid the cornerstone, church members "and their friends" dedicated the new John Street Church in October 1891. The Gothic wood structure was built for $3,500, $2,000 of which had been raised "from members of the society and its friends," and the remainder contributed by the Baptist Board of Worcester. Church members "and their friends," reported the local press, "had the pleasure of witnessing the consummation of their hopes building a neat and commodious house of worship." Several white patrons contributed to the building, with the Norcross Brothers construction firm donating the pink granite cornerstone and a local citizen providing a new pulpit set.[27]

Even though the church constructed an independent, black southern Baptist identity, the John Street Church cooperated with the city's other black churches in various spiritual and social events. As historian James Grossman found in the much larger community of black Chicago in the early twentieth century, black churches managed to bridge differences within their community. As he notes, "Although the fissures were significant, they were neither as deep nor as wide as the gap separating black and white." Because theirs was such a small community and they were such an extreme minority, numbering only 524 in 1880 and 763 in 1890, black Worcesterites likely moved more easily among churches and bridged gaps of difference even more readily than their counterparts in Chicago. Allen Parker, a member of the Pleasant Street Baptist Church, for example, regularly attended the John Street Church. Moreover, as a generally poor group, they had to pool resources to support and participate in community events across denominational lines. Soon after he arrived in Worcester to pastor Mount Olive, for example, the Reverend Conway presented a sermon at the AME Zion Church's revival meetings. The city's black churches also held joint Sunday school picnic excursions to Wawshacum Lake. Reporting on one such event for the *Boston Advocate*, the city's black newspaper, the Worcester correspondent noted that "in union, there is strength, for it astonished the citizens of Worcester to see the out-pouring of the people."[28]

"Worcester Whittlings"

Churches provided just one site of community cooperation that created a common space for both black Yankee and southern migrant. Worcester's black community teemed with voluntary organizations and activities, which were regularly reported on in the "Worcester" column of the *Boston Advocate* and the "Worcester Whittlings" column of the *Boston Guardian*. Worcester's people of color annually celebrated two Emancipation Days. Continuing the pre–Civil War tradition of celebrating West Indian Emancipation Day on 1 August, they also commemorated the emancipation of American slaves on 1 January. Serving as an annual reminder to both black and white Worcesterites of the importance of the emancipation story, the January event sometimes featured prominent speakers, such as William Wells Brown, who gave a speech titled "The Heroism and Fidelity of the Colored People During the War." The August celebration featured a picnic, often held at Lake Quinsigamond, complete with clam chowder.[29]

Although the celebrations appear to have diminished in the 1880s, by the 1890s, the community had revived the annual events. It is probably not a coincidence that the community restored American Emancipation Day celebrations just as southern states began dismantling black civil rights established during Reconstruction. In 1890, in defiance of the 14th and 15th Amendments, Mississippi disfranchised its black voters, setting a trend that would be followed by every southern state by 1908. At the same time, segregation laws, which were upheld by the Supreme Court in 1896, went into effect in many southern states. To make matters worse, beginning in the 1880s and continuing in the 1890s, lynchings of blacks in the South increased dramatically.

The January 1891 Emancipation Day celebration was typical of such celebrations: it served to remind the community — both white and black — of
the centrality of the freedom story amidst deteriorating race relations. The
celebration prodded white Worcesterites to remember the role that white
liberators played in emancipation while stressing to the black community
the richness of its heritage and the importance of its defense. While a street
parade had to be canceled due to inclement weather, 150 children from the
city's three black churches presented a concert at Horticultural Hall. Portraits
of Lincoln, Charles Sumner, and John Brown adorned the walls. The children
opened the concert with the song, "Out of Bondage."[30]

Along with annual Emancipation Day celebrations, Memorial Day took
on special significance for Worcester's black community. The day that was
originally designated for remembering the Civil War dead served as another
opportunity to remind local citizens of the centrality of slavery to the war.
Educator Sarah Ella Wilson, daughter of migrants who came north from
Virginia with missionary teacher Sarah Chase, organized an annual Memorial Day program at the Belmont Street School, where she taught. Wilson's
program, recalled one of her students, featured three southern-born black
women — Louise Jones, Minnie Lee, and Maria Bryant — singing "Plantation
Songs, War Songs, and the Spirituals." They punctuated their rich, resonant
singing with background stories about the songs. A fellow teacher remembered that Wilson did not confine her heritage lessons to Memorial Day:
"I remember that she spent many recesses with the older Black pupils teaching them Spirituals. She wanted them to know their heritage. I recall her
saying that she wanted them to be proud of their race." For migrant Robert
Morse, who came to North Brookfield with Dr. Warren Tyler after the Civil
War, "Memorial Day was always a favorite," and "it was a very great privilege
and pleasure for him" to "decorate the graves of comrades." Memorial Day
commemorations placed African Americans at the center of the Civil War
story, as the community celebrated its southern heritage while memorializing
its past.[31]

Fraternal lodges and auxiliaries provided another show of community
strength and self-help. For a community of its size, Worcester supported an
unusually large number of fraternal lodges and auxiliaries as early as the mid-
1870s. As historian Nick Salvatore notes in his study of Worcester's Amos
Webber, the level of organization among the city's small black community
was truly "striking." Convened by Civil War veteran Amos Webber in 1868,
the North Star Lodge No. 1372, Grand United Order of Odd Fellows, marked,
Salvatore argues, "an important turning point in the city's collective black

life," as this lodge, like the many that followed it, served as "a self-conscious instrument of both individual and collective black self-help." The King David Lodge No. 16 of the Prince Hall Masons was established in 1874, along with a women's auxiliary, the Household of Ruth. A second Odd Fellows lodge, Integrity Lodge No. 1768, appeared in 1876. By the time Mount Olive/John Street became the third black church in Worcester, black Worcesterites established two more fraternal/sororal organizations, the Knights of Pythias, U. S. Grant Lodge, and the Ebenezer Lodge of Good Samaritans and Daughters of Samaria. Fraternal and sororal organizations attracted both black Yankees and southern migrants. Salvatore found that far from being elitist, lodges were inclusive in their membership. Half of the lodge members found in the census were southern-born. In addition, it appears that there were no identifiably "southern" lodges. Fraternal and sororal organizations bridged differences among Worcester's black community. These organizations would have been especially important vehicles for migrants, introducing them to other members of the community, providing them networks for jobs and housing, and infusing them with an ethos of self-help and community activism.[32]

Just as southern black Baptists had been discouraged from establishing a third black church in such a small community, the founders of the Knights of Pythias lodge received a similar response. Community leader and lodge member Amos Webber warned that "most of our well thinking men are of the opinion that it will be injurious to our citizens, as most of them belong to the four branches of Odd Fellows, and the same of Masonic and a lodge of Good Samaritans and Daughters of Samaria." He warned, "These are about as much as we can sustain and pay our honest bills, and be honorable in the community."[33]

Yet this lodge, as well as the other social and religious institutions that preceded it, flourished in the 1880s. The "Worcester" columns in area black newspapers attest to the beehive of activity that was black Worcester. Women of the AME Zion Church held a "Rainbow festival," while their sisters at Bethel sponsored a "Clothes-Pin party." The Household of Ruth and the Knights of Pythias cooked up annual turkey dinners. The genteel Sixteen Associates sponsored a monthly Ladies Day, while the Mount Zion Commandery held a dress ball, featuring dancing and live music.[34]

Churches and fraternal and sororal organizations provided black Worcesterites a sense of the important role they played in the larger African American community. They linked Worcester's small community to black New England and beyond, creating regional and even national networks for both social and political purposes. The AME Zion denomination's "connection," its church network, tied the Worcester congregation to sister churches nationally. Local black lodges sent delegations to regional and national conventions, and Worcester lodges held annual excursions to out-of-state destinations, such as Rocky Point, Rhode Island, where they met up with their Providence counterparts.[35]

George Ward Post 10, Grand Army of the Republic, also played a vital role in the lives of many black Worcesterites and connected them to both regional and national networks. Moreover, the post helped sustain the memory of the Civil War and of the role of its black veterans in the Union triumph. At least nine of Worcester's southern migrants belonged to the local post. Founded in 1867, Post 10 was unusual in its acceptance of black veterans, which totaled around twenty. Although the GAR officially established a color-blind membership policy, allowing many black veterans to join the organization, most black veterans belonged to segregated posts. In large cities, such as Philadelphia, historian Stuart McConnell found that black and white veterans maintained separate, segregated posts, with black veterans consequently "accorded separate and unequal status."[36]

Yet the issue of race nearly imploded Post 10 in its infancy. In 1870, Bazzell Barker, a black veteran of the 54th Massachusetts regiment, found himself blackballed when he applied for membership. According to one member, he had not been admitted because of his race. However, the post already had two black members, Amos Webber, of the 5th Massachusetts Volunteer Cavalry, the state's only black cavalry unit, and New Bern native Thomas Waples, brother of Sarah Waples Mero, who had served in the 11th New York Colored Regiment. After a second ballot came back unfavorably for Barker, the post held a meeting that led to the adoption on 9 June 1870 of resolutions stating, without equivocation, that "the only requisites we deem essential to eligibility to membership of this Post are: That the applicant shall be of good character, have served in the Army or Navy for the suppression of the rebellion, and to have been honorably discharged therefrom" and, notably, "that with these qualifications no inquiry as to race, color, or nationality of any applicant should, or by right ought to be made, wither by any Committee or by this Post." A subsequent vote on Barker again came back negative, and several members threatened the end of the post "if the colored man was not allowed in it." When still another vote rejected Barker, the commander of the post, who supported Barker's membership, resigned, along with two other white officers of the post.[37]

Barker never became a member, but Post 10 ultimately accepted approximately eighteen black veterans, both northern- and southern-born, in addition to Webber and Waples. North Carolina migrants Emory Phelps, who served in the 54th Massachusetts, and Allen Parker, a U.S. Navy landsman, joined the post. Virginians Alfred Edwards, of the 5th Massachusetts Cavalry, and Charles Fisher, a master's mate in the U.S. Navy, as well as Charleston, South Carolina, native Charles Clark, who served in both the U.S. Army and Navy, were active members of Post 10.[38]

Membership in the GAR bestowed a plethora of benefits to its members, not the least of which was that it was a powerful vehicle for political participation. As historian McConnell shows, the GAR was much more than a potent Republican political organization; it "wore several masks: fraternal lodge, charitable society, special-interest lobby, patriotic group, political club." The GAR also played a crucial role in securing pensions for its members, guaranteeing their appropriate burial, and providing relief funds for their family members. It was no accident that many of the political leaders in Worcester's black community in the late 1860s, 1870s, and 1880s were Civil War veterans, whose military service not only gave them status in the community but also educated them in the political process and provided them a platform for political participation. As Nick Salvatore shows, in the 1870s and 1880s, Civil War veterans — most notably Amos Webber, George Scott, and William Gardner — served as the core of a "leadership cohort." Gilbert Walker, Isaac Mason, and William Jankins, although not veterans, helped recruit locally for African American regiments during the Civil War. All of these men were active members of fraternal organizations, where they became, in Salvatore's words, "seasoned, proven leaders."[39]

Probably more than any single group, black veterans kept the "patriotic vision" of the Civil War alive. They served as living examples of the sacrifices that blacks had made to save the Union and the citizenship rights that they had earned through their sacrifice. In 1884, led by Amos Webber, black veterans of Massachusetts units formed the Massachusetts Colored Veterans Association of Worcester. Through parades in the city and their participation in national black veterans' reunions, they articulated a powerful message to those who would forget their contributions. At an August 1887 national reunion of black Massachusetts regiments, the assembly passed a series of resolutions that demanded "full and equal protection of the laws" and vowed political support only to those "who have been faithful" to the constitutional amendments passed in Reconstruction. In addition, they insisted that a monument be built in the nation's capital as a reminder of "the patriotic negro soldier and his kin who came to the rescue of an imperiled nation." They had "so nobly earned" full citizenship "in the dark days of the rebellion." Reconciliation between North and South, they asserted, should not come at the expense of black civil rights: "Conciliation and peace with enemies are grand" but only when "coupled with justice to faithful allies."[40]

"The majority are not prosperous"

Despite the effervescence of community activity in the 1880s and 1890s, Worcester's black community stagnated economically. In his *Dictionary of Worcester and Its Vicinity*, published in 1893, Franklin Rice made the following blunt assessment: "The social condition of this race has not improved here during the past forty years. In fact, Negroes are not treated with the consideration they were before the war, when Worcester was thought a paradise for the fugitive from oppression." He continued, "There are a few well-to-do colored men here, but the majority are not prosperous."[41]

While many first-generation southern migrants enjoyed the patronage of influential, sympathetic whites, subsequent generations did not benefit from the same personal networks forged in the crucible of the Civil War. Indeed, white sympathy and patronage, as Rice suggested, dramatically faded as Civil War veterans and the abolitionist generation, the "benevolent sympathizers," in fugitive slave Isaac Mason's words, passed from the scene.

While Rice's depiction of black Worcester's decline from a "paradise" to a stagnant poverty was an overstatement, he nonetheless captured a shift in sentiment — both locally and nationally — of white northerners toward their black counterparts. Even as individual patrons remained, as George Whitney's speech indicated, Worcester had drifted away from its abolitionist heritage and commitment to black rights. While Worcester's Senator George Frisbie Hoar remained a stalwart advocate — and often a lone voice in the U.S. Senate — for black civil rights, most of the city's white men and women who had cut their teeth on antislavery activism and participated in the struggle for freedpeople's rights had been replaced by a new generation of men and women far removed from the momentous struggles that had shaped the nation in the 1850s and 1860s. Even the Republican Party, whose radicals boldly fought for — and established in the Constitution — full-fledged citizenship and rights for black Americans, had quickly moved to the right, replacing concern for freedpeople with laissez-faire economics and denying African Americans patronage positions they had surely earned through their loyalty to the party of Lincoln. While willing to "wave the bloody shirt" to win national elections, white Republicans, like many white Americans, chose to erase slavery and emancipation from their memory of

the Civil War. They constructed instead a sentimental narrative that emphasized the reconciliation of North and South and honored the southern "Lost
Cause." In the process, they expunged the horrific story of human slavery,
the liberation of slaves, and the radical vision of equality that the war had
engendered.[42]

Industrial employment was one crucial area in which blacks sorely felt
a lack of "consideration," in Rice's words. African Americans migrated as
Worcester evolved into a major manufacturing center. As early as 1870,
Worcester emerged as the second largest city in the state and boasted hundreds of manufacturing establishments and over 10,000 workers. By 1890,
Worcester ranked as the thirteenth largest manufacturing city in the country.
Unusual in their diversity, Worcester's largest industries specialized in machinery manufacture and wire-making, but they also produced leather belts,
boots, shoes, corsets, and even shredded wheat. But local industrialists pre-
ferred to hire the European immigrants who also flocked to the city. By 1900,
nearly 25,000 workers labored in the city's numerous and diverse factories.
Yankee industrialists often complained of labor shortages as they tried to fill
the ranks of their manufactories. Yet most Worcester firms limited their hiring to whites. In an era when local employers constructed a hierarchy of the
most desirable industrial workers among those of European descent — with
the Protestant Swedes at the top of the list, followed by the French Canadians,
and then the Irish at the bottom — African Americans received little or no
consideration.[43]

Lack of access to industrial jobs had significant ramifications for social
mobility and the wealth and well-being of the city's black community. The advantages enjoyed by the first generation of southern migrants through Civil
War–era patronage networks did not continue for subsequent migrants. An
examination of property ownership in 1900 starkly reveals this fact. Of 184
African American households in the city of Worcester in 1900, only 21 occupied homes that they owned either outright or through a mortgage. Of these,
14 were occupied by southern migrants. But, notably, 6 of the 14 were occupied by first-generation Civil War–era migrants and their children. They included Virginian Bethany Veney and her daughter, Charlotte, and son-in-law,
Aaron Jackson; New Bern native Jane Waples Mero, who accompanied General and Mrs. A. B. R. Sprague to Worcester at the end of the war; Mero's son,
Charles Sumner Mero; and Christopher Bryant, a member of the original New
Bern contraband family. The remainder of the city's southern-born homeowners in 1900 were skilled workers, such as South Carolina–born Joseph
Clark and brick mason Augustus Raiford, a native of Georgia. The hand-

ful of northern-born homeowners included custodian Amos Webber, world cycling champion Marshall "Major" Taylor, and upholsterer Charles Brown, who ran the business established by his father, William, before the Civil War. Despite the burning desire of many ex-slaves to own property, very few managed to do so in Worcester; neither did their northern-born compatriots, as African Americans remained largely barred from industry and mired in the lowest-paying jobs.[44]

A comparison of southern black migrants' situation with that of French Canadian immigrants casts the economic stagnation of Worcester's black community into sharp relief. Arriving at the same time as southern blacks, beginning in the Civil War years, with their numbers increasing dramatically in the 1870s, French Canadians, like their black counterparts, came from a rural, nonindustrial background. While early southern migrants generated some sympathy as refugees of the Civil War and victims of slavery, many local citizens, by contrast, held French Canadians in contempt, viewing them with suspicion, as they seemed unusually clannish and unwilling to assimilate. French Canadians worked for low wages, insisted on maintaining their language, and immediately set up their own separate schools and Catholic parishes as the cornerstones of their ethnic communities. In a highly publicized report, Carroll D. Wright, chief of the Massachusetts Bureau of Statistics of Labor, went as far as labeling the French Canadians "the Chinese of the East." But as people of European descent, with the doors of Worcester's industries open wide to them, they managed to advance rapidly from unskilled to skilled positions, particularly as operatives in boot and shoe factories, as iron- and steelworkers, and as machinists. Over 66 percent of French Canadian workers in 1900 engaged in manufacturing and mechanical occupations, and only 9.5 percent labored in unskilled jobs. Skilled jobs could also be handed down to sons and daughters, ensuring economic security and a better chance at upward mobility.[45]

By contrast, Worcester's black population remained mired in the same domestic service and unskilled occupations that they held years before. In a city where over half the workforce labored in manufacturing and mechanical pursuits, less than 20 percent of blacks held such jobs. Well over half of the city's black working population — 57.9 percent — toiled as unskilled laborers in domestic and personal service. Black women found Worcester's industries even less welcoming than their male counterparts. Whereas 40 percent of the city's white working women labored in the manufacturing sector, less than 10 percent of black women did so. The city's corset-making industry, boot and shoe factories, and textile mills, which employed thousands of white women, many of them French Canadian and Irish, did not employ a single black woman. Instead, black women toiled overwhelmingly as domestic workers: 165 of the city's 195 black working females (84.6 percent) worked as domestics.[46]

Even Irish workers, who complained about job discrimination by Worcester's manufacturers, had far more job opportunities than blacks. Only 20 percent of Irish workers labored in unskilled positions, and they found work in all of the city's manufactories. Irish men concentrated in machine shops, iron- and steelworks, and wireworks; and although 38 percent of Irish women worked as domestics, Worcester's clothing manufacturers, corset makers, textile mills, and other industries provided them opportunities unavailable to black women.[47]

Access to skilled jobs in manufacturing provided the economic grounding for a prosperous and rapidly growing French Canadian community in Worcester. As one local French Canadian resident noted, "In 1869 we had nothing to speak of," but by 1882 the community had built "a French convent and a French church," constructed at a cost of $80,000. The city's French Canadian community boasted a benevolent society as well as several other clubs and even a French-language newspaper. A walk through Worcester revealed an emerging middle class: "French grocers on every street" and "three French doctors," as well as "French clerks in every first-class store." The community's leaders seemed well aware of the value of their whiteness. In response to Carroll Wright's negative portrayal of the French, a local leader demanded a meeting with the labor bureau chief to "show him that we are white people, and that we have been well brought up." Possibilities for advancement seemed so certain for French Canadians in Worcester that, by 1900, they made up the city's second-largest foreign-born population, consisting of over 14,000 people.[48]

By contrast, southern blacks trickled into the city of Worcester. The community that had grown to only 1,100 by 1900 lacked both the wealth and the population simply to sustain the numbers of cultural institutions that the French Canadians managed to establish in a short period of time. Like their counterparts in other northern cities, most African Americans in Worcester found their chances of economic security — and those of their children — significantly diminished due to racist hiring practices. In their study of Pittsburgh, which compared the experiences of black and Polish workers from 1900 to 1930, John Bodnar, Michael Weber, and Roger Simon found that southern migrants faced especially harsh discrimination: they were "particularly unwanted because they were thought to be 'inefficient,' 'unstable,' and unsuitable for the heavy pace of mill work." Worcester's blacks appear to have faced the same "urban racism and structural inequality" that severely limited the upward mobility of blacks in Pittsburgh. It is likely that, like their Pennsylvania counterparts, they were "unable to overcome racial hostility and pass job skills on to their children."[49]

Worcester's color bar was not limited to industrial jobs. Historian Timothy Meagher points out that clerical opportunities for white men and women expanded significantly in the city between 1880 and 1900, with the number of white males in clerical jobs increasing "by almost double the growth of the overall male workforce in those two decades" and the number of women in clerical jobs increasing "by an astonishing 928 percent, seven times the proportionate growth in the female workforce from 1880 to 1900." Yet blacks found themselves unable to take advantage of these jobs as well. The example of Joseph Rollins provides insight into the obstacles they faced. Rollins, who aspired to the white-collar position of stenographer in a local business, found his path barred when a local shorthand school refused to enroll him. "An intelligent young colored man," according to the local press, Rollins worked for Joseph H. Walker, a boot manufacturer in the city. When, in response to a newspaper ad, he applied to Gaffey's shorthand school in April 1888, the school refused the "ambitious young fellow" admission. Challenging his rejection, Rollins was told that the school's policies forbade the admission of "colored pupils."[50]

The *Worcester Telegram*, in reporting the incident, noted a sea change in the city. "The color line has never existed in Worcester until now," the newspaper argued. "A negro has enjoyed every privilege a white man has enjoyed." While Worcester's people of color would not have agreed with such an exaggerated statement, the press nevertheless accurately assessed the change in race relations in the city as white residents' collective memory of the Civil War as a war for emancipation faded. The school's proprietor "seemed to have got an idea that he was doing business in Mississippi," the newspaper noted, and "he had forgotten that the war of the rebellion had been fought, and that the negro had a lawful right to every privilege enjoyed by his white brother, at least in states where law has any force."[51]

On the fringes of Worcester's industrial economy, the city's blacks seem to have been especially hard hit by the severe economic depression of the 1890s. In 1894, the John Street Baptist Church noted in its annual report to the Worcester Baptist Association, "Our members have felt the pressure of the times, for most of them were without work last winter, especially the male portion."[52]

In addition to struggling to find a firm economic footing in the city, Worcester's blacks also found themselves grappling with unofficial Jim Crow. African
Americans were barred from residency in the city's homes for the elderly.
As the *Worcester Telegram* so delicately put it, such institutions "in the city
have always drawn the line on the race questions with distinctness." In re-
sponse, twelve women from the AME Zion Church organized "the Woman's
Progressive Club, of Worcester, Mass.," in October 1898 and incorporated the
organization two years later. Like the city's many fraternal organizations, the
Progressive Club incorporated both southern- and northern-born members.
Of the twelve founders, three were from the South: Jane Collins hailed from
North Carolina, and Ella Edwards and Narcissa Tossit were born in Washington. Two additional Edwards women, Emma and Gertrude, were among
the founders. The object of the club was "to secure co-operation among its
members, mutual improvement, and the establishment of a Day Nursery and
Home for the Needy." Renting a house at 6 Liberty Street, the club had established both the day nursery and home for "aged and frail colored women" by
the summer of 1900. The following year, the club purchased 10 Liberty Street
as its new home.[53]

The Progressive Club was part of the black clubwomen's movement emerging in towns and cities across the country. Black women first tackled problems of race and gender discrimination and poverty at the local level before
organizing regionally and nationally. As historian Deborah Gray White notes,
despite some regional variations, "the guiding principle behind all the clubs
was racial uplift through self-help. Black clubwomen believed they could help
solve the race's problems through intensive social service focused on improving home life and educating mothers." Organizations like the Progressive
Club provided a "vehicle for race leadership" to women, who enthusiastically
embraced their role in community uplift.[54]

The same year that the Progressive Club purchased its home on Liberty
Street, a rival association appeared: the Lucy Stone Club. Named after the
Worcester County abolitionist and feminist, the Lucy Stone Club "resulted
from dissension in the ranks" of the Progressive Club when Mrs. Walter
Coshburn, the club's first treasurer and its second president, resigned in protest over the outcome of the club's third set of elections. Forming the competing club, she adopted the same aims as the Progressive Club, and, according
to the local press, "every move of the Woman's progressive club has been

swiftly followed through all the months succeeding," including the purchase of a property at 43 Liberty Street from Amos and Lizzie Webber.[55]

The local press enjoyed reporting on the rivalry of the two black women's groups in Worcester's small community. The *Worcester Evening Post* labeled the conflict a "Modern Day War of the Roses" and reported that a member of the Progressive Club referred to the rival organization as a "secessionist movement." The *Telegram* depicted the two clubs "putting forward every effort to outdo the other in good works and honor." But press reports also indicate that more was at play than petty jealousies. The *Telegram* noted that the two clubs "have worked by different methods." The Progressive Club aimed "first to raise among its members and through its efforts, a good nucleus, and then, with this behind them, to show their earnestness and sincerity, the members intended to appeal to the rich citizens of Worcester." By holding lawn parties, fund-raising entertainment, and parties in their homes, and by collecting dues regularly, members managed to raise $100 for their new home, "every cent of which has come from the pockets of the colored people of Worcester." By contrast, the Lucy Stone Club solicited money first by making personal petitions for funds; as the *Evening Post* reported, "The Lucy Stone association appealed to the white people for money and got it." Mailing a subscription circular "to the charitable men and women of Worcester," it managed to raise an amount that "passed the expectations of the promoters." The Lucy Stone Club printed a long list of contributors in the *Evening Post*. Some of the city's most prominent citizens and businesses, including Stephen Salisbury and the Denholm, McKay Company, were among the contributors. In response, a Progressive Club member proudly noted that her club "is able to look out for the colored race without appealing to the sympathies of white people."[56]

The so-called War of the Roses soon fizzled out, and the two clubs made their peace. Along with a third black women's club, the Standard Social Club, the organizations helped host the annual convention of the Northeastern Federation of Colored Women's Clubs in August 1904. Speaker Sylvia Kennard, a founder of the Progressive Club, welcomed the convention on behalf of all three clubs. Unable to cast their votes in political elections, the clubwomen nevertheless made their voices heard in a series of resolutions at the convention condemning "lynch law and mob violence" and Jim Crow railroad cars as "inhuman, as un-American, as unconstitutional."[57]

For southern-born members of the women's clubs, many of whom still had kin in the South, these resolutions would have taken on an especially personal meaning. Since members stood in firm agreement on the urgency of these issues, the clubs' past disagreements faded into insignificance. But the conflict between the Progressive Club and the Lucy Stone Club over strategy pointed to an ongoing dilemma for Worcester's small and resource-poor black community. Aspiring to independence and seeking to define the agenda for their own community, Worcester's blacks nevertheless continually found themselves, out of necessity, regularly seeking the support of the city's wealthier white citizens. Their aspirations for autonomy and the establishment of a self-reliant community were continually frustrated by the small size of their community and a lack of resources. Nowhere was this more evident than in local politics.

"Remember that every ballot you cast for a Democrat means additional negro hardships, more lynching, more riots"

By the 1890s, community leadership and goals changed markedly, shaped by both local and national events and a generational shift. Young southerners provided fresh leadership and more aggressive strategies in response to the changing racial climate locally and nationally. They began to replace the older generation of leaders who had shaped community activism since before the Civil War.

By comparing the names of African American political activists mentioned in the local press in the 1890s to those listed in census and vital statistics records, a clear portrait of the new leadership cohort emerges. Twenty-two of 28 men mentioned in local newspapers between 1896 and 1900 could be identified in censuses or vital statistics records. A total of 16 of the 22 identified activists either were born in the South or were the children of Civil War–era southern migrants. Eleven activists were southern-born, with Robert H. Johnson — the Maryland-born truckman who aided the first contrabands in Worcester — the lone representative of pre–Civil War Worcester. Five Massachusetts-born activists were children of southern migrants who arrived in the Civil War era. Brothers Charles and Walter Scott were the Worcester County–born sons of Edward and Catherine Scott, migrants from Virginia in the 1860s. William Beckton, who came to Worcester at the age of fifteen in 1865 from Washington, North Carolina, and his Worcester-born son, George, were both Republican activists. Daniel Edwards, like Beckton, arrived in Worcester as a teenager in the early 1870s as part of the Civil War–era migration. Virginia-born ministers Hiram Conway of John Street Baptist Church and L. H. Taylor of the AME Zion Church also provided consistent leadership. By the 1890s this group of activists — most of whom were in their forties or early fifties — emerged as the new generation of leadership.[58]

While not Civil War veterans, as the previous generation had been, the new generation of leaders were, as Horace James put it so many years before during the war, "the children of this revolution." The Civil War and the protection of its legacy strongly informed their politics. As many were born into slavery and liberated by the war, and then reached maturity during the heady days of Reconstruction, when black Americans were promised full equality, they refused to lower their expectations. Even as race relations worsened in the 1890s, both locally and nationally, they demanded to be heard and treated as equals, and they insisted on respect and representation in local government. Whereas white politicians continually waved "the bloody shirt" of the Civil War through the late nineteenth century to win elections, the black activists' constant allusion to the war had a far deeper meaning. As children of the revolution, they, like many other African Americans in this era, fought to maintain an emancipationist vision of the Civil War. They insisted that the nation remember the true meaning of the Civil War, the sacrifices black Americans made for the Union cause, and the Radical Republican vision of full equality. They adamantly refused any compromise of the war's meaning and legacy. With their roots in Dixie, with family and friends suffering there, and with resilient migration networks providing a fresh, personal perspective on the South's worsening climate, they boldly spoke out against injustice in the North and the South, particularly the rise of Jim Crow laws and the disfranchisement of black voters.[59]

In the aftermath of the Civil War, Worcester's black community continued the tradition of political activism established in the prewar era. As Nick Salvatore shows, Worcester's political activists, led by Amos Webber and Gilbert Walker, among others, insisted on a voice in both local and national politics. They organized black voters through rallies and election parades. They generally remained committed to the Republican Party — the party of emancipation — even when local white Republicans refused them membership in their organizations. Creating a "Colored Grant and Colfax Club" in support of U. S. Grant's presidential campaign in 1868, they bravely campaigned, amidst vicious attacks, for Grant and did so again in 1872. Webber and his fellow leaders also rallied the black community to commemorate the death of Senator Charles Sumner and to support of the Civil Rights Bill of 1875. In 1878 and 1883, the "Colored Republicans" boldly opposed Democrat Benjamin Butler in his race for the governorship.[60]

By the late 1880s, as Salvatore notes, a generational shift in leadership took place with the establishment of the Massachusetts Citizens Equal Rights Association. Founded by representatives from across the Bay State, with a branch in Worcester established in 1890, the association had a clear-cut agenda: to guarantee "to all Americans the full right and enjoyment of natural, essential, inalienable rights, guaranteed to them by the constitution of the United States" and to commemorate annually the Emancipation Proclamation. The celebration, once an annual event in Worcester, faded in the 1870s and 1880s. Its revival provided a way to jar the nation from its amnesia regarding the war's legacy. The new organization's leaders, notes Salvatore, "indicated the sea change" in leadership "then underway." While an aged Isaac Mason participated, a new leadership cohort had emerged, which included the Reverend Hiram Conway of John Street Baptist, along with George Alfred Busby, a Barbados-born tailor who came to Worcester from Boston in 1884. The older generation of leaders either were too old to participate or had passed away. William Jankins, Isaac Mason, and Amos Webber, for example, were all aged, and Gilbert Walker died in 1888. (Jankins died in the late 1890s, Mason in 1898, and Webber in 1904.) Having nobly served their community, they now yielded to a new generation of leaders.[61]

The establishment of the Citizens Equal Rights Association signaled a shift toward a more aggressive political strategy in the 1890s. The city's previous black activists had never hesitated to assert themselves, sometimes at the risk of bodily harm, but much of their energy had focused on supporting white Republican candidates through Colored Republican clubs and activities. Black Republicans in Worcester, as well as in the rest of the nation, had grown weary of getting so little in return for their loyal support. They demanded representatives of their own race in political office as well as the patronage positions handed out by elected officials. In addition, a new set of crises confronted African Americans, and the Republican Party remained unresponsive. Having abandoned southern blacks in 1877, with the end of Reconstruction, the party failed to address the disfranchisement of southern black voters, begun in Mississippi in 1890, and turned a blind eye to the rise of Jim Crow laws and a surge in lynching. Angry for being abandoned and tired of being taken for granted as sure votes for the Republican Party, some black leaders began to advocate a strategy of independence to force both major parties to vie for their votes and to make political gains.[62]

The new generation of Worcester's black activists, much like their antebellum counterparts, waged the war for equal rights both locally and nationally. In the early 1890s, they formed the Colored Republican Protective Association as the vehicle for this war. The name itself suggested the need for more forceful action to protect African Americans' rights. In 1896, members of the Colored Protective Association met in the Grange Hall and broke with the past tradition of supporting white candidates. Instead — for the first time — they endorsed two members of their own community for city offices: the Reverend Hiram Conway, who was running for a seat on the Worcester School Committee, and tailor George Alfred Busby, who was running for common council. As the *Telegram* noted in a front-page story, "For the first time in the history of Worcester colored men will stand as candidates before the coming caucuses for city offices."[63]

The two men represented the aspirations of the city's black community for recognition and representation. George Potter, who chaired the meeting, explained, "The colored man has been always found on the side of the right, for sound money and the principles of protection, and all that makes for greater liberty and the advancement of the community. But he has never been recognized as having claims to a part in the government." However, he added, "This year we propose to do something that will show our strength and win recognition from the people as a strong element in the community."[64]

Just as the Irish, French Canadians, Swedes, and "Hebrews," as the local press referred to them, organized to show their political clout, demanding a place at the governmental table and the political patronage that went with it, so, too, did Worcester's blacks. While still small in number compared to the city's other ethnic communities, they now believed that they had the critical mass to move forward with their own candidates. In 1896, the city had roughly 500 registered African American voters, still a fraction of the number of Irish, French Canadian, or Swedish voters. But, as Hiram Conway asserted at the meeting, "It is a fact that we will never get anything unless we make an effort to get it." "I believe in making an effort," he continued, "in allowing it to be seen that we have a desire to be represented by our own people," adding that he promised to "make the best fight I can."[65]

Notably, Ward One encompassed the city's largest black enclave, the John Street Church neighborhood, the largely southern-born community west of Highland Street. Yet black voters were still a minority in Ward One, a fact that the Colored Republican Protective Association was well aware of. For their candidates to win, they needed not only, as barber Daniel Gaines noted at the meeting, to "unite the colored voters" but also to "get as many of the white voters to support" them as possible: "As a people, united we stand, divided we must fall."[66]

Both Conway and Busby appeared to be especially viable candidates, with the potential to attract the white votes necessary to win. As pastor of the John

Street Baptist Church, Conway was well known to local white Baptists, some of whom had helped send him to a Virginia theological seminary. Highly educated and well-spoken, he had already demonstrated his outstanding leadership abilities by guiding his church from its origins as a tiny flock of former slaves meeting in rented rooms to a flourishing congregation in a new edifice on John Street. Busby, as the owner and operator of a tailoring business on Main Street that specialized in fine men's suits, was also familiar to many prominent white Worcesterites. As Virginia-born Daniel Edwards noted at a rally in 1896, Busby "has a fine figure, speaks his words distinctly and carries himself with utmost ease."[67]

But polished presentations and sterling reputations proved not to be enough for either candidate. At the Republican caucuses held to nominate the party's candidates, Busby garnered only 62 votes compared to the 214 cast for Albert H. Inman, a local businessman and president of the YMCA. Conway did not fare much better, losing to candidate Austin Garner 241 to 95.[68]

However, the unsuccessful vote proved to be only part of the story. Four days after the caucuses, the Colored Republican Protective Association held "an indignation meeting" at the Grange Hall to express its outrage at a remark allegedly made by Albert Inman, Busby's victorious opponent. Inman, several members charged, urged a voter to cast his ballot for him by "denouncing his opponent as nothing but a nigger." Several attendees questioned the truthfulness of the account. William R. Anderson, a Maryland-born coachman in the city, and Isaac Mason's brother argued that insults were the cost of political involvement and that the remark was something that "could have been applied to a Swede or any other nationality." In response, an angry Daniel Gaines, a local barber whose parents had been slaves in Virginia, replied, "We are colored voters of Worcester. We have been oppressed ever since we were born. There are those though their skins be white, their hearts are blacker than the 'nigger' of whom it was said don't vote for him." He continued, "I want to say to the colored voters of Worcester, it is time to wake up from slumber and let him know that we are to be respected or we won't amount to anything. . . . If he were here I would tell him, though he may have all the advantages, yet the colored man is his superior. They at least have manners. When the strength of the colored voter is learned, then he will be respected." Gaines went on to remind the gathering about the history of their hard-earned freedom: "There is no race in the past 30 years that has made such advancement, left, too, as we were at the end of the war, without a home or without a cent. It was on the battlefield that the confederates said, 'Take your black faces from the field and we will lick you.'" Gaines demanded that his fellow citizens fight with the same resolve, that "we will show him we are here to fight."[69]

Chairman Potter continued the debate by setting Inman's alleged remark against the backdrop of the widening color line both locally and nationally: "It is . . . the matter of drawing the color line. If President Inman will draw the color line in politics, he will draw it in the Young Men's Christian Association, you may be sure." Busby himself agreed: "If it is wrong for the people of Louisiana or Mississippi and other southern states to discriminate against us, it is wrong for them to do it in Massachusetts." A week later, they passed and published a series of resolutions condemning Inman and seeking his resignation as president of the YMCA. Denouncing Inman as "dishonorable and cheap" for "placing his opponent's color, which God is responsible for, before them in order to secure the nomination," they asserted, "It is the opinion of this Republican protective association that no man ought to be elected or defeated on account of his color." They called upon "all fair minded voters to repudiate Albert H. Inman as being unfit and a disgrace to this fair state, and especially to the voters of ward 1." Finally, they asked that the YMCA sever ties with Inman since the organization "stands for all that is good and pure" and should not have as an officer one "who loses all reverence for God and shows no respect for his commandments."[70]

Neither Albert Inman nor the Republican leaders responded publicly to the charges and resolutions of the Colored Republicans. Perhaps black votes were too insignificant in number to warrant a public acknowledgment. In any case, Inman went on to win a seat on the common council from Ward One, despite the indignation of the city's black voters.[71]

From 1896 through 1900, Worcester's blacks continued to nominate candidates for local office, seeking representation as well as political patronage. But success eluded them. Busby ran annually for common council, along with Walter Coshburn, who ran unsuccessfully from Ward Seven in 1897. W. R. Ringalls articulated the frustration of the city's blacks, who were barred from not only industrial jobs but also political patronage positions that offered steady work at decent wages: Street Commissioner Stone had solicited votes by "saying that he would employ colored men when he got into office," but "he had failed to see brown faces at work on the roads. Instead, he found the Irishmen, the ones who voted against [him]." The Irish were employed, he charged, because they "are banded together and their demands count for something." Raymond Jones agreed: "The only way that other nationalities got representation was through uniting." Virginia native Rev. L. H. Taylor of the AME Zion Church agreed, arguing that "representation and recognition would come if the colored people proved themselves united and in earnest," a strategy endorsed by his fellow minister Hiram Conway.[72]

But Worcester's black voters, already handicapped by small numbers, never attained the unity necessary to become a viable political force. Like their counterparts across the nation — and especially in the South — they divided in the 1890s over their loyalty to the Republican Party. Tired of their shabby treatment, some blacks began to assert their political independence from the party of Lincoln, arguing that they could make more gains, especially with patronage positions, if they gave their votes to the party that promised them the most — even voting for Democrats if necessary. Splitting their votes, they argued, would force both parties to take them seriously. To most Worcester blacks, defection to the Democratic Party was nothing short of heresy, especially given the racial politics of the Democratic South. And while most stuck doggedly with the Republican Party, infighting with Democratic "apostates" weakened an already meager voting bloc.[73]

For black Republican loyalists — who made up the overwhelming majority of voters in Worcester as well as in the rest of the country — the Civil War, Reconstruction, and Jim Crow Democratic politics provided the main justification for sticking with the party. For most activists — especially those with southern roots — defection to the Democrats was unthinkable, and they articulated variations of Frederick Douglass's famous refrain: "The Republican Party is the ship, all else is the ocean."[74]

The 1900 election brought this fundamental division to a dramatic head. With Republican William McKinley running for reelection against Democrat William Jennings Bryan, and with Republican Charles Washburn seeking to unseat incumbent Democratic congressman John R. Thayer, the election, in the eyes of many of the city's blacks, also served as a referendum on the disfranchisement of black voters and violence against them in the South.

The Colored Republicans kicked off the heart of their campaign at a "rousing rally" held at Horticultural Hall in late October. It was "one of the best meetings of the campaign," according to the *Worcester Daily Spy*. And although the city's black women could not cast their votes, they took great interest in this election. The press noted the women seated in the hall and galleries and that they "appeared to enjoy the program." As the resolutions of the Northeastern Federation of Colored Women's Clubs convention held in Worcester several years later revealed, black women, like their male counterparts, spoke out boldly against the white supremacy steam engine rolling across the South.[75]

Henry Clay Elliot, a Worcester barber and recent migrant from South

Carolina, made the first speech at the rally. He noted that the basic question presented by the election on 6 November was simple: "whether the party of Tillman, Jones, Croker and Bryan is to govern this country, or the party of Grant, Lincoln, Douglass and McKinley." Elliot then recited South Carolina's Senator Benjamin Tillman's proud claim that in addition to stuffing ballot boxes in recent elections, "we bulldozed niggers, we shot niggers, and we are not ashamed of it!" After South Carolina's disfranchisement of black voters, Tillman-style, Elliot noted, North Carolina adopted a constitutional amendment, "a method they thought cheaper than the South Carolina method." Other southern states, he pointed out, had successfully stripped blacks of their voting rights through similar methods. To the charge that the Republican Party had done little for blacks, Elliot reminded his listeners, "In 1861 the Republican party instituted a campaign to free 4,000,000 souls in slavery." Moreover, "it has placed colored men in responsible positions." In voting for Republican candidates, he added, "you will have done your duty toward yourself and your race and freedom."[76]

W. R. Davis, a politician from New York, followed Elliot at the podium. Recounting a tale that would have resonated with many attending the rally, Davis said, "I was born in North Carolina, and the first light I ever beheld that was real light, I got from Massachusetts. From a little town in this State a worthy maiden lady came and taught me my alphabet." He continued, "Since then I have had too much light to vote for anything that looks like or feels like a Democrat." He condemned "Democratic imperialism," which had been revived when "they began to burn us at the stake, to shoot us, to bulldoze us. Would you vote for such a party as that? . . . Show us one thing that the Democratic party ever did for the negro, or even for a yellow dog." He then demanded that Worcesterites oust their Democratic congressman and vote for Charles Washburn.[77]

Cultivating this theme, P. B. S. Pinchback, the renowned Reconstruction governor of Louisiana, then spoke, denouncing, in the harshest terms, any black man who would vote with the Democratic Party: "If a colored man should tell me he was a Democrat, I should tell him he was a liar. . . . There is nothing for you to do but to vote for that grand old party which emancipated you, which made you free and will keep you so."[78]

Two local white men — both with antislavery credentials — then made speeches, reinforcing the theme of the evening. David Manning, a Republican state senator, laid out his pedigree for his African American audience: "My father was one of the first free soilers and my grandfather's house was a refuge for escaped slaves." He then pleaded for support for the McKinley administration. Then Colonel William A. Gile, who had served as a captain in the 117th U.S. Colored Troops during the Civil War, spoke. Bryan and his party, he asserted, would take away African Americans' liberties; his war experience had shown him that black men were capable voters and would vote to defend their rights.[79]

But not all of Worcester's black voters were swayed by these appeals. A small number of blacks cast their lot with the Democrats and organized the city's first Colored Democratic Club in late October 1900. At its first meeting, Carl F. Randall explained that he "converted to Bryanism" after losing his job during a Republican administration. Charles E. Scott explained that he had become a Democrat seven years earlier and that he "will never vote the republican ticket until the party changes from its present policy of tyranny." He charged, "Never was a race so tied down as the negroes." The city's black voters, he challenged, "should not vote the republican ticket this fall, for they will forget you after the election." However, he pointed out, "I don't expect to convert the old, hard-shelled colored voters; it is the younger generation, who are beginning to understand what it is to be a republican and live under republican rule." Clifford H. Plummer, a black Democrat from Boston, then urged Worcester blacks "to be loyal to each other," so that both parties would respect and "bow" to them as they did to the Irish: "In Worcester, the colored men vote the Republican ticket and the jobs go to the Murphys, the O'Haras and the Maguires." Asserting that "we can make or break any candidate we choose," Plummer asked, "How many of you here tonight ever received any help from Mayor Dodge's administration? How many of you can go to city hall when the city needs men for the highway, the police department or elsewhere, and receive a position from the republicans now holding Worcester in its power?" Too often, Plummer added, "the Irish citizen steps off with the prize." Interestingly, Plummer then blamed the McKinley administration for the rise in "outrages in this country" and for denying true protection to blacks in the South: "Before election, the republicans say 'Help us.' After they are given power over us all, where is the protection they promised us?"[80]

In the midst of Plummer's plea, Robert H. Johnson could no longer contain himself. The elderly Maryland-born truckman and former slave who had played a key role in settling contrabands in Worcester jumped up from behind a stove and angrily interrupted Plummer: "You know, Mr. Speaker, that your face or my face cannot get justice in the South; therefore, you are wrong." Johnson continued, "Sir, when you remember what the republican party has done for our people; when you remember what the war of rebellion brought about; when you remember what that great friend of every colored man, Abraham Lincoln[,] did for the generation of 1861, and that of today, Mr. Speaker, how could you turn from us?"[81]

According to the local press, Johnson's "short speech brought down the house." Plummer brushed off the old man with an aside to the audience that dripped with condescension: "This gentleman has spoken the best he knows how." Plummer's comment only infuriated Johnson even more, as he swore, "I'll give you some more." Plummer then replied that he was not in Worcester "to convert old men, but he wanted to reach the young colored voters." Insulted, the seventy-year-old Johnson once again leapt to his feet, retorting, "I'm not so very much older than you." Plummer attempted to pick up where he left off, passionately defending the Democrats. In the middle of his plea to the crowd to "join with me tonight," Johnson jumped to his feet again, screaming, "Never!" Plummer then left the platform for a tête-à-tête with Johnson, in an attempt to pacify him. But Johnson sent up a cheer for McKinley as a parting shot.[82]

Whereas Johnson disrupted the meeting of the Colored Democrats in defense of the Republican Party, D. W. Bell, president of the Colored Republican Club of Ward One, made an impassioned plea in the local press. In a letter addressed "to the colored voters of Worcester county," he reminded them of the dire consequences of their vote — especially for their brothers and sisters in the South. Born in Mississippi in 1857, the forty-two-year-old hairdresser migrated to Massachusetts around 1880. Bell recounted a long list of white abuses, including "stakeburned negroes" and Ben Tillman's statement that "a negro has no rights a white man is bound to respect." He then argued that the best defense against further violence against blacks was a Republican Congress. To that end he urged that blacks vote for Republican congressional candidate Charles Washburn. A vote for his Democratic opponent, he warned, "would help to swell the Democratic majority in Congress, and a Democratic victory means negro oppression." "Stop and reflect," he urged. "Can you, a colored man, afford to ignore the rights of your people? Are you willing to help jeopardize the existence of the southern negro because you have the protection of the north? Are you willing to be recorded as a traitor to your race? Remember that every ballot you cast for a Democrat means additional negro hard-ships, more lynching, more riots."[83]

The Reverend Hiram Conway used the power of his pulpit and the support of his southern congregation to remind voters of their duties in preserving the legacy of the Civil War. The press reported on the Sunday evening before the election, "John Street Baptist church was filled to the doors by members of the parish and a delegation from the Colored republican club" who were there to hear Conway "deliver a special address to the voters on their duties on election day." The minister argued that a vote for the Democrats guaranteed the continued oppression of the nation's blacks. "At the present time," Conway said, "the negro is in the scales. This nation is weighing him politically." The black voter faced two key questions: "Does he realize his manhood and independence, and set a right value on the freedom he enjoys?" and "Is he honoring the blood of his fathers and brethren who fell in battle for his liberty?" "The race must vindicate itself by its actions," Conway asserted. As one who fought for the advancement of his people, Conway added, "I cannot take side with those who advocate a return to former darkness and slavery." He continued, "It has been through the Republican party that the freedom and rights which we now enjoy have come. The Democratic party has done nothing for us. . . . Under whose policy has the negro been more blessed. Lincoln's or Jeff Davis'?" While McKinley was far from perfect, he had, at least, handed out far more patronage positions to African Americans than any president before: "We had better try him for four more years than experiment with Bryan and Ben Tillman." The minister directly countered the claims made at the Colored Democratic Club rally a few days before. Remember, he said, "when you go to the polls Tuesday . . . that in the South, that fairest country in the world, our brethren are being driven about like sheep by men who are proud to call themselves democrats." Conway related newspaper reports from Virginia in which Democrats referred to blacks "as wharf rats and crapshooters." Yet Democrats still expected blacks in the North to vote for them "and thus aid them in their attempts to disfranchise our brethren in the South." Democrats in the South "are pursuing a steady policy of disfranchisement," which meant "a virtual return to slavery." He continued, "Our vote should be given to the party that has done the most good to our race." Simply put, he concluded, "For the Negroes in the North to vote the Democratic ticket is to strengthen the Democrats of the South in oppressing our brothers."[84]

Conway challenged his listeners to continue to fight the good fight after the election. He made a special plea to the women in the audience: "Mothers, wives, sisters, get your sons, husbands and brothers to vote for William McKinley and the Republican party." "To the Colored Republican Club," he concluded, "I would say, don't disband when the election is over and McKinley is president for another term. . . . Keep up your organization. Engage in social activity, get into some business. Don't mistrust each other. Believe that your fellow means what he says, until the contrary is proved. Above all, don't find fault with the white man for trying to protect his own. Let us bend our energies toward getting something to protect ourselves."[85]

Conway's remarks alluded to other growing divisions in Worcester's black community — beyond party loyalty — over dependence on white patronage as well as who in the community best represented its interests. A week after Robert Johnson disrupted the black Democrats' rally, he published a revealing letter in the *Spy* reproaching the city's black community. "It has often been a source of wonderment to me," he began, "that the colored people of this city are not more united and more harmonious on questions which would not only be of benefit to them, but would have a tendency to place them before the public in a different light." Compared to other ethnic groups in the city, Worcester's blacks, he argued, had difficulty staying unified and sustaining social and political organizations. Especially troublesome was a dependence on "subscriptions from white people of the city who perhaps are willing to help them." The result, asserted Johnson, was "then we simply become the prey of other nations, simply because of our lack of ambition."[86]

Johnson pointed out an uncomfortable truth, that the city's black community could not truly assert its independence as long as it continued to rely on white patronage. Conway's John Street Church had been built with the aid of white supporters, and, as all black political activists knew all too well, the election of a black official would be impossible without white votes. Both were good reasons for Conway to appeal as he did before the election to community members to be less critical of their white counterparts. Whereas Johnson contended that dependence on whites continued "because of our lack of ambition," Conway viewed the cultivation of white support as a necessary means to achieve the end of strengthening Worcester's black community.

Johnson scathingly addressed a second issue in his "reproach": the black community's growing resentment of some of its leaders. Johnson took aim at "four gentlemen of our race who have been so thoughtful of their existence that they imagine without their presence at a public meeting, it is a failure." These same men, Johnson charged, "on no occasion take any interest in the welfare of the colored people's interest whatever; their intellectual faces are never seen in our colored churches, fairs, and other celebrations." Perhaps they felt themselves "better than the race they represent. . . . What we want is a man who is willing to associate with us through the twelve months of the year, and not who has charms for only two months." Johnson challenged them to "come and put themselves amongst organizations which are trying to do for them and the race," rather than "trying to pose as individual gods."[87]

Although Johnson never identified the "four gentlemen" he targeted for his disdain, one of them may have been Democrat Charles E. Scott and certainly one of them was George Alfred Busby. One of the few West Indians in the city, the Barbados-born Busby cultivated relationships with prominent whites through his tailoring business. In 1893, nine years after moving to Worcester from Boston, he married Jennie Clough, one of the first black schoolteachers in the city and the daughter of a well-known black Yankee family engaged in the hairdressing business. He belonged to the elite, predominantly white All Saints Episcopal Church, and he was the only black man appointed to the executive committee of the Worcester Republican Club. While he was a member of King David Lodge and Integrity Lodge, his name rarely appears in reports of community activities found in the Worcester columns of Boston's black newspapers.[88]

Johnson was not the only critic of Busby. A few years earlier, when he became the first black man nominated to run for common council, Busby had come under attack for his aloofness. Colored Republican Protective Association member Daniel Gaines asserted in a public meeting that "Mr. Busby . . . is a man who don't associate with his people, and only comes around when there is a turkey to eat or an axe to grind." Gaines contended that Busby "does not attend the meetings of the association [the Colored Republican Protective Association] and now he asked for our support at the caucus."[89]

Divisions over strategies and leadership seriously hampered efforts by black voters to gain recognition and the spoils of patronage. Although McKinley won handily in Worcester in 1900, local Republicans did not manage to oust John Thayer from his congressional seat or elect a Republican mayor.

Debate over political affiliation continued into the new century. Reflecting a frustration with the lack of political advancement, several previously rabid Republican black activists broke with the old party. The rock-ribbed Republican Daniel Gaines surrendered his party loyalty, announcing in the local press that although he remained in the party of Lincoln, "the only way for the two parties to realize the strength of the black vote" was for the black voter "to absent himself from one or the other in order to get the recognition which he may desire." Gaines pointed out that "the republican party has been promising [us] things" but all they had gained was "one fireman out at Burncoat street." As loyal Republicans, he added, "our votes are counted before being cast." North Carolina–born Henry Whitfield made a similar argument, asserting that "it was necessary that the race should look out for itself and not be used as a tool for any party, but vote the right way."[90]

Local white Democrats responded to black voters' vocal and highly publicized disillusionment by attempting to court them. In 1901, in the tight race for a state senate seat, for example, Democrat David Walsh of Clinton pursued the city's black voters. At a meeting of the Roger Wolcott Club (formerly the Colored Democratic Club), Walsh pleaded with black voters to cast their ballots for candidates who would "best serve their interests": "If there are 2500 colored people in the city of Worcester, as I am informed, you should be a power. You are in a position to be recognized. You have the right to demand representation just as any other man of any race, or creed or nationality or color. I am surprised that you are not represented in Worcester city hall." Charging that they must "unite as one man," Walsh held up the example of "the Germans of Clinton," who "get what they want because they are organized, they stand together, they swing the balance of power in that town. . . . Their vote is neither always democratic or republican, yet they swing the decision in elections. This same position is within your grasp in Worcester."[91]

Daniel Gaines and Charles E. Scott, who were running for common council from Ward Two, echoed Walsh's message. Gaines asserted that it was high time that blacks stopped "asking and begging." Acting together would "show our strength and get [us] into the position where we can demand what we want." Scott complained that the city's black voters were "continually pulling apart" and that "we do not urge our demand and we get nothing." "The first thing we know," he predicted, "we will have an Armenian mayor in Worcester before there is a colored man employed in city hall." George Alfred Busby, running once again for common council from Ward One, refused to respond to the speakers.[92]

Several weeks later, though, at a Colored Republican rally, Busby defended Republican loyalty. Once again defeated in the Republican caucus, Busby nevertheless remained loyal to the party. Endorsing Republican mayoral candidate Edward F. Fletcher, Busby asked, "Do you think because I was defeated I am going to stand by and see my party stabbed in the heart? Certainly not." Other black Republicans spoke harshly of their black Democratic counterparts. William George Beckton, who migrated as a teenager to Worcester from eastern North Carolina in 1865, claimed that "the colored man who voted the democratic ticket in Worcester was a dog below the Mason Dixon line." Years ago, he noted, he had tried to get a position on the city police force and had almost landed the job when Democratic mayor John Thayer "had his application tabled with the remark that they did not want a colored policeman." His job petition "remained tabled to this day," as far as he knew. Beckton concluded, "If the colored men want to be recognized, they must vote for the republican candidate or do as the colored voter of the South, 'go way back and sit down.'"[93]

In the election, the Republicans triumphed in both the state senate race

and the city's mayoral race. The outspoken Daniel G. Gaines, who had supported Walsh, found himself dropped from the Republican Party by local officials. In a public explanation, Gaines made clear that he had supported several Democratic candidates in order to teach the local party a lesson, that he
was tired of black voters being "the tail end of the G.O.P.," with their votes "all
counted before being cast." He reminded local Republicans that "the colored
voters are free to act, free to think, and under the Australian ballot system
free to vote to suit themselves." Not giving an inch, he concluded, "You need
our votes and in order to hold them you must listen to us and in the future,
acts, not promises, will be our guide."[94]

This time Gaines's argument did not fall on the deaf ears of Republican
leaders. According to Gaines, who recounted his story at a reelection rally
for Fletcher the following year, Fletcher "has stood by the colored people."
Gaines claimed that although supporting Democrat Walsh for state senate,
he worked for Edward F. Fletcher, the Republican candidate for mayor. After
his election, Gaines met with Fletcher, who asked him what he wanted in
return for his support. "Any old thing," Gaines responded, "so long as you
recognize the race." After a few months and a second appeal, the mayor, explained Gaines, "had two of our race appointed janitors." Raymond Jackson
and Benjamin Walker were hired as custodians in the public schools.[95]

The following year, after seven attempts — beginning in 1896 — George
Alfred Busby finally won a seat on the common council from Ward One,
becoming the first black man elected to citywide office in Worcester. Part of
a near Republican sweep that kept Mayor Fletcher in office, Busby beat out
his Democratic opponent by 461 votes. Notably, unlike every year before in
which he had been defeated in the caucus, Busby ran unopposed, his road to
victory apparently paved by local Republicans, who handed him the nomination without opposition.[96]

Initially, then, the strategy to split the black vote, as advocated by Gaines
and Scott, seemed to pay dividends for Worcester's black community. Convinced that custodian jobs represented just the beginning of political patronage for the city's blacks, Gaines called the appointments "the stepping stone
to better things." But the "stepping stone" led nowhere. Worcester's blacks
received nothing beyond the few token, low-level positions granted by Fletcher
in his first term. The black vote, according to postelection analysis, did not
seem to be a factor in the mayor's election. While a local newspaper noted
that the "French vote" did not turn out for Fletcher's opponent, O'Connell,
and that the Swedish Republicans, "who deserted their party last month in the
congressional election," returned to the fold, the black vote received no men-

tion. Granted a few crumbs from the feast of political patronage in 1902, blacks soon learned that their meager serving would be all they would receive.[97]

The following year, incumbent George Alfred Busby did not even obtain the Republican nomination for reelection to common council. Worcester's Republican leaders apparently felt that they had done enough for the city's black voters, and Busby served for just one term. Blacks in Worcester would not have another representative in local government until 1926, when Charles E. Scott, who as a young man broke ranks with the Republican Party and threw his support to the Democratic Party in 1893, finally reaped his reward with election, after several attempts, to the common council from Ward Three. Scott held his seat until his death in 1938. Worcester would not elect another black city councillor for over half a century, when in 1997, Democrat Stacey A. DeBoise was elected to the city council. Reporting on her election, the *Worcester Telegram and Gazette* noted that she was the third African American to serve on the city council. It also published an extensive article on "Black trailblazer" Charles Scott. As for the city's first black councilman, Busby, "little is known about him." The noble fight of black Republicans for recognition and respect, begun a century before, had receded entirely from local memory.[98]

"Our lives are largely composed of sorrow and joy"

Between 1889 and 1895, three former slaves who made Worcester their home played a key role in strengthening bonds of southern identity and community in Worcester by preserving historical memory. Bethany Veney's *The Narrative of Bethany Veney, A Slave Woman* (1889), Isaac Mason's *Life of Isaac Mason as a Slave* (1893), and Allen Parker's *Recollections of Slavery Times* (1895) all told the stories of the authors' dramatic journeys from bondage to freedom. While each narrative tells a unique story, all had a common aim: to prod readers to remember the horrors of slavery; the price paid by blacks in enslavement; and the inimitable strength blacks demonstrated in overcoming the evils that slavery inflicted. In an era of historical amnesia and worsening race relations, these narratives placed black Americans at the center of the national story. And in their own way, each reminded white Americans of the promises they had made to blacks and had broken. At the same time, the narratives not only reminded black readers of their heritage but also provided lessons in strength and courage to a community struggling in a climate of frustration and disappointment.[99]

The narratives of Veney, Mason, and Parker recounted the historical experiences of many of the black community's elders, who by the 1890s, were quickly passing from the scene. While the personal stories of Veney, Mason, and Parker seem to have been well-known among their friends and acquaintances, their publication gave a permanency to the authors' sagas, ensuring that future generations would know the sacrifices and triumphs of their forebears. The narratives provided valuable guideposts for the younger generation who had never experienced bondage. They reminded younger members of the community of their southern roots and encouraged pride in what had been accomplished by the first generation out of slavery. As B. Eugene McCarthy and Thomas L. Doughton, who have analyzed the Worcester narratives in depth, argue, the stories provide "models of black success," tracing the authors' trajectory from the chains of southern slavery to freedom in the North. At the same time, the stories are often bittersweet: even in the North, freedom did not come without struggle.[100]

The authors were well-known personages in the city. The connections that they built with prominent white citizens helped make their publications possible; some provided letters and statements published with the narratives that attested to the veracity of the stories and the character of the writers. Veney, a lifelong church member, was active in a number of churches in Worcester, including Bethel A M E Church, Park Street Methodist Church, and Trinity Methodist Church. She worked as a domestic and later established a successful business selling "blueing" to housewives in the city. The *Worcester Evening Gazette* reported her death on its front page. "Few women in Worcester," it noted, "were better known than Aunt Betsy." Mason had long been a community leader with many connections to prominent whites that went back to antebellum days. Mason counted U.S. senator George Frisbie Hoar among his many friends. Mason's work, as a carpet cleaner and custodian, also took him into the homes and offices of the city's leading citizens. Mason, the *Worcester Telegram* reported at the time of his death, "has for years been looked up to by his people as a counselor and friend, and his voice and judgment have been followed on any occasions." Parker, whose death also received front-page notice, was described in the *Telegram* as "one of the best known colored men in Massachusetts." He had worked as a carpet cleaner in Worcester and was widely known for the popcorn and homemade candies he sold in Worcester factories, schools, and offices. Allen "Pop" Parker was a Civil War veteran, active in the G A R, and a member of the Pleasant Street Baptist Church.[101]

The introductions to the narratives stressed the publications' central purpose: to remind a nation that had willfully forgotten about the centrality of the story of slavery and emancipation and to inform a generation too young to remember. The preface to Veney's narrative explains that slavery "in our national history is largely overlooked, and to the generation now coming upon the stage of action is almost unknown." Similarly, an anonymous editor introduced Parker's story by noting that "one-third of a century has passed since slavery ceased forever in our land, and to the generation that has grown up in that time, it hardly seems possible that such an institution as slavery could have existed in this free land."[102]

Each author describes the slavery experience and passage to freedom in vivid detail. At the same time, each author tells his or her story with a unique voice and emphasis. Bethany Veney's story tells the wrenching tale of the destruction of her family in slavery and her success in reconstructing family life after the war. Her religious faith also provides an organizing theme; her strong faith allowed her not only to endure the most heart-wrenching aspects of slavery but also to forgive her former master, with whom she meets after the war. By contrast, Parker's narrative catalogs the details of slave life in Chowan County, North Carolina, and recounts his escape from his plantation to a Union gunboat for his freedom and his subsequent service in the Union navy during the Civil War. Mason also describes his harrowing escape to freedom. But Mason devotes a significant portion of his narrative to life in the North after emancipation, which neither Veney nor Parker does. Life in the free North, he emphasizes, presented its own set of difficult challenges, namely, unemployment; the Fugitive Slave Law, which sent him fleeing to Canada; and disappointment when a plan to emigrate to Haiti fell through. "Our lives are largely composed of sorrow and joy," he writes, "but my cup, it seems to me, has been full to overflowing with sorrow, but God has been my strength." Mason's clear-eyed and honest depiction of the hardships faced by African Americans, even in the Bay State, would have resonated with his community in the 1890s, faced as it was with a multitude of frustrations.[103]

"Worcester . . . is failing to offer to the Negro an opportunity to earn a living as a free laborer"

After an influx of migrants to Worcester between 1880 and 1900, Worcester's black population languished in the first half of the twentieth century, never exceeding 2 percent of the overall population until 1980. Even the Great Migration, which brought millions of southern blacks to northern cities when wartime shortages of white labor gave them access to industrial jobs, bypassed Worcester. Ella L. Vinal, who conducted a sociological study of Worcester's black community in the 1920s, noted that it was "not a migrant" community, as was typical in many northern cities during and after the Great Migration. Instead, she wrote, "it is almost a stagnating one." Historian Timothy Meagher agrees, pointing out that Worcester's economy was "reaching maturity by the late nineteenth century" and had grown sluggish. Even as the state's black population grew by nearly 20 percent between 1910 and 1920 — increasing at an even faster rate than the overall population — Worcester saw barely any increase at all, growing by only 0.7 percent. Meanwhile, Springfield's black population increased by 80 percent, Brockton's increased by 50 percent, and Boston's increased by 20.5 percent. It is likely that the city had earned a reputation as an inhospitable place, which would not have been surprising given its negative attitude toward black labor. Vinal came to the same conclusion. "Since population normally follows economic and industrial opportunities," she wrote, "the failure of Worcester's negro population to grow is indicative of a lack of opportunity for livelihood even as compared with other cities in the same state."[104]

Long after the First World War dismantled the color bar in other northern cities, it still stood in Worcester industry. Surveying 98 industries, Vinal found that of the 30,610 people employed in Worcester's many, diverse industries, only 40 were black; "according to their percentage in the population," she estimated, "there should [have been] at least 214." Moreover, Vinal found numerous examples of outright prejudice on the part of employers and she noted that many educated and skilled blacks in the city worked in jobs for which they were clearly overqualified. "The trained worker," she concluded, "does not easily find an opening in the City of Worcester," and many simply "go elsewhere to work." The city that once attracted fugitive and emancipated slaves alike because of its reputation for "benevolent sympathizers" now had a reputation for its paucity of kindness. Vinal also noted this remarkable shift. "Worcester, birthplace of one of the earliest abolitionist movements," she concluded, "apparently is failing to offer to the Negro an opportunity to earn a living as a free laborer."[105]

IN THE LAST QUARTER of the nineteenth century, southern migrants built a vibrant and active community, giving the city's black community a decidedly southern cast. The experience of slavery and the Civil War served as the foundation of southern community identity and increasingly that of the larger community as a whole. In the era of segregation, disfranchisement, and lynching, the patriotic memory of former slaves and their children in the North propelled them to vigilantly defend their brothers and sisters in the South. Moreover, it provided the inspiration to fight against a worsening racial climate in the once-welcoming city of Worcester. As Worcester's blacks wielded their history as a weapon to defend themselves and assert civil rights, north and south, many white Worcesterites — the heirs of an abolitionist tradition that had aided migrants seeking a more complete freedom in the North — chose to forget theirs. Like much of the rest of the country, they chose instead to marginalize African Americans and erase the memory of their central role in the nation's story. Facing discrimination in politics and employment, Worcester's black community survived but languished. While the city still offered more than the deteriorating Jim Crow South of the late nineteenth and early twentieth centuries, it generally failed to live up to its mythical reputation as "free Massachusetts" for the many men and women who went there in search of full-fledged citizenship.

Epilogue

Historian William McFeely, in *Sapelo's People*, his masterful portrait of a Georgia Sea Island community, writes, "African-Americans' anger may derive as much from the broken promises of Reconstruction as from slavery itself. So much promise was held out, so much withdrawn, that the sting is still there." While referring specifically to the federal government's broken promises, McFeely's assertion could easily apply to northern communities such as Worcester, the destination of southern migrants who journeyed to the city in search of equal treatment and full citizenship. Worcester held out its own set of pledges to fleeing war refugees and freedpeople, which was fulfilled for some but not for many. Desperately seeking to define their own freedom, whether in the initial aftermath of emancipation or in the age of Jim Crow, many southern black migrants found their "manhood" and "womanhood" circumscribed. The color bar in local industry conspired to marginalize Worcester's black community and undermine the independence that its members so deeply treasured, keeping the community small, with little political clout, and resource-poor. At the same time, for "the children of this Revolution, the promising first fruits of the war," as Horace James labeled them, and for their descendents, their southern heritage would remain a source of pride and strength well into the twentieth century.[1]

Despite the many frustrations blacks faced in Worcester, the city at least promised jobs with higher wages than those in the South, education for children in integrated schools, and an escape from the legacies of slavery that continued to cast a long shadow across much of the "New" South. In 1938, as a child, Edna Spencer migrated from Tennessee with her mother to Worcester, where they joined her uncle and grandfather; subsequently, all but one of her family members followed. She notes that southern-born parents and grandparents like her own stressed independence through property ownership, just as earlier southern migrants to Worcester had, although most were frustrated in their efforts. Owning your own piece of land, she explained, is "what Southerners did." "My grandfather bought a house," she explained, "he started his own business, he was working for the railroad, he was a hard-working man—loved it. And one of the things my grandfather emphasized to his children, 'You must own a piece of land.' And they passed it on to me. . . . He wound up in Upton [Worcester County] and bought land out there. . . . They came in, they worked, they bought a piece of land. You had to have your own piece of land."

Worcester's southern migrants stamped a lasting imprint on the city's black community in other ways. When Spencer migrated to Worcester, she felt as though she had practically returned to the South: black Worcester had a distinctive "southern village atmosphere." Like rural Tennessee, she said, "we all knew one another. . . . Everybody knew everybody. Everybody knew everybody's kids." Moreover, "there was that camaraderie, that connection when I came here." She explains, "There was such a dependence on one another for survival, there was such a need for support. . . . There was no way that you could survive alone in the South. So that camaraderie was there: a matter of survival, a matter of survival—very simple." In addition, family remained central to identity: "The Afro-Americans in the Worcester area recognized one another as residents and members of particular families." If you met someone in the street, Spencer recalled, "they automatically spoke. This was also an extension of southern custom."[2]

The John Street Baptist Church, where she was a member, played a key role in maintaining and sustaining southern culture in Worcester. The church "retained more of the atmosphere of the old church, especially in the rural South," which is still evident even to this day: John Street's service, Spencer notes, retains its "southern-style worship." She recalls that when she first started attending, some of the first members of the church were still alive. Reflecting pride in their origins and a lasting sense of identity, the city's migrants also formed a "North Carolina Club," a "Virginia Club," and a "South Carolina Club." These social clubs "would give dinners, fried chicken dinners, and picnics and whatnot."[3]

Spencer points out the ways that southerners in the twentieth century—like their earlier counterparts—were part of a larger black community but at the same time retained a separate identity. Annual "East Side–West Side" picnics at Beaver Brook Park, which still occasionally take place, always included a baseball game pitting the two neighborhoods against each other. Given that mostly southern-born blacks settled in west-side residential enclaves during the Civil War era, this gathering may have originated as a way to bring west-side southerners together with east-side black Yankees. The picnic created unity while at the same time acknowledging and celebrating cultural differences through a friendly rivalry.[4]

Just as the East Side–West Side picnics brought black Yankees and southerners together, so did Emancipation Day celebrations. Like the picnics, Emancipation Day, as it had in the decades following the Civil War, continued to provide a reason to socialize as well as to remember distinctive origins. Before the Civil War, black Yankees and white abolitionists traditionally celebrated August 1st, West Indian Emancipation Day. After the emancipation of slaves in the United States in 1863, the city's black community often celebrated both days. By the 1880s, the January 1st celebrations seem to have died out, but they were revived again as a powerful statement in the darkening days of Jim Crow America. But in the harsh climate of New England, August 1st as a holiday had a clear advantage over January 1st. In the end, the old Yankee celebration won out. Yet by the twentieth century, Emancipation Day celebrations had become an amalgam of old and new traditions, of pre–Civil War black Worcester and its postwar southern migrants. Even though the annual celebration fell on West Indian Emancipation Day, southerners enthusiastically participated and used the day to celebrate the liberation of their ancestors. Spencer recalls that the North Carolina, Virginia, and South Carolina Clubs "were a big part of the Emancipation Proclamation celebration that we had each August 1st." Like their nineteenth-century counterparts, Worcester's black Elks "connected with churches and organizations in Boston and Springfield and Rhode Island," and the community "would all converge at Crescent Park" for a big dance and carnival rides.[5]

The struggle for equality in the workplace continued well into the twentieth century. Just as late-nineteenth-century black Worcesterites found themselves barred from decent-paying jobs in Worcester's industries, their descendents faced similar discrimination for decades. According to Spencer, "Things didn't start opening up here until the 50s." She continues, "I can think of a couple of black male college graduates who did work as maintenance workers because they could not find work." Some black women "who were very, very lucky got jobs as stitchers" in factories, and "you could do piecework and you could make a few extra dollars." But "for the most part women ran elevators, they cleaned, they were domestics, some got jobs cooking and the like, but that was about all that was available." Worcester had its own "unofficial Jim Crow. . . . 'Blacks Only' and 'Whites Only' existed right here in New England; they just didn't have the signs." Jim Crow, she notes, was alive and well in the city's hotels, restaurants, and theaters, even though forbidden by Massachusetts law. At the same time, she points out, "when whites wanted to go slumming," they went to black establishments "like the Elks and the Chicken Shack." Members of the black community, she adds, did not have the same privilege to attend "whites only" clubs and restaurants.[6]

Perhaps it was no accident that the John Street Baptist Church and its ministers played a leading role in civil rights struggles in the 1950s and 1960s. The church's minister, the Reverend Dr. Toussaint L. Davis, served as the president of the local chapter of the NAACP in the 1960s and helped to establish the Worcester Fair Employment Committee to address racial discrimination in hiring practices. He also led the fight for fair housing in the city. In 1963, Davis linked Worcester civil rights activists to the southern movement, organizing pickets of Woolworth's and Walgreens to protest their discriminatory policies in Birmingham. Following in the footsteps of the Reverend Hiram Conway and his compatriots, who, in the 1890s, insisted that they had to fight for what was rightfully theirs, Davis and others, through their hard-earned victories in the 1960s, provided a fitting tribute to the men and women who fought the same fight generations before.[7]

Echoing Bethany Veney, who wrote about her experiences as a southern migrant to Worcester over a hundred years earlier, Edna Spencer explains that for her and her generation, the South "will always be home." Perhaps, as she notes, subsequent generations "don't have the same interest" in their southern roots and many have left Worcester for better opportunities elsewhere. But for migrants themselves, such as Spencer and her husband, and those old enough to have had direct contact with the earliest southern migrants, their connection with the South remains vital and resilient: "You don't go down South," says Spencer, "you go home, although you've been here for forty years. That's home."[8]

$$\mathscr{Appendix}$$

TABLE A.1 Population, Worcester County, 1860–1900

	1860	1870	1880	1890	1900
White	158,881	191,550	225,452	279,304	345,139
Colored	769	1,136	1,398	1,483	1,819
Southern-born	69	269	272	NA	369
Percentage southern-born	9	23.7	19.4	NA	20.3
Total	159,650	192,686	226,850	280,787	346,958

Source: U.S Bureau of the Census, Manuscript Census Schedules,
Worcester County, Massachusetts, 1860–1900

TABLE A.2 Population, City of Worcester, 1860–1900

	1860	1870	1880	1890	1900
White	24,688	40,588	57, 524	83,679	117,206
Colored	272	524	763	944	1,104
Southern-born	46	181	172	NA	255
Percentage southern-born	17	34.5	22.5	NA	23.1
Percenatage adult colored population southern-born	22	46.6	31.5	NA	45
Total	24, 960	41, 112	58,287	84,623	118,310

Source: U.S Bureau of the Census, Manuscript Census Schedules,
Worcester County, Massachusetts, 1860–1900

TABLE A.3 Southern-born Population, City of Worcester, 1860–1900

Birthplace	1860	1862–1870	1870–1880	1880–1900
Virginia	1	128	123	104
North Carolina	4	68	72	120
Maryland	35	26	37	20
South Carolina	NA	20	13	36
Washington, DC	1	14	16	15
Georgia	NA	12	15	11
Louisiana	NA	9	4	3
Other (TX, MO, TN, MS, KY, FL)	1	58	16	11
Total	82	335	296	320

Sources: See Table A.1; Massachusetts Manuscript Census, Worcester County, 1865; Birth, Marriage, and Death Records, City of Worcester, 1860–1900

Notes

INTRODUCTION

1 "Arrival of a Contraband," *Worcester Daily Spy*, 28 June 1862.

2 "Letter from Chaplain James," *The Congregationalist*, 10 October 1862.

3 Michael P. Johnson, "Out of Egypt: The Migration of Former Slaves to the Midwest during the 1860s in Comparative Perspective," in *Crossing Boundaries: Comparative History of Black People in Diaspora* (Bloomington: Indiana University Press, 1999), 228. For two classic studies of the Great Migration, see Florette Henri, *Black Migration: Movement North, 1900–1920* (Garden City, NY: Anchor Press, 1975); and Gilbert Osofsky, *Harlem: The Making of a Ghetto, Negro New York, 1890–1930* (New York: Harper and Row, 1966). Clyde Vernon Kiser's *Sea Island to City: A Study of St. Helena Islanders in Harlem and Other Urban Centers* (New York, 1932) briefly examines the post–Civil War migration of a small number of Sea Islanders to the North, connecting the migration to the Civil War experience. Seth Scheiner, *Negro Mecca: A History of the Negro in New York City, 1865–1920* (New York: New York University Press, 1965), discusses the migration from the South Atlantic states that increased the city's black population by nearly 27 percent between 1865 and 1870 and 54 percent between 1870 and 1880 without much attention to Civil War–era migration networks. James Grossman's *Land of Hope: Chicago, Black Southerners, and the Great Migration* (Chicago: University of Chicago Press, 1989); Albert Broussard's *Black San Francisco: The Struggle for Racial Equality in the West, 1900–1954* (Lawrence: University of Kansas Press, 1993); Quintard Taylor's *The Forging of a Black Community: Seattle's Central District from 1870 through the Civil Rights Era* (Seattle: University of Washington Press, 1994); and Lillian Serece Williams's *Strangers in the Land of Paradise: The Creation of African American Community, Buffalo, New York, 1900–1940* (Bloomington: Indiana University Press, 1999), all include minimal discussions of pre-1900 migrations. For an excellent overview of the historiography of black migration, see Joe William Trotter, "Black Migration in Historical Perspective: A Review of the Literature," in *The Great Migration in Historical Perspective: New Dimensions of Race, Class, and Gender*, ed. Joe William Trotter (Bloomington: Indiana University Press, 1991), 13–17; also see Lillian Serece Williams, *Strangers in the Land of Paradise*, xii–xiv.

4 Isaac Mason, *Life of Isaac Mason as a Slave* (Worcester: n.p., 1893), 66.

5 Thomas Wentworth Higginson, *Massachusetts in Mourning! A Sermon, Preached in Worcester, on June 4, 1854* (Boston: James Munroe and Company, 1854), 14.

6 I arrived at overall migrant numbers by combining census information with birth, marriage, and death records for the city of Worcester. These numbers are conservative, most certainly an underestimate. Worcester County people of color, like their counterparts elsewhere in the United States, were regularly undercounted in nineteenth-century censuses. Historians estimate, for example, that the 1880 census undercounted black Americans by 9 percent. Elizabeth Pleck estimates that Boston's blacks, in the same period as this study, were undercounted by as much as 33 percent. See Elizabeth Pleck, *Black Migration and Poverty: Boston, 1865–1900* (New York: Academic Press, 1979), 215. Vital statistics for Worcester from 1860 to 1900 include many names of African Americans not included in any census records, suggesting a significant undercount. For more on census undercounting, see Miriam L. King and Dianna L. Magnuson, "Perspectives on Historical U.S. Census Undercounts," *Social Science History* 19 (Winter 1995): 455–66; and Richard A. Steckel, "The Quality of Census Data for Historical Inquiry: A Research Agenda," *Social Science History* 15 (Winter 1991): 579–99. For a specific discussion of the problems implicit in determining migration statistics, see "Appendix A: About Migration Statistics" in William Cohen, *At Freedom's Edge: Black Mobility and the Southern White Quest for Racial Control, 1861–1915* (Baton Rouge: Louisiana State University Press, 1991), 299–300.

7 Nell Irvin Painter's *Exodusters: Black Migration to Kansas after Reconstruction* (New York: Knopf, 1977) still stands as the key study of the Kansas migration. One of many studies from the 1960s and 1970s that sought the origins of black poverty, Pleck's book argues that "in the short run, the move from the South to the North strengthened traditional slave folkways, but in the long run residence in the city gave blacks access to the American Dream without the economic progress that was supposed to go with it." Differing in important ways from historians such as Stephan Thernstrom, Pleck nevertheless concluded that "the nineteenth-century city was destructive," as black migrants could not overcome barriers of "exclusion and unsuccessful competition" placed by employers, white workers, and unions (Pleck, *Black Migration and Poverty*, 3–11). See Cohen, *At Freedom's Edge*; Carol Faulkner, *Women's Radical Reconstruction: The Freedmen's Aid Movement* (Philadelphia: University of Pennsylvania Press, 2004); Robert Harrison, "Welfare and Employment Policies of the Freedmen's Bureau in the District of Columbia," *Journal of Southern History* 72 (2006): 75–110.

8 V. Jacque Voegeli, *Free But Not Equal: The Midwest and the Negro during the Civil War* (Chicago: University of Chicago Press, 1967); Johnson, "Out of Egypt"; Leslie A. Schwalm, *Emancipation's Diaspora: Race and Reconstruction in the Upper Midwest* (Chapel Hill: University of North Carolina Press, 2009).

9 Schwalm, *Emancipation's Diaspora*, 15–23, 26; Joanne Pope Melish, *Disowning Slavery: Gradual Emancipation and "Race" in New England, 1780–1860* (Ithaca: Cornell University Press, 1998), xiii–xiv.

10 Schwalm, *Emancipation's Diaspora*, 44–45.

11 *Ninth Census of the United States: The Statistics of the Population of the United States* (Washington: Government Printing Office, 1872). Between 1860 and 1870, for example, Vermont's black population increased by 30 percent, Rhode Island's by 26 percent, and Maine's by 21 percent. Both Johnson and Schwalm note the difficulty of estimating numbers of migrants. Johnson points out the southern migrants "more than doubled the black population" in the Midwest between 1860 and 1870. See Johnson, "Out of Egypt," 228; Schwalm, *Emancipation's Diaspora*, 45; and Leslie A. Schwalm, "'Overrun with Free Negroes': Emancipation and Wartime Migration in the Upper Midwest," *Civil War History* 50 (2004): 152.

12 V. Jacque Voegeli, "A Rejected Alternative: Union Policy and the Relocation of Southern 'Contrabands' at the Dawn of Emancipation," *Journal of Southern History* 49 (November 2003): 765–89.

13 Schwalm, *Emancipation's Diaspora*, 157–74, 137–43.

14 Ibid., 175–80.

15 Both Willie Lee Rose, in her landmark study, *Rehearsal for Reunion: The Port Royal Experiment* (New York: Oxford University Press, 1964), and Leslie A. Schwalm, in *A Hard Fight for We: Women's Transition from Slavery to Freedom in South Carolina* (Urbana: University of Illinois Press, 1997), cite numerous examples of cruelty and abuse. Rose emphasized the "demoralizing influence" on blacks in the Sea Islands of Union soldiers who regularly pillaged the countryside of scarce resources and regularly engaged in drunken, violent attacks on blacks, beat men, and attempted to rape women. See Rose, *Rehearsal for Reunion*, 64–65, 177, 240–41. Schwalm (*Hard Fight for We*, 102) echoes Rose's depictions of the abuse of blacks at the hands of Union soldiers in the Sea Islands.

16 Voegeli, *Free But Not Equal*, 2–3; Schwalm, *Emancipation's Diaspora*, 29, 31–32; Johnson, "Out of Egypt," 228; *Ninth Census of the United States: Population*. For example, Taylor, *Forging of a Black Community*, notes a post–Civil War black migration to Seattle as a result of oppression in the South but does not explore migration networks. Similarly, Scheiner's *Negro Mecca* attributes a 27 percent increase in New York's black population between 1865 and 1870 and a 54 percent increase between 1870 and 1880 to economic and social problems in the postwar South but does not explore migration networks.

CHAPTER ONE

1 Thomas Wentworth Higginson, *Cheerful Yesterdays* (Boston: Houghton, Mifflin and Company, 1898), 245; "Troops Ordered Into Service," *Worcester Daily Spy*, 16 April 1861. For an in-depth description of Worcester during the Civil War, see Abijah P. Marvin, *History of Worcester in the War of Rebellion* (Cleveland: A. H. Clark, 1880).

2 John L. Brooke, *The Heart of the Commonwealth: Society and Political Culture in Worcester County, Massachusetts, 1713–1861* (New York: Cambridge University Press, 1989), 30, 294, 389; Timothy J. Meagher, *Inventing Irish America: Generation, Class, and Ethnic Identity in a New England City, 1880–1928* (Notre Dame,

IN: University of Notre Dame Press, 2001), 20, 22–24; *Eighth Census of the United States: Manufactures of the United States in 1860* (Washington: Government Printing Office, 1865), 251; *Ninth Census of the United States: The Statistics of Wealth and Industry of the United States, Volume III* (Washington: Government Printing Office, 1872), 678; Joshua Chasan, "Civilizing Worcester: The Creation of Institutional and Cultural Order, Worcester, Massachusetts, 1848–1876" (Ph.D. diss., University of Pittsburgh, 1974), 15–16; Nick Salvatore, *We All Got History: The Memory Books of Amos Webber* (New York: Times Books, 1996), 103.

3 "The War Feeling in the City," *Worcester Daily Spy*, 17 April 1861.

4 "What It Means," *Worcester Daily Spy*, 16 April 1861.

5 "War Meeting," *Worcester Daily Spy*, 18 April 1861.

6 James Eugene Mooney, "Antislavery in Worcester County, Massachusetts: A Case Study" (Ph.D. diss., Clark University, 1971), 3; Cushing quoted in John D. Cushing, "The Cushing Court and the Abolition of Slavery in Massachusetts: More Notes on the Quock Walker Case," *American Journal of Legal History* 5 (April 1961): 133; Mooney, "Antislavery in Worcester County," 10–15. Joanne Pope Melish notes that even with Cushing's decision, "the institution of slavery was not fully extinguished," although no slaves were reported in the state in the first federal census, taken in 1790. See Joanne Pope Melish, *Disowning Slavery: Gradual Emancipation and "Race" in New England, 1780–1860* (Ithaca: Cornell University Press, 1998), 65, 76.

7 Albert Von Frank argues that Worcester's uncommon antislavery activism was rooted in the identification of slavery as a labor problem, tied to free labor, free soil, and white advancement: "One of the reasons why Worcester was so forward in the Burns matter and in antislavery in general was the presence there of a vital culture of artisans, mill workers, and shopkeepers. From the moment of Burns's arrest it was understood that help was to be looked for not from fashionable Boston, where capital and corporations held sway, but from 'the country,' particularly Worcester, 'the Heart of the Commonwealth'" (Albert Von Frank, *The Trials of Anthony Burns: Freedom and Slavery in Emerson's Boston* [Cambridge, MA: Harvard University Press, 1998], 158). For more on Higginson and Stowell, see ibid.

8 For more on Worcester's role in Kansas emigration, see Eli Thayer, *The New England Emigrant Aid Company* (Worcester: Franklin P. Rice, 1887) and *A History of the Kansas Crusade: Its Friends and Its Foes* (New York: Harper and Brothers, 1889); Mooney, "Antislavery in Worcester County," 264; and "The Execution of John Brown, Commemoration of the Event in Worcester & Vicinity," *Massachusetts Spy*, 7 December 1859.

9 Higginson, *Cheerful Yesterdays*, 247–48.

10 *Worcester Daily Spy*, 19 April 1861.

11 Higginson, *Cheerful Yesterdays*, 146; "The Late 'Prof.' Walker," *Worcester Evening Gazette*, 17 December 1890; Isaac Mason, *Life of Isaac Mason as a Slave* (Worcester: n.p., 1893), 1–2, 49–52, 55–56.

12 U.S. Bureau of the Census, Manuscript census schedules, Worcester County, Massachusetts, 1850. Census takers did not recognize the ethnic and racial complexities of Worcester's people of color, designating them merely as "black," "mulatto,"

or "Indian." But extensive research done by local historian Thomas L. Doughton has shown that the "black," "mulatto," and "Indian" census designation obscures the multiethnic descent of many of Worcester's citizens who claimed both Native American and African American heritage. See Doughton's "Unseen Neighbors: Native Americans of Central Massachusetts, A People Who Had 'Vanished,'" in *After King Philip's War: Presence and Persistence in Indian New England*, ed. Colin G. Calloway (Hanover, NH: University Press of New England, 1997), 207–30. In the 1850s, for example, Gilbert Walker married Sarah E. Richardson, a Hassanamisso (Grafton) Indian, yet Sarah Walker and the Walker children were designated as "black" in the 1860 census and "mulatto" in 1870. See "Death of Gilbert Walker," *Worcester Spy*, 17 December 1890; *Worcester City Directory*, 1850–1856; and Worcester County Registry of Deeds, Books 516/383, 523/196, and 533/157, Worcester County, Massachusetts, Courthouse.

13 "Great Meeting in Worcester!" *Worcester Daily Spy*, 9 October 1850.

14 Mason, *Life of Isaac Mason*, 56; Von Frank, *Trials of Anthony Burns*, 122–24; "Another Sims Case in Boston," *The Liberator*, 2 June 1854.

15 "Another Sims Case in Boston," *The Liberator*, 2 June 1854; Von Frank, *Trials of Anthony Burns*, 138–39.

16 "Great Excitement in Worcester," *Worcester Daily Spy*, 31 October 1854; "More Excitement in Worcester," *National Aegis*, 1 November 1854. Butman's reason for his visit to Worcester remains unclear to this day. In an article written almost a quarter century after the event, the Reverend Albert Tyler claimed, as the city's African Americans and many of its white abolitionists did at the time, that Butman came to Worcester in pursuit of Jankins. See Tyler, "The Butman Riot," *Worcester Society of Antiquity Publications* 1 (1879): 85–89. In his autobiography, Higginson states that Butman's "purpose, real or reputed," was "looking for evidence against those concerned in the [Burns] riot." See Higginson, *Cheerful Yesterdays*, 162. George Frisbie Hoar concluded in his autobiography, "It was believed that he [Butman] was in search of information about fugitive negroes who were supposed to be in Worcester, and I suppose that to be the fact, although it was claimed that his errand was to summon witnesses against persons concerned in the riot which took place when Burns was captured." See George Frisbie Hoar, *Autobiography of Seventy Years, Vol. 1* (New York: Scribner's, 1903), 182.

17 Letter to "Friend Garrison," *The Liberator*, 3 November 1854; "Great Excitement in Worcester," *Worcester Daily Spy*, 31 October 1854; "Mob Violence," *Worcester Daily Transcript*, 31 October 1854.

18 "Great Excitement in Worcester," *Worcester Daily Spy*, 31 October 1854; "Mob Violence," *Worcester Daily Transcript*, 31 October 1854.

19 "Great Excitement in Worcester," *Worcester Daily Spy*, 31 October 1854; "Mob Violence," *Worcester Daily Transcript*, 31 October 1854.

20 For more on black Worcester's antebellum activism, see Salvatore, *We All Got History*, 107–9.

21 Melish, *Disowning Slavery*, 262.

22 Ibid., 265; "Celebration of the First of August," *The Liberator*, 15 August 1862.

23 U.S. Bureau of the Census, Manuscript census schedules, Worcester County, Massachusetts, 1860; Salvatore, *We All Got History*, 109. For more on black abolitionism and the antebellum convention movement, see James Oliver Horton and Lois E. Horton, *Black Bostonians: Family Life and Community Struggle in the Antebellum North* (New York: Holmes and Meier, 1979), 115–28.

24 Letter quoted in B. Eugene McCarthy and Thomas L. Doughton, eds., *From Bondage to Belonging: The Worcester Slave Narratives* (Amherst: University of Massachusetts Press, 2007), xxvi–xxvii; Thomas Wentworth Higginson, *Massachusetts in Mourning! A Sermon, Preached in Worcester, on June 4, 1854* (Boston: James Munroe and Company, 1854), 14.

25 "Hattie Rogers," in George P. Rawick, ed., *The American Slave: A Composite Autobiography*, vol. 15, North Carolina Narratives, pt. 2 (Westport, CT: Greenwood Publishing Company, 1972), 229.

26 "Andrew Boone," in Rawick, ed., *American Slave*, vol. 14, pt. 1, 136; "Henry Rountree," ibid., vol. 15, pt. 2, 234.

27 Ira Berlin, Barbara J. Fields, Thavolia Glymph, Joseph P. Reidy, and Leslie Rowland, *Freedom: A Documentary History of Emancipation, 1861–67: The Destruction of Slavery*, ser. 1, vol. 1 (New York: Cambridge University Press, 1985), 8–9.

28 James McPherson, *Battle Cry of Freedom: The Civil War Era* (New York: Ballantine Books, 1988), 285.

29 "City and County," *Worcester Daily Spy*, 20 April 1861; Andrew E. Ford, *The Story of the Fifteenth Regiment, Massachusetts Volunteer Infantry in the Civil War, 1861–64* (Clinton, MA: W. J. Coulter, 1898), 14–15; "The Military Movement," *Worcester Daily Spy*, 22 April 1861.

30 Ford, *Story of the Fifteenth Regiment*, 26.

31 *Worcester Daily Spy*, 14 June 1861; "The Disaster," *Worcester Daily Spy*, 23 July 1861; "A Discourse," *Worcester Daily Spy*, 29 July 1861.

32 Devens quoted in Ford, *Story of the Fifteenth Regiment*, 13; Ford, *Story of the Fifteenth Regiment*, 11; "City and County: Departure of the Fifteenth Regiment," *Worcester Daily Spy*, 8 August 1861.

33 "Col. Upton's Regiment," *Worcester Daily Spy*, 8 October 1861; *Worcester Daily Spy*, 19 September 1861; Henry S. Washburn, "Respectfully Dedicated to Col. Edwin Upton and His Command," in J. Waldo Denny, *Wearing the Blue in the Twenty-fifth Massachusetts Volunteer Infantry* (Worcester: Putnam & David, 1870), 26–27.

34 *Worcester Daily Spy*, 21 September 1861; Denny, *Wearing the Blue*, 20–21.

35 "Rev. Mr. Richardson's Sermon," *Worcester Daily Spy*, 28 September 1861.

36 Horace James, *An Oration Delivered in Newbern, North Carolina, Before the Twenty-fifth Regiment, Massachusetts Volunteers, July 4, 1862* (Boston: Brown and Company, 1862).

37 Horace James, *Our Duties to the Slave: A Sermon Preached Before the Original Congregational Church and Society in Wrentham, Massachusetts on Thanksgiving Day, November 26, 1846* (Boston: Richardson and Filmer, 1847); Eli Thayer, *A History of*

the *Kansas Crusade: Its Friends and Its Foes* (New York: Harper and Brothers, 1889), 133; *Worcester Daily Spy*, 7 December 1859; *Worcester Daily Spy*, 28 October 1861.

38 "Rev. Mr. James Accepts the Chaplaincy of the Twenty-fifth Regiment," *Worcester Daily Spy*, 10 October 1861.

39 "The Twenty-fifth Regiment," *Worcester Daily Spy*, 1 November 1861; David L. Day, *My Diary of Rambles with the Twenty-Fifth Massachusetts Volunteer Infantry* (Milford, MA: n.p., 1883), 5. Day notes that the 25th saw "a little something of the peculiar institution" in Annapolis, on their way to North Carolina, as "there are a great many Negroes strolling around the camps, most of them runaways, and as Maryland is supposed to be a loyal state, we have no right to take sides and offer them protection." However, he noted that when masters appeared, seeking out their slaves, the soldiers "put them on the wrong track and then run the boys into other camps, and then run them into the woods" (Day, *My Diary*, 11–12).

40 Thomas Wentworth Higginson, ed., "Preface," in *Harvard Memorial Biographies*, vol. 1 (Cambridge: Sever and Francis, 1866), iii.

CHAPTER TWO

1 Andrew E. Ford, *The Story of the Fifteenth Regiment, Massachusetts Volunteer Infantry in the Civil War, 1861–64* (Clinton, MA: W. J. Coulter, 1898), 99–100; John Hapgood Brooks, "About Josiah Allen, a colored slave who was here in 1871," in possession of George N. Blanchard, Brooks's grandson. I owe a special debt to Mr. Blanchard for sharing this account with me. Written on an envelope by Brooks, whose father employed Allen, the account mistakenly refers to Allen as "Josiah." All of the details of the letter support the fact that Brooks actually wrote about Isaiah Allen.

2 Allen Parker, *Recollections of Slavery Times* (Worcester: Charles Burbank & Company, 1895), 78–87.

3 "Mary Barbour: Ex-Slave Story," in George P. Rawick, ed., *The American Slave: A Composite Autobiography*, vol. 14, North Carolina Narratives, pt. 1 (Westport, CT: Greenwood Publishing Company, 1972), 79–81.

4 "Sarah Harris," ibid., 376.

5 "Letter from Newbern," *Worcester Daily Spy*, 26 April 1862.

6 Quoted in Ford, *Story of the Fifteenth Regiment*, 58.

7 Ibid., 57, 58.

8 James McPherson, *Battle Cry of Freedom: The Civil War Era* (New York: Ballantine Books, 1988), 355–56.

9 Ambrose E. Burnside, *The Burnside Expedition* (Providence: N. Bangs Williams and Company, 1882), 7; General A. B. R. Sprague, "Burnside's Expedition to North Carolina: The Capture of Roanoke Island," *Proceedings of the Worcester Society of Antiquity for the New Year, 1907*, vol. 23 (Worcester: Worcester Society of Antiquity, 1908), 112, 128; John G. Barrett, *The Civil War in North Carolina* (Chapel Hill: University of North Carolina Press, 1963), 74–81, 89.

10 Burnside, *Burnside Expedition*, 8, 13–14.

11   Ibid., 22; Sprague, "Burnside's Expedition," 113–14, 116; William Green to Green family, 22 January 1862, 23 January 1862, 24 January 1862, Green Family Papers, American Antiquarian Society, Worcester, MA.

12   Barrett, *Civil War in North Carolina*, 74–81.

13   "Another Glorious Victory," *New York Times*, 19 March 1862; "Burnside's Operations on the North Carolina Coast," *New York Times*, 19 March 1862; "News from Washington," *New York Times*, 19 March 1862; "Newbern in Our Hands," *Worcester Daily Spy*, 20 March 1862.

14   William F. Draper, *Recollections of a Varied Career* (Boston: Little, Brown, and Company, 1908), 65–67; Sprague, "Burnside's Expedition," 125; *New Bern Weekly Progress*, 18 January 1862; Allen Watson, *A History of New Bern and Craven County* (New Bern: Tryon Palace Commission, 1987), 379; W. A. Curtis, "A Journal of Reminiscences of the War," *Our Living and Our Dead* 1, no. 3 (May 1875): 288.

15   Frederick G. Brown, William O. Dupuis, and Norman H. French, eds., *Boylston, Massachusetts, in the Civil War: The Letters Home of Pvt. John W. Partridge with Biographical Sketches of Other Boylston Soldiers* (Bowie, MD: Heritage Books, Inc., 1995), 33; "Letter from Chaplain James," *The Congregationalist*, 18 April 1862; A. E. Burnside to E. M. Stanton, 21 March 1862, *The War of the Rebellion: A Compilation of the Official Records of the Union and Confederate Armies* (hereafter *Official Records*), series 1, vol. 9 (Washington: Government Printing Office, 1883), 199.

16   A. E. Burnside to E. M. Stanton, 21 March 1862, *Official Records*, ser. 1, vol. 9, 199.

17   Joe A. Mobley, *James City: A Black Community in North Carolina, 1863–1900* (Raleigh: North Carolina Department of Cultural Resources, Division of Archives and History, 1981), 5; Vincent Colyer, *Report of the Services Rendered by the Freed People to the United States Army, in North Carolina* (New York: Vincent Colyer, 1864), 6; Dr. R. R. Clarke to John G. Metcalf, 21 April 1862, in Scrapbook of John G. Metcalf, M.D., Civil War Collection, American Antiquarian Society, Worcester, MA.

18   McPherson, *Battle Cry of Freedom*, 355–56.

19   Colyer, *Report of the Services Rendered*, 5. Historians have disagreed about the nature of antislavery sentiments of Union soldiers. For example, James M. McPherson has argued that such sentiments were "more pragmatic than altruistic" and Joseph Allan Frank has posited that antislavery was more an attack on the southern ruling class than the promotion of black rights. The New Bern example suggests that while pragmatic, antislavery sentiments among Union soldiers consisted of a great deal of altruism as well. See James M. McPherson, *For Cause and Comrades: Why Men Fought in the Civil War* (New York: Oxford University Press, 1997), 19, 199–23, and Joseph Allan Frank, *With Ballot and Bayonet: The Political Socialization of American Civil War Soldiers* (Athens: University of Georgia Press, 1998), 67.

20   John Cross to John G. Metcalf, 19 September 1862, in Scrapbook of John G. Metcalf, M.D., Civil War Collection, American Antiquarian Society, Worcester, MA.

21   "The New England Anti-Slavery Convention," *The Liberator*, 6 June 1862.

22   "Letter from Newbern," *Worcester Daily Spy*, 26 April 1862.

23   Ibid.

24 Ibid.

25 "What a Soldier Thinks," *Worcester Daily Spy*, 20 May 1862; W. P. Derby, *Bearing Arms in the Twenty-seventh Massachusetts Regiment of Volunteers Infantry during the Civil War, 1861–65* (Boston: Wright and Patterson, 1883), 96; "Extracts from a Soldier's Letter," *Worcester Daily Spy*, 7 July 1862; "From the Fifty-first Regiment," *Worcester Daily Spy*, 19 February 1863.

26 Colyer, *Report of the Services Rendered*, 9, 33; Horace James, "The Governor Stanly Imbroglio," *The Congregationalist*, 20 June 1862; Derby, *Bearing Arms*, 163; James A. Emmerton, *A Record of the Twenty-third Regiment Massachusetts Volunteer Infantry during the Civil War, 1861–65* (Boston: William Ware & Company, 1886), 95.

27 Colyer, *Report of the Services Rendered*, 6, 33; Barrett, *Civil War in North Carolina*, 127.

28 Colyer, *Report of the Services Rendered*, 9; "Contrabands and Their Services," *The Liberator*, 11 July 1862. Official correspondence of Union officers in eastern North Carolina contains numerous references to the contributions of contrabands. See, for example, *Official Records*, ser. 1, vol. 9, 208, 286, 354. See also "General Orders, No. 2," *Official Records*, ser. 1, vol. 9, 369–70, and A. E. Burnside to E. M. Stanton, 27 March 1862, *Official Records*, ser. 1, vol. 9, 373–74.

29 Emmerton, *Record of the Twenty-third Regiment*, 95; Derby, *Bearing Arms*, 163.

30 Emmerton, *Record of the Twenty-third Regiment*, 95.

31 Thomas J. Jennings to "Kind Friend," Federal Soldiers Letters, New Bern Occupation Papers, Southern Historical Collection, University of North Carolina, Chapel Hill; Samuel H. Putnam, *The Story of Company A, Twenty-fifth Regiment, Massachusetts Volunteers, in the War of the Rebellion* (Worcester: Putnam, David, and Company, 1886), 130–31, 172.

32 "Letter from Chaplain James," *The Congregationalist*, 18 April 1862.

33 Horace James to "My Dear Friends of the Old South Sabbath School," 21 June 1862, Horace James Papers, American Antiquarian Society, Worcester, MA; Horace James, "The Governor Stanly Imbroglio," *The Congregationalist*, 20 June 1862; Colyer, *Report of Services Rendered*, 43–44. For a thorough account of James's vision of a new social order for the South, see Stephen Edward Reilly, "Reconstruction through Regeneration: Horace James's Work with the Blacks for Social Reform in North Carolina, 1862–1867" (Ph.D. diss., Duke University, 1983).

34 "Letter from Newbern," *Worcester Daily Spy*, 1 April 1862; Reid Mitchell, *The Vacant Chair: The Northern Soldier Leaves Home* (New York: Oxford University Press, 1993), 21.

35 Horace James to "My Dear Friends of the Old South Sabbath School," 21 June 1862, Horace James Papers, American Antiquarian Society, Worcester, MA.

36 Brown et al., eds., *Boylston, Massachusetts, in the Civil War*, 38.

37 Colyer, *Report of the Services Rendered*, 44.

38 Draper, *Recollections of a Varied Career*, 66; Mrs. Frederick C. Roberts, "Historical Incidents," *Carolina and the Southern Cross* 2, no. 1 (April 1914): 5.

39 Roberts, "Historical Incidents," 5; Brown et al., eds., *Boylston, Massachusetts, in the Civil War*, 34.

40 Barrett, *Civil War in North Carolina*, 126–27; Edward Stanly, *A Military Governor Among Abolitionists* (New York, 1865), 26–27; Edwin M. Stanton to Major-General Ambrose E. Burnside, 20 May 1862, *Official Records*, ser. 1, vol. 9, 391; William C. Harris, "Lincoln and Wartime Reconstruction in North Carolina, 1861–1863," *North Carolina Historical Review* 63 (1986): 156.

41 Stanly, *Military Governor Among Abolitionists*, 26–27. The content of the conversation between Colyer and Stanly remains unclear to this day as both participants gave different accounts that changed significantly over time. While Colyer initially claimed that Stanly ordered the black schools closed, Stanly claimed that he did not want any action taken abruptly. Yet when Colyer immediately closed the schools, Stanly thanked him for doing his duty. See Norman D. Brown, *Edward Stanly: Whiggery's Tarheel "Conqueror"* (University: University of Alabama Press, 1975), 207–8. Stanly later claimed that he had no intention of closing the schools, and Colyer also withdrew his earlier claim that Stanly ordered the schools closed immediately. See Harris, "Lincoln and Wartime Reconstruction in North Carolina," 159, and "The Stanly-Colyer Controversy," *The Liberator*, 4 July 1862.

42 "Closing the Schools for Contrabands," *New York Times*, 21 May 1862.

43 Ibid.; Horace James, "The Governor Stanly Imbroglio," *The Congregationalist*, 20 June 1862. Larned quoted in Brown, *Edward Stanly*, 209.

44 "Sending Back the Blacks," *New York Times*, 31 May 1862; Brown, *Edward Stanly*, 208; "Civil Rule in North Carolina," *New York Times*, 4 June 1862.

45 Dr. R. R. Clarke to Dr. Metcalf, 5 June 1862, in Scrapbook of John G. Metcalf, M.D., Civil War Collection, American Antiquarian Society, Worcester, MA; "Sending Back the Blacks," *New York Times*, 31 May 1862.

46 Dr. R. R. Clarke to Dr. Metcalf, 5 June 1862, in Scrapbook of John G. Metcalf, M.D., Civil War Collection, American Antiquarian Society, Worcester, MA; *New York Times*, 31 May 1862; "An Officer's Opinion," *Worcester Daily Spy*, 17 June 1862; "Civil Rule in North Carolina," *New York Times*, 4 June 1862.

47 Dr. R. R. Clarke to John G. Metcalf, 5 June 1862, in Scrapbook of John G. Metcalf, M.D., Civil War Collection, American Antiquarian Society, Worcester, MA; "An Officer's Opinion," *Worcester Daily Spy*, 17 June 1862.

48 Letter of "a clergyman of Northern birth and association," quoted in Stanly, *Military Governor Among Abolitionists*, 21–22. Stanly quoted this letter to provide evidence that he and other whites in New Bern were actually in danger of an attack by blacks.

49 Dr. R. R. Clarke to John G. Metcalf, 5 June 1862, in Scrapbook of John G. Metcalf, M.D., Civil War Collection, American Antiquarian Society, Worcester, MA.

50 Ibid.

51 "Gov. Stanly and His Barbarous Proceedings in North Carolina," *The Liberator*, 20 June 1862; Harris, "Lincoln and Wartime Reconstruction in North Carolina," 162.

52 Horace James, "The Governor Stanly Imbroglio," *The Congregationalist*, 20 June 1862; *Worcester Daily Spy*, 9 June 1862.

CHAPTER THREE

1 "From the Fifty-first Regiment," *Worcester Daily Spy*, 10 December 1862.

2 "Arrival of a Contraband," *Worcester Daily Spy*, 28 June 1862.

3 Vital Statistics for the City of Worcester, Marriage Records, January 1863.

4 Vincent Colyer, *Report of the Services Rendered by the Freed People to the United States Army, in North Carolina* (New York: Vincent Colyer, 1864), 9.

5 "The New England Anti-Slavery Convention," *The Liberator*, 6 June 1862.

6 "Arrival of a Contraband," *Worcester Daily Spy*, 28 June 1862; Leslie A. Schwalm, *Emancipation's Diaspora: Race and Reconstruction in the Upper Midwest* (Chapel Hill: University of North Carolina Press, 2009), 96–97.

7 U.S. Bureau of the Census, Manuscript census schedules, Worcester County, Massachusetts, 1860; James Oliver Horton and Lois E. Horton, *Black Bostonians: Family Life and Community Struggle in the Antebellum North* (New York: Holmes and Meier, 1979), 7; James Oliver Horton, *Free People of Color: Inside the African American Community* (Washington: Smithsonian Institution, 1993), 26–27. The city's reputation as the center of abolitionism likely attracted more migrants to Boston. While the 1860 census undoubtedly undercounts southern blacks, since runaway slaves would have avoided a census listing, especially after 1850, the census nonetheless confirms that most Worcester blacks were northern-born and southern blacks were small in number. Notably, using census data to reveal the racial composition of a town or county is fraught with problems, but it is one of the few sources available for this kind of documentation. Census takers received no specific directions for determining racial classification. Moreover, many Worcester County residents of African descent intermarried with Native Americans before the Civil War; some of these individuals are classified as black, some mulatto, and still others as Indian. At best, for people of color, the census paints a community portrait with a broad brushstroke. For more on the problems inherent in using the census to study northern blacks before the Civil War, see Horton, *Free People of Color*, 28.

8 Thomas Wentworth Higginson, *Massachusetts in Mourning! A Sermon, Preached in Worcester, on June 4, 1854* (Boston: James Munroe and Company, 1854), 14; U.S. Bureau of the Census, Manuscript census schedules, Worcester County, Massachusetts, 1860; *Worcester Almanac, Directory and Business Advertiser*, 1862. In the 1865 Massachusetts census, R. H. and Mary Johnson listed three Massachusetts-born children, the oldest ten years old.

9 For more on black Worcester's antebellum activism, see Nick Salvatore, *We All Got History: The Memory Books of Amos Webber* (New York: Times Books, 1996), 107–9, and Albert Von Frank, *The Trials of Anthony Burns: Freedom and Slavery in Emerson's Boston* (Cambridge, MA: Harvard University Press, 1998), 122.

10 *Worcester Almanac, Directory, and Business Advertiser*, 1863.

11 Worcester County Registry of Deeds, Grantor-Grantee Index, Books 562/538, 562/539, and 571/370, Worcester County, Massachusetts, Courthouse; Isaac Mason, *Life of Isaac Mason as a Slave* (Worcester: n.p., 1893), 1–2, 49–52. Mason gave this account of his coming to Worcester at his seventy-fifth birthday party, reported in

"Isaac Mason's Celebration," in the *Worcester Telegram* on 15 May 1897. The reporter recorded Mason as referring to "a man named Store, one of the most uncompromising anti-slavery and freesoil men in all this vicinity," as helping bring him to Worcester. Mason later remarked that Store emigrated to Kansas and died there. He then recounted that he had recently visited with Store's widow, a Mrs. Kimball, who had remarried and lived in New Hampshire. Mason's discussion of Mrs. Kimball confirms that Store was indeed Martin Stowell, who died not in Kansas but in Tennessee during the Civil War. According to Civil War pension records, Stowell's widow remarried a man named Kimball and resided in New Hampshire. (Thanks to the late Robert Cormier for sharing his research on Stowell with me.)

In his autobiography, Mason gave a slightly different — but not contradictory — account of his arrival in Worcester, claiming that Hayden (a close abolitionist associate of Stowell) sent him to Worcester with a letter of introduction to William Brown, a prominent black upholsterer, and that Brown helped him secure housing with another black Worcesterite, Ebenezer Hemenway. See Mason, *Life of Isaac Mason*, 55–56. Mason's freedom proved to be tenuous even in Worcester. In 1852, he recalled in his autobiography, as a result of the Fugitive Slave Law, "hunting slave fever got so high that our sympathizing friends advised me to leave at once to go to Canada." After a brief sojourn in Montreal and then Toronto, Mason returned to Worcester — walking from Rochester, New York, for lack of train fare.

12 Mason, *Life of Isaac Mason*, 66; Worcester County Registry of Deeds, Grantor-Grantee Index, Books 562/538, 562/539, and 571/370, Worcester County, Massachusetts, Courthouse.

13 Joshua Chasan, "Civilizing Worcester: The Creation of Industrial and Cultural Order, Worcester, Massachusetts, 1848–1876" (Ph.D. diss., University of Pittsburgh, 1974), 16. Chasan estimates that in 1860, 82 percent of city residents did not own real property. "Isaac Mason's Funeral: Senator George F. Hoar Pays a Tribute to His Character," *Worcester Daily Spy*, 30 August 1898. In 1863, the Masons deeded the property at 62 Union to Rice, Barton, and Faler (see Worcester County Registry of Deeds, Book 683/503, Worcester County, Massachusetts, Courthouse), apparently unable to pay their mortgage on the property, although they did pay off their loan to Wilson.

14 "Isaac Mason's Funeral," *Worcester Daily Spy*, 8 August 1898; *Worcester Almanac, Directory, and Business Advertiser*, 1861.

15 *Worcester Almanac, Directory, and Business Advertiser*, 1863, 1864.

16 V. Jacque Voegeli, "A Rejected Alternative: Union Policy and the Relocation of Southern 'Contrabands' at the Dawn of Emancipation," *Journal of Southern History* 49 (November 2003): 765–89; "Nigger on the Brain," *Worcester Daily Spy*, 31 October 1862. Voegeli notes Lincoln's surprise at Andrew's rejection of the refugees and that "hostility toward black migration in Massachusetts" had long-term consequences since it "helped shape Union policy toward southern freedpeople," making the North "off-limits to the army's resettlement of substantial numbers of freedpeople" (786).

17 Schwalm, *Emancipation's Diaspora*, 86.

18 "An Act to Suppress Insurrection, to Punish Treason, to Seize and Confiscate the Property of Rebels, and for Other Purposes," *U.S. Statutes at Large, Treaties, and Proclamations of the United States of America*, vol. 12 (Boston, 1863), 589–92; Norman D. Brown, *Edward Stanly: Whiggery's Tarheel "Conquerer"* (University: University of Alabama Press, 1975), 212–13.

19 Joe A. Mobley, *James City: A Black Community in North Carolina, 1863–1900* (Raleigh: North Carolina Department of Cultural Resources, Division of Archives and History, 1981), 14–15; Brown, *Edward Stanly*, 228; "From North Carolina," *Worcester Daily Spy*, 26 August 1862; "Letter from the Army," *The Congregationalist*, 26 September 1862.

20 *The Congregationalist*, 30 January 1863.

21 "Letter from the Fifty-first," *Worcester Daily Spy*, 2 February 1863; George F. Weston letter, 15 February 1863, New Bern Occupation Papers, Southern Historical Collection, University of North Carolina, Chapel Hill; "Letter from Chaplain James," *The Congregationalist*, 10 October 1862.

22 *The Congregationalist*, 30 January 1863.

23 Circular from Horace James, "To the Public," 27 June 1863, Horace James Papers, Massachusetts Historical Society, Boston.

24 "City and County," *Worcester Daily Spy*, 18 July 1863.

25 "Letter from Horace James," *Worcester Daily Spy*, 13 March 1864.

26 "The 'Contrabands,'" *Worcester Daily Spy*, 27 December 1861; "An Appeal," *Worcester Daily Spy*, 22 November 1862. For an in-depth study of the antebellum activism of Worcester's women, see Carolyn J. Lawes, *Women and Reform in a New England Community, 1815–1860* (Lexington: University Press of Kentucky, 2000).

27 See, for example, reports of "Freedman's Relief," *Worcester Daily Spy*, 15 January 1863, 10 October 1863, 12 January 1864, 3 March 1864.

28 Carol Faulkner, *Women's Radical Reconstruction: The Freedmen's Aid Movement* (Philadelphia: University of Pennsylvania Press, 2004), 34–35.

29 "Relief for the Contrabands," *Worcester Daily Spy*, 8 March 1862; "The Contrabands at Port Royal," *Worcester Daily Spy*, 31 March 1862.

30 "Relief for the Contrabands," *Worcester Daily Spy*, 8 March 1862; "Mr. Wayland's Letter," *Worcester Daily Spy*, 3 April 1862.

31 For more on these competing visions after the Civil War, see Faulkner, *Women's Radical Reconstruction*, 38–66.

32 Lunsford Lane, *The Narrative of Lunsford Lane, Formerly of Raleigh, North Carolina*, 2nd ed. (Boston: J. G. Torrey, 1842), 8–9, 15, 21, 25, 34, 37–38, 41, 52; The Rev. William G. Hawkins, *Lunsford Lane; or, Another Helper from North Carolina* (Boston: Crosby & Nichols, 1863), vi–vii, 82, 147–55, 194; "Lunsford Lane," in William S. Powell, ed., *Dictionary of North Carolina Biography*, vol. 4 (Chapel Hill: University of North Carolina Press, 1991), 14.

33 Lane quoted in Hawkins, *Lunsford Lane*, 202–7.

34 Ibid., 206.

35 "An Appeal," *Worcester Daily Spy*, 22 November 1862; "City and County: Letter from Mrs. Horace James to the Colored People of Worcester," *Worcester Daily Spy*, 27 April 1864; Faulkner, *Women's Radical Reconstruction*, 67.

36 "City and County: Letter from Mrs. Horace James to the Colored People of Worcester," *Worcester Daily Spy*, 27 April 1864; U.S. Bureau of the Census, Manuscript census schedules, Worcester County, Massachusetts, 1850 and 1860; *Worcester Daily Spy*, 20 January 1862.

37 "City and County: Letter from Mrs. Horace James to the Colored People of Worcester," *Worcester Daily Spy*, 27 April 1864.

38 Horace James to the Old South Sunday School, 25 May 1863, Horace James Papers, American Antiquarian Society, Worcester, MA.

39 Horace James, *Annual Report of the Superintendent of Negro Affairs in North Carolina, 1864* (Boston: W. F. Brown and Company, 1865), 38–42; U.S. Bureau of the Census, Manuscript census schedules, Worcester and Middlesex counties, Massachusetts, 1860.

40 Patricia C. Click, *Time Full of Trial: The Roanoke Island Freedmen's Colony, 1862–1867* (Chapel Hill: University of North Carolina Press, 2001), 55; "Ministers and Churches," *Worcester Daily Spy*, 1 January 1864; "From Newbern, N.C.," *The Congregationalist*, 12 February 1864.

41 "From the Fifty-first Regiment," *Worcester Daily Spy*, 10 December 1862; American Missionary Association Archives, Amistad Research Center, North Carolina Letters (hereafter NC Letters), Reel 2; "November Report of Committee on Teachers," *The National Freedman*, 15 November 1865; H. S. Beals to George Whipple, 21 May 1866, NC Letters, Reel 2; "From Newbern, N.C.," *The Congregationalist*, 12 February 1864.

42 "List of Teachers Now in Service," *The Freedmen's Record*, April 1865, December 1865, December 1866, December 1867.

43 Henry L. Swint, ed., *Dear Ones at Home: Letters from Contraband Camps* (Nashville: Vanderbilt University Press, 1966), 4–7, 105, 142, 145. Lucy and Sarah Chase recorded several visits to fellow Worcesterites in the New Bern area, visiting not only with Helen and Horace James but also with Colonel A. B. R. Sprague, the Reverend Briggs, and fellow teacher Anne Merriam. See, for example, letters, 18 January 1864, 15 January 1865, 3 March 1865, Chase Family Papers, American Antiquarian Society, Worcester, MA.

44 Horace James to Secretaries of the American Missionary Association, 20 October 1865, NC Letters, Reel 1.

45 William T. Briggs, "Annual Report of the Superintendent of Colored Schools in North Carolina," 1865, NC Letters, Reel 1; Horace James to L. B. Russell, 12 June 1863, NC Letters; Emily Frances Thomas, "'To Make Another New England of the Whole South': Massachusetts Freedpeople's Teachers, 1862–1900" (M.A. thesis, Clark University, 1998), 7, 15; *The Freedmen's Record*, May 1865.

46 Roper quoted in Click, *Time Full of Trial*, 83.

47 William T. Briggs, "Annual Report of the Superintendent of Colored Schools in North Carolina," 1865, NC Letters, Reel 1.

48 Elizabeth James to George Whipple, 19 December 1863, NC Letters, Reel 1; H. S. Beals to S. Hunt, 19 December 1865 and 29 June 1866.

49 William T. Briggs, "Annual Report of the Superintendent of Colored Schools in North Carolina," 1865, NC Letters, Reel 1.

50 Ibid.; *The Freedmen's Record*, September 1865.

51 NC Letters, February 1864, Reel 1; William Briggs to George Whipple, 27 April 1864, NC Letters, Reel 1.

52 George M. Fredrickson, *The Black Image in the White Mind: The Debate On African-American Character and Destiny* (New York: Harper & Row, 1971), 107, 110. Fredrickson sums up romantic racialism: "As characteristically put forth by whites . . . it often revealed a mixture of cant, condescension, and sentimentality not unlike the nineteenth-century view of womanly virtue, which it so closely resembled" (125).

53 Thomas, "'To Make Another New England of the Whole South,'" 37–39; Oliver Howard, letter to *The Freedmen's Record*, November 1865.

54 William T. Briggs, "Annual Report of the Superintendent of Colored Schools in North Carolina," 1865, NC Letters, Reel 1; "The Freedmen of Carolina," *The Congregationalist*, 22 January 1864.

55 "Letter from Chaplain James," *The Congregationalist*, 11 September 1863; "Practical Reflections, by Rev. B. W. Pond," *The National Freedman*, 15 August 1866.

56 Hawkins, *Lunsford Lane*, 196–97.

57 The Rev. B. W. Pond to Rev. William G. Hawkins, 19 July 1865, *The National Freedman*, 1 August 1865.

58 "Schools in North Carolina," *Worcester Daily Spy*, 29 March 1866. The report from Lane reprinted in the *Spy* was dated 16 June 1865.

59 William T. Briggs, "Annual Report of the Superintendent of Colored Schools in North Carolina," 1865; Sarah A. Beals to Rev. S. Hunt, 30 April 1866; and Sarah A. Beals to Rev. S. Hunt, 19 June 1866 and 20 July 1866, all in NC Letters, Reel 1.

60 *The Freedmen's Record*, 9 March 1867; Helen M. Dodd to Rev. S. Hunt, 29 November 1865, NC Letters, Reel 1.

61 Roper quoted in Click, *Time Full of Trial*, 116; Lucy Chase to Sarah Chase, 15 January 1865, Chase Family Papers, American Antiquarian Society, Worcester, MA.

62 *The Liberator*, 9 October 1863; Susie Taylor, *A Black Woman's Civil War Memoirs: Reminiscences of My Life in Camp with the 33rd U.S. Colored Troops, Late 1st South Carolina Volunteers*, ed. Patricia Romero (New York: Markus Weiner, 1988), 137.

63 H. S. Beals to E. P. Smith, 15 February 1867; and S. J. Whiton to E. P. Smith, 16 February 1867, NC Letters, Reel 3. For a more complete discussion of the controversy in Beaufort, see Maxine D. Jones, "The American Missionary Association and the Beaufort, North Carolina, School Controversy, 1866–67," *Phylon* 48, no. 2 (2nd Quarter 1987): 103–11.

64 S. J. Whiton to E. P. Smith, 16 February 1867, NC Letters, Reel 3.

65 "Memorial to the AMA from the Col'd. citizens of Beaufort," 4 March 1867, NC Letters, Reel 3.

66 Hyman Thompson to George Whipple, March 1867, NC Letters, Reel 3.

67 Letter from George W. Jenkins (freedman) to "Miss Sarah," 29 June 1864, NC Letters, Reel 1.

68 "Anniversary Celebration of the President's Proclamation at Newbern by an Eyewitness," *The Freedmen's Record*, February 1865.

69 *North Carolina Daily Times*, 24 March 1865; "Extracts From Monthly Reports of the Teachers at Newberne, N.C. for Month of March," *The Freedmen's Record*, May 1865.

70 James, *Annual Report*, 47–48.

71 *North Carolina Daily Times*, 28 March 1865, 18 April 1865.

72 Mrs. Frederick C. Roberts, "The Aftermath," *Carolina and the Southern Cross* (February 1914): 4; Bryan quoted in Alan D. Watson, *History of New Bern and Craven County* (New Bern: Tryon Palace Commission, 1987), 457; Mrs. Frederick C. Roberts, "Historical Incidents," *Carolina and the Southern Cross* 2, no. 1 (April 1914): 10–12.

73 Roberts, "Historical Incidents," 12; Eric Foner, *Reconstruction: America's Unfinished Revolution, 1863–1877* (New York: Harper and Row, 1988), 81.

74 William T. Briggs, "Annual Report of the Superintendent of Colored Schools in North Carolina," 1865, NC Letters, Reel 1; James, *Annual Report*, 5.

75 Foner, *Reconstruction*, 69.

76 Click, *Time Full of Trial*, 129–36.

77 Ibid., 153–76.

78 Watson, *History of New Bern and Craven County*, 402; James, *Annual Report*, 11; *North Carolina Daily Times*, 8 August 1865.

79 Watson, *History of New Bern and Craven County*, 450; *North Carolina Daily Times*, 7 June 1865; "Mass Meeting of the Colored People," *North Carolina Daily Times*, 29 August 1865, 28 August 1865.

80 Watson, *History of New Bern and Craven County*, 429; "Mass Meeting of the Colored People," *North Carolina Daily Times*, 28 August 1865.

81 "Mass Meeting of Colored Citizens," *North Carolina Daily Times*, 30 August 1865.

82 Ibid.

83 Ibid.

84 Watson, *History of New Bern and Craven County*, 462.

85 *North Carolina Daily Times*, 24 May 1865; "A Colored Man's Letter," *North Carolina Daily Times*, 22 December 1865.

86 "The Next Year in North Carolina," *The Freedmen's Record*, September 1866; "Letter from Rev. Horace James," *The Congregationalist*, 8 December 1865.

87 Mobley, *James City*, 58–59, 60–61.

88 "Letter from Horace James," *The Congregationalist*, 8 December 1865; Mobley, *James City*, 36–38; "Letter from North Carolina," *The Congregationalist*, 23 February 1866.

89 Click, *Time Full of Trial*, 193–94; Horace James, *Trial before a Special Military Commission, Convened by Direction of Andrew Johnson, President of the United States, in Sept., 1866* (Washington: n.p.); *Worcester Daily Spy*, 10 June 1875; J. Waldo Denny, *Wearing the Blue in the Twenty-fifth Massachusetts Volunteer Infantry* (Worcester: Putnam and David, 1879), 442.

CHAPTER FOUR

1 *Worcester Daily Spy*, 6 July 1865.

2 Linking birth, marriage, and death records for the city of Worcester with the state manuscript census for 1865 and the federal census for 1870 yielded a total of 336 southern-born migrants between 1862 and 1870, 196 of them from Virginia and North Carolina. Given the perennial problem of undercounting of African Americans in the census, the southern-born population was likely greater than the 336 who can be documented. See Thomas L. Doughton, ed., *Births, Deaths, Marriages of People of Color: Worcester, Massachusetts, 1849–1890* (Worcester: Nipnet Press, 1990); Massachusetts Manuscript Census, Worcester County, 1865; and U.S. Bureau of the Census, Manuscript census schedules, Worcester County, Massachusetts, 1870.

3 See, for example, Doughton, ed., *Births, Deaths, Marriages*, 9, 12, 33, 51, 55, 63, 82–83; and Massachusetts Manuscript Census, Worcester County, 1865.

4 *Worcester Daily Spy*, 8 April 1865; "The Death of the President," *Worcester Daily Spy*, 14 April 1865.

5 "Solemnities in Worcester," *Worcester Daily Spy*, 20 April 1865; "Retribution," *Worcester Daily Spy*, 18 April 1865.

6 *Worcester Daily Spy*, 6 July 1865.

7 Ibid.

8 Ibid.

9 Ibid. Walker received authorization to recruit for the state's black regiment in February 1863. See Samuel A. Stone to Adjutant General Schouler, 26 February 1863, Adjutant General's Correspondence, January–February 1863, Massachusetts Military Museum and Archive, Worcester, MA.

10 "Frederick Douglass in Worcester," *Worcester Daily Spy*, 6 April 1865.

11 *Worcester City Directory*, 1865.

12 Ibid., 1866, 1867; *Worcester Daily Spy*, 28 October 1869. In both the 1865 Massachusetts census and the 1870 federal census, Mary Bryant is listed as "keeping house."

13 Massachusetts Manuscript Census, Worcester County, 1865; U.S. Bureau of the Census, Manuscript census schedules, Worcester County, Massachusetts, 1870; Doughton, ed., *Births, Deaths, Marriages*, 49. Julia Ann Bryant listed her birthplace as New Bern and her parents as William and Hager Bryant in her marriage record. William Bryant listed Henry Johnson as a partner in the advertisement published in the *Worcester Daily Spy* on 28 October 1869.

14 Alan D. Watson, *A History of New Bern and Craven County* (New Bern: Tryon Palace Commission, 1987), 428, 433, 442, 446–47.

15 U.S. Bureau of the Census, Manuscript census schedules, Worcester County, Massachusetts, 1870 and 1880; *Worcester City Directory*, 1870–80.

16 Allen Parker, *Recollections of Slavery Times* (Worcester: Charles Burbank and Company, 1895), 86–90; Allen Parker Civil War Pension File, National Archives, Washington, DC.

17 *Worcester City Directory*, 1869; *Worcester Daily Spy*, 20 March 1869; "Old 'Pop' Parker Is Forever Free," *Worcester Evening Post*, 18 June 1906.

18 Worcester County Registry of Deeds, Grantor-Grantee Index, Books 709/22 and 746/444, Worcester County, Massachusetts, Courthouse.

19 *Worcester Daily Spy*, 27 and 29 April 1869; *Worcester Evening Gazette*, 27 April 1869. The last listing for William Bryant is in the 1870 city directory.

20 "A Letter from North Carolina," *The National Freedman*, 1 March 1865.

21 Massachusetts Manuscript Census, Worcester County, 1865; U. S. Bureau of the Census, Manuscript census schedules, Worcester County, Massachusetts, 1870; "Worcester Whittlings," *Boston Guardian*, 14 February 1904.

22 Leslie A. Schwalm, *Emancipation's Diaspora: Race and Reconstruction in the Upper Midwest* (Chapel Hill: University of North Carolina Press, 2009), 85–86.

23 "North Brookfield," *Worcester Daily Spy*, 10 January 1872.

24 Ibid.

25 James Phinney Munroe, *A Life of Francis Amasa Walker* (New York: Henry Holt and Company, 1923), 64–65; "North Brookfield," *Worcester Daily Spy*, 10 January 1872.

26 George Frisbie Hoar, "Tribute to Francis A. Walker," typewritten manuscript (no date), American Antiquarian Society, Worcester, MA; Josiah H. Temple, *History of North Brookfield* (n.p., 1887), 285, 478–79; Mark E. Ellis and Linda V. Hart, "The Church Across the Street," *Quaboag Plantation, Special Commemorative Issue*, 1987; "North Brookfield," *Worcester Spy*, 10 January 1872. The church split left deep wounds in North Brookfield that would have still been fresh at the time of David Allen's arrival. While the Walkers seemed sincere in their guardianship of Allen, their "adoption" of him may have provided a way to confront the shoe manufacturers' pro-southern sentiments, another act of defiance in a small-town civil war.

27 U.S. Bureau of the Census, Manuscript census schedules, Worcester County, Massachusetts, 1870 and 1880; "Death of Robert Morse," *North Brookfield Journal*, 31 May 1912; "Robert Morse Goes to Answer Last Call," *Worcester Telegram*, 30 May 1912, Association of Colored Peoples Papers, Worcester Historical Museum, Worcester, MA; Temple, *History of North Brookfield*, 339.

28 Evidence regarding Allen's status before the Civil War is contradictory, although the weight of evidence indicates that he was a slave and not free. Whereas Allen claimed he was free-born when he enlisted in the U.S. Army in 1863, his pension records include an affidavit from a woman, "Mrs. E. S. C. Head," who swore under oath after the Civil War that Allen had been owned by her mother in Leesburg and that "he lived after the war at my mother's home until the death of my mother about ten years ago." Head was likely Eliza S. Gover, the daughter of Sarah J. Gover, who would have been Allen's owner. Consistent with Head's sworn statement, Allen is listed in the 1880 U.S. Manuscript Census as living in the Gover household, made up of Sarah and Eliza S. Gover, in Loudon County, Virginia. In addition, he does not appear in the 1860 U.S. Manuscript Census as a free person of color. The Reverend Alonzo Hill referred to Allen as "a freeman of color" in his appendix to Spurr's funeral sermon, but several accounts written after the war, including a brief statement by a member of the Worcester family who employed Allen after Spurr's death, claim that Allen had been a slave. Allen also told stories at a reunion of the 15th Massachusetts in 1871 about his escape from slavery, from Leesburg to Poolesville.

In addition, veterans visiting Virginia who looked up Allen referred to him as a "contraband." Perhaps the conflicting evidence regarding Allen's status reflects the ambiguity of the law regarding contrabands before 1863. Given Spurr's strict adherence to federal policy in 1862, Allen may have claimed he was free in order to secure employment with Spurr as well as fend off any attempts to have him returned to his master. Ultimately, most local citizens seemed to view and remember Allen as a freed slave. For references to Allen's prewar status, see, for example, John Hapgood Brooks, "About Josiah Allen, a colored slave who was here in 1871," in possession of George M. Blanchard, Worcester, MA; Isaiah Allen Civil War Pension File, National Archives, Washington, DC; Alonzo Hill, *A Discourse Preached in Worcester, October 5, 1862, on Lieutenant Thomas Jefferson Spurr, Fifteenth Massachusetts Volunteers* (Boston: J. Wilson, 1862), 29; "Military Reunion," *Worcester Daily Spy*, 23 October 1871; and *History of the Excursion of the Fifteenth Massachusetts Regiment and Its Friends to the Battlefields of Gettysburg, Antietam, Ball's Bluff and the City of Washington, DC, September 14–20, 1900* (Worcester: O. B. Wood, 1901).

29 Thomas Spurr to Mary A. Spurr, 28 January 1862, 2 February 1862, 27 February 1862, 16 March 1862, George Frisbie Hoar Papers, Massachusetts Historical Society, Boston, MA.

30 Stephen Sears, *Landscape Turned Red: The Battle of Antietam* (New Haven: Ticknor and Fields, 1983), 228. Regimental historian Andrew Ford estimated that the Fifteenth lost 57 percent of its men at Antietam. See his *The Story of the Fifteenth, Massachusetts Volunteer Infantry in the Civil War, 1861–64* (Clinton, MA: W. J. Coulter, 1898), 200–201, 228. Sears notes that the 15th Massachusetts lost the largest number of troops of any regiment in the battle while the 12th Massachusetts, which lost 224 of 334 men, earned "the terrible distinction of suffering the highest casualty rate (67 percent) of any Federal regiment on that bloody day" (Sears, *Landscape Turned Red*, 190).

31 S. F. Haven, Jr., to S. F. Haven, 24 September 1862, Haven Family Papers, American Antiquarian Society, Worcester, MA.

32 Anonymous, "Notes on Thomas Sparr's last moments," September 1862, George Frisbie Hoar Papers, Massachusetts Historical Society, Boston, MA. The notes are in Hoar's handwriting.

33 Hill, *Discourse Preached in Worcester*, 30.

34 Brooks, "About Josiah Allen"; Henry W. Draper to George Frisbie Hoar, 10 October 1862, George Frisbie Hoar Papers, Massachusetts Historical Society, Boston, MA. Henry W. Miller owned a hardware store on Main Street that featured "tin, copper, and iron work to order." Albert Tolman owned a carriage and harness shop on Exchange Street, and John H. Brooks ran a blacksmith shop on his farm at Nelson Place in Worcester. See *Worcester City Directory*, 1862.

35 Brooks, "About Josiah Allen"; Richard Reid, "Raising the African Brigade: Early Black Recruitment in Civil War North Carolina," *North Carolina Historical Review* 70 (July 1993): 266, 285–87.

36 Isaiah Allen to George Frisbie Hoar, 28 January 1868, 3 February 1868, George Frisbie Hoar Papers, Massachusetts Historical Society, Boston, MA.

37 Brooks, "About Josiah Allen"; "Military Reunion," *Worcester Daily Spy*, 23 October 1871.

38 Henry A. Willis, *The Fifty-third Regiment, Massachusetts Volunteers* (Fitchburg, MA: Blanchard and Brown, 1889), 70, 81; C. Peter Ripley, *Slaves and Freedmen in Civil War Louisiana* (Baton Rouge: Louisiana State University, 1976), 20, 82.

39 Willis, *Fifty-third Regiment*, 99–100; Massachusetts Manuscript Census, Worcester County, 1865. Littler does not appear in subsequent censuses.

40 Willis, *Fifty-third Regiment*, 99–100; Massachusetts Manuscript Census, Worcester County, 1865; U.S. Bureau of the Census, Manuscript census schedules, Worcester County, Massachusetts, 1880.

41 Massachusetts Manuscript Census, Worcester County, 1865; D. Hamilton Hurd, *History of Worcester County with Biographical Sketches of Its Pioneers and Prominent Men*, vol. 2 (Philadelphia: J. W. Lewis and Company, 1889), 1004, 1035–36, 1169; George W. Powers, *The Story of the Thirty-Eighth Regiment of Massachusetts Volunteers* (Cambridge, MA: Dakin and Metcalf, 1866).

42 Massachusetts Manuscript Census, Worcester County, 1865; Schwalm, *Emancipation's Diaspora*, 97; "Worcester Whittlings," *Boston Guardian*, 14 February 1904. Schwalm also notes that the "employment of newly arrived black women as domestics and farmworkers introduced complicated dynamics into the relationship between servants and the women who hired them," and especially generated resentment from white men, who "repeatedly asserted their right and intention to defend the racial purity of the white household and the family it sheltered" (*Emancipation's Diaspora*, 99–100).

43 J. Waldo Denny, *Wearing the Blue in the Twenty-fifth Massachusetts Volunteer Infantry* (Worcester: Putnam and David, 1879), 224; "North Carolina: From New Berne," *The Freedmen's Record*, April 1866; "Newbern," *The National Freedman*, 15 November 1865.

44 U.S. Bureau of the Census, Manuscript census schedules, Worcester County, Massachusetts, 1870 and 1880; *Worcester City Directory*, 1876–90.

45 Corrine Bostic, *Go Onward and Upward!: An Interpretive Biography of the Life of Miss Sarah Ella Wilson* (Worcester: Commonwealth Press, 1974), 41–42; letter from Sarah E. Chase, *The Freedmen's Record*, May 1865.

46 Bostic, *Go Onward and Upward!*, 41; American Missionary Association Archives, North Carolina Letters, Reel 2; Massachusetts Manuscript Census, Worcester County, 1865; Doughton, *Births, Deaths, Marriages*, 55, 57.

47 "For the Sunday School," *Freedmen's Advocate*, October 1864; Massachusetts Manuscript Census, Worcester County, 1865; U.S. Bureau of the Census, Manuscript census schedules, Worcester County, Massachusetts, 1870.

48 U.S. Bureau of the Census, Manuscript census schedules, Worcester County, Massachusetts, 1870.

49 Massachusetts Manuscript Census, Worcester County, 1865; "Letter from Mrs. James to the Colored People of Worcester," *Worcester Daily Spy*, 27 April 1864; Doughton, *Births, Deaths, Marriages*, 12; U.S. Bureau of the Census, Manuscript census schedules, Worcester County, Massachusetts, 1870.

50 Michael P. Johnson, "Out of Egypt: The Migration of Former Slaves to the Midwest during the 1860s in Comparative Perspective," in *Crossing Boundaries: Comparative History of Black People in Diaspora*, ed. Darlene Clark Hine and Jacqueline McLeod (Bloomington: Indiana University Press, 1999), 233.

51 For more on these racial notions, see George M. Fredrickson, *The Black Image in the White Mind: The Debate on African-American Character and Destiny* (New York: Harper and Row, 1971), 107, 110.

52 Bethany Veney, *The Narrative of Bethany Veney, A Slave Woman* (Boston: George H. Ellis, 1889), 13–14; U.S. Bureau of the Census, Manuscript census schedules, Worcester County, Massachusetts, 1870. By 1870, in the city of Worcester, 50 percent of black migrants lived in independent households, 83 percent of which were male-headed; in the county, 41 percent lived in independent households, 90 percent of which were male-headed. Regarding freedpeople in the South, Eric Foner argues, "The desire to escape from white supervision and establish a modicum of economic independence profoundly shaped blacks' economic choices during Reconstruction," with landownership as the chief means to guarantee their independence, a desire, he points out, found among former slaves in all postemancipation societies. See Eric Foner, *Reconstruction: America's Unfinished Revolution, 1863–1877* (New York: Harper and Row, 1988), 104.

53 "North Brookfield," *Worcester Daily Spy*, 10 January 1872; letter to the author from Professor Robert T. Brown, professor of history, Westfield State College, 19 June 1996. Brown culled information about Allen's academic career from the records and archives of Westfield State. U.S. Bureau of the Census, Manuscript census schedules, Worcester County, Massachusetts, 1880 and 1900.

54 Vital Statistics, Marriage Records, North Brookfield, Massachusetts, 15 November 1871; "Death of Robert Morse," *North Brookfield Journal*, 31 May 1912. On 24 May 1912, the *North Brookfield Journal* reported on a joint meeting of the GAR, the Sons of Veterans, and the Women's Relief Corps at New Braintree, Massachusetts, in which "Miss Isabelle Morse" provided "two selections, A Modern Sermon, and The Gallant Soldiers." The 1900 federal census notes that Morse owned his home outright and that he was mortgage-free. See U.S. Bureau of the Census, Manuscript census schedules, Worcester County, Massachusetts, 1900; and "Funeral of Mr. Robert Morse," *North Brookfield Journal*, no date, Association of Colored Peoples Papers, Worcester Historical Museum, Worcester, MA.

55 U.S. Bureau of the Census, Manuscript census schedules, Worcester County, Massachusetts, 1880 and 1900.

56 Andrew Mero Military Pension File, National Archives, Washington, DC; Doughton, *Births, Deaths, Marriages*, 47; "Worcester Whittlings," *Boston Guardian*, 14 February 1903; *Worcester City Directory*, 1865–80.

57 Franklin Rice, ed., *The Worcester of 1898: Fifty Years as a City* (Worcester: F. S. Blanchard Company, 1899), 47–49.

58 "A Good Citizen," *Worcester Magazine* 13 (1910): 160–61; will of Jane Waples Mero, probated 10 February 1903, Worcester County, Massachusetts, Courthouse.

59 Worcester County Registry of Deeds, Book 923/266, Worcester County, Massachusetts, Courthouse; *Worcester City Directory*, 1874–80; U.S. Bureau of the Census, Manuscript census schedules, Worcester County, Massachusetts, 1870 and 1880.

60 "Worcester Whittlings," *Boston Guardian*, 14 February 1903.

61 Veney, *Narrative of Bethany Veney*, 40.

62 Ibid., 40–42, 44.

63 Ibid., 38–39.

64 "Worcester Whittlings," *Boston Guardian*, 14 February 1903; Bostic, *Go Onward and Upward!*, 42.

65 Bostic, *Go Onward and Upward!*, 49.

66 Deborah Gray White, *Too Heavy a Load: Black Women in Defense of Themselves* (New York: W. W. Norton, 1999), 27, 28; Sieglinde Lemke, introduction to *Lifting as They Climb*, by Elizabeth Lindsay Davis (New York: G. K. Hall, 1996), xviii.

67 Stanley Holmes Gutridge, *For God and Humanity: A Documentary History How Twelve Women in 1898 Served the Community and Emerged as the Association of Colored Peoples* (Worcester: published by author, 2004), 23, 1-B; Davis, *Lifting as They Climb*, 298; "The Family at 63 Parker Street," *Worcester Sunday Telegram*, 8 October 1933.

68 Davis, *Lifting as They Climb*, 298; Bostic, *Go Onward and Upward!*, 38–39.

69 "Sarah Wilson Dies; Teacher 49 Years," *Worcester Telegram*, 2 November 1955.

70 Bostic, *Go Onward and Upward!*, 31, 11.

71 Interview of Stanley Gutridge by the author, 12 July 2006, Worcester, MA; Charles Nutt, *History of Worcester and Its People*, vol. 2 (New York: Lewis Historical Publishing Company, 1919), 794–95; Rice, ed., *Worcester of 1898*, 484–85.

72 Stanley Gutridge interview; Doughton, ed., *Births, Deaths, Marriages*, 64; *Worcester City Directory*, 1870–1918; A. S. Roe, "Twenty Years of Harvard Street," *Proceedings of the Worcester Society of Antiquity*, vol. 47 (Worcester: Worcester Society of Antiquity, 1897), 275.

73 Rice, ed., *Worcester of 1898*, 733–35; A. S. Roe, *Worcester Classical and English High School: A Record of Forty-seven Years* (Worcester: published by author, 1892), 43; Roe, "Twenty Years of Harvard Street," 266.

74 Roe, "Twenty Years of Harvard Street," 275.

75 Roe, *Worcester Classical and English High School*, 87–88; Stanley Gutridge interview.

76 *Worcester City Directory*, 1878–1900; U.S. Bureau of the Census, Manuscript census schedules, Craven County, North Carolina, 1870; *Worcester City Directory*, 1883–1910; record for Elizabeth Braddock listing brother George Hollister Wiggins "at North" and sister "Louisa, married to Martin Smith. Mother is Matilda Wiggins," in Freedman's Savings and Trust Records, New Bern, National Archives, Washington, DC; Roe, "Twenty Years of Harvard Street," 284.

77 Stanley Gutridge interview.

78 Ibid.

79 Elizabeth Pleck estimates that census takers undercounted Boston's black population by as much as 33 percent between 1870 and 1900. See her *Black Migration and*

Poverty: Boston, 1865–1900 (New York: Academic Press, 1979), 215. Isaiah Allen's story illustrates the difficulty of measuring persistence with any accuracy. Allen never appeared in the census, city directories, or local vital statistics, but other sources document that he lived in Worcester after Antietam, from 1862 to mid-1863; served in the army from 1863 to 1866; lived in New Bern until around 1869; returned to Worcester, where he lived for at least a few more years; and ultimately migrated back to Leesburg. Similarly, Joseph and Nellie Fowle, who lived in Worcester in the 1870s and 1880s, never appear in local census records but showed up in vital statistics upon the birth of their two children. See Brooks, "About Josiah Allen"; Isaiah Allen to George Frisbie Hoar, 3 February 1868, George Frisbie Hoar Papers, Massachusetts Historical Society, Boston, MA; and Doughton, ed., *Births, Deaths, Marriages*.

80 *Worcester Daily Spy*, 27 September 1867, 6 April 1868.

81 Josephine Griffing to Col. J. Eaton, Jr., Assistant Commissioner of the Bureau of Refugees, Freedmen, and Abandoned Lands, Washington, 31 August 1865, Records of the Bureau of Refugees, Freedmen, and Abandoned Lands (hereafter RBRFAL), RG 105, M1055, Roll 14, Target 1, "Monthly Reports from Visiting Agents, August 1865–February 1866; *Worcester Daily Spy*, 15 December 1869, 8 March 1869, 20 April 1869, 25 November 1872. Leslie Schwalm (*Emancipation's Diaspora*, 97–100) also notes an outbreak of "wench fever," as it was called in the upper Midwest, and suggests that having a black servant "imparted a new aura of status."

82 Lowell quoted in Robert Harrison, "Welfare and Employment Practices of the Freedmen's Bureau in the District of Columbia," *Journal of Southern History* 72 (February 2006): 100.

83 "Letter to Mrs. May," in Henry Swint, ed., *Dear Ones at Home: Letters from Contraband Camps* (Nashville: Vanderbilt University Press, 1966), 162; "Union Freedmen's Aid and Intelligence and Employment Agency," *The Freedmen's Record*, May 1865; Lois Elaine Horton, "The Development of Federal Social Policy for Blacks in Washington, D.C., After Emancipation" (Ph.D. diss., Brandeis University, 1977), 85, 93–95.

84 William H. Williams, *The Negro in the District of Columbia during Reconstruction* (Washington, DC: Howard University Studies in History, No. 5, 1924), 7; "The Freedmen in Washington," *Freedman's Journal*, February 1865.

85 "Union Freedmen's Aid and Intelligence and Employment Agency," *The Freedmen's Record*, May 1865.

86 Harrison, "Welfare and Employment," 75–110; Carol Faulkner, *Women's Radical Reconstruction: The Freedmen's Aid Movement* (Philadelphia: University of Pennsylvania Press, 2004), 117–31; William C. Cohen, *At Freedom's Edge: Black Mobility and the Southern White Quest for Racial Control, 1861–1915* (Baton Rouge: Louisiana State University Press, 1991), 78–89.

87 Letter of permission from Rebecca Brown, 21 August 1867, RBRFAL, RG 105, M1055, Roll 18; "Miss Carter's Report," *The Freedmen's Record*, October 1866; Lois Horton, "Development of Federal Social Policy," 94.

88 Faulkner, *Women's Radical Reconstruction*, 119–27.

89   Harrison, "Welfare and Employment," 95; Cohen, *At Freedom's Edge*, 83; Faulkner, *Women's Radical Reconstruction*, 117.

90   J. G. Johnson to Josephine S. Griffing, 10 September 1867, RBRFAL, RG 105, Box 5, "District of Columbia, Office of Local Superintendent, Descriptive Lists of Freedpeople Granted Transportation"; H. M. Wilson to Charles Howard, 20 July 1867, RBRFAL, RG 105, M1055, Roll 13, Target 4, "Reports of Operations, Annual, Quarterly, and Monthly Reports," August 1865–December 1868; Josephine S. Griffing to Charles Howard, 9 October 1866, RBRFAL, RG 105, M1055, Roll 14, Target 3, "Tri-monthly and Monthly Reports from Employment Offices," August 1865–November 1867; H. G. Stewart to S. N. Clark, 4 February 1867, RBRFAL, RG 105, M1055, Roll 14, Target 3.

91   Pleck, *Black Migration and Poverty*, 27; Anna Lowell, "Report of the Howard Industrial School," 1 November 1866–1 August 1867, RBRFAL, RG 105, M1055, Roll 14, Target 1; H. G. Stewart to S. N. Clark, 31 October 1867, RBRFAL, RG 105, M1055, Roll 14, Target 3; Diane M. Boucher, "The Howard Industrial School for Colored Women and Children," unpublished seminar paper, Clark University, 2008.

92   RBRFAL, RG 105, M1055, Roll 14, Target 1, "H. L. Smith, Reports of Employment Obtained for Freedpeople," June and August 1867; RBRFAL, RG 105, M1055, Roll 17, Target 6, "Records Relating to Transportation of Freedmen and Bureau Personnel," Vol. 1, July 1865–January 1866, and Vol. 2, April 1866–November 1868; RBRFAL, RG 105, M1055, Roll 18, Target 2, "Subordinate Field Offices, District of Columbia, Employment Register," Vol. 68, July 1867–October 1868, and Roll 18, Target 3, "Subordinate Field Offices, Local Superintendent for Washington and Georgetown, Records Relating to Employment for Freedmen, Employment Registers from Wisewell Barracks," Vol. 1, August 1866–August 1868.

93   U.S. Bureau of the Census, Manuscript census schedules, Worcester County, Massachusetts; RBRFAL, RG 105, M1055, Roll 18, Target 2, "Subordinate Field Offices, District of Columbia, Employment Register," Vol. 68, July 1867–October 9, 1868; RBRFAL, RG 105, M1055, Roll 14, Target 1, "H. L. Smith, Reports of Employment Obtained for Freedpeople," June 1867.

94   U.S. Bureau of the Census, Manuscript census schedules, Worcester County, Massachusetts, 1870; RBRFAL, RG 105, M1055, Roll 17, Target 6, "Records Relating to Transportation of Freedmen and Bureau Personnel," Vol. 2, April 1866–November 1868.

95   RBRFAL, RG 105, M1055, Roll 18, Target 2, "Subordinate Field Offices, District of Columbia, Employment Register," Vol. 68, July 1867–October 1868; City of Worcester, Resolution in Honor of Edward Earle, 21 May 1877, Edward Earle Papers, American Antiquarian Society, Worcester, MA; New England Yearly Meeting of Friends Committee to Maj. Gen. O. O. Howard, 15 July 1865 and 7 December 1865, Edward Earle Papers, American Antiquarian Society, Worcester, MA.

96   RBRFAL, RG 105, M1055, Roll 17, Target 6, "Records Relating to Transportation of Freedmen and Bureau Personnel," Vol. 2, April 1866–November 1868; RBRFAL, RG 105, M1055, Roll 18, Maria Lewis permission letter, 15 October 1867. Carol Faulkner notes that Ann Earle wrote several letters on behalf of Brooks concerning the whereabouts of Brooks's daughter, Kitty. Distressed that Kitty had been separated from her mother when she was sent by the bureau to work in New York, Earle

demanded that the bureau locate the girl and angrily asserted that bureau employment agent Josephine Griffing had "clearly kidnaped [*sic*] little Kitty as if she had been a slave trader" (Faulkner, *Women's Radical Reconstruction*, 127).

97 Cohen, *Freedom's Edge*, 95–96, 86; "Monthly Earnings with Board of Farm Laborers by Region," *Historical Statistics of the United States: Millennial Edition Online*; Massachusetts Manuscript Census, Worcester County, 1865; U.S. Bureau of the Census, Manuscript census schedules, Worcester County, Massachusetts, 1870. In her study of Freedmen's Bureau migrants to Boston, Pleck (*Black Migration and Poverty*, 66) found that many workers migrated seasonally and returned home.

98 "A Conflict of Races," *Worcester Daily Spy*, 11 March 1868.

99 "Assault with a Pistol," *Worcester Daily Spy*, 17 May 1869. Henry Walker appears in the 1880 and 1900 censuses and would have been twenty years old in 1869.

100 "Disturbance in Church," *Worcester Daily Spy*, 20 September 1869; Schwalm, *Emancipation's Diaspora*, 104, 117, 141. Schwalm notes that the Irish in the upper Midwest were specifically blamed for attacking black workers. For other examples of Irish workers' protest against and violence toward blacks in the era of the Civil War, see Jacqueline Jones, *American Work: Four Centuries of Black and White Labor* (New York: W. W. Norton, 1998), 290–91, who cites a walkout of Boston caulkers in protest of a black caulker from Baltimore; and Williston H. Lofton, "Northern Labor and the Negro during the Civil War," *Journal of Negro History* 34 (July 1949): 251–73, who cites examples of violence perpetrated by Irish workers in Cincinnati, Chicago, Buffalo, and New York City.

101 "Stabbing Affray," *Worcester Daily Spy*, 17 May 1869; "Kennary Inquest," *Worcester Daily Spy*, 23 July 1869. J. L. Libbey applied to the Freedmen's Bureau in August 1867 seeking workers. The newspaper report on the stabbing incident noted that Washington was twenty-nine years old and "came from Maryland since the war, and has been in the city one or two years." See RBRFAL, RG 105, M1055, Roll 18, Target 2, "Subordinate Field Offices, District of Columbia, Employment Register," Vol. 68, July 1867–October 1868.

102 Carol Faulkner argues that by "pushing domestic service as a route to economic independence, [Anna] Lowell and other female agents recreated the race, class, and gender relations of the plantation household in Northern homes" (*Women's Radical Reconstruction*, 127). But as the Worcester story shows, some female migrants, such as Sarah Waples Mero, did manage to attain an autonomous household and sponsor additional family members in Worcester after first working as live-in domestic servants. See Pleck, *Black Migration and Poverty*, 65–66.

103 "The Evening Schools," *Worcester Daily Spy*, 27 November 1869.

104 Veney, *Narrative of Bethany Veney*, 14.

CHAPTER FIVE

1 "Mt. Olive Corner Stone Laid," *Worcester Evening Telegram*, 23 June 1891.

2 Ibid. See also "In New House of Worship," *Worcester Evening Telegram*, 24 October 1891.

3 David W. Blight, *Race and Reunion: The Civil War in American Memory* (Cambridge, MA: Belknap Press of Harvard University Press, 2001), 300–301, 319. Blight notes "several strains of black Civil War memory" in addition to "patriotic memory": a view of the slave past "as paralytic burden; a celebratory-accommodationist mode of memory" best characterized in Booker T. Washington's philosophy; a Pan-African/millennialist interpretation of the past; and "a tragic vision of the war" as the nation's journey through catastrophe from an old to a new order.

4 Leslie A. Schwalm shows that for blacks in the upper Midwest, "wartime conflicts over emancipation's consequences launched an unprecedented era of regional activism and organizing." Schwalm, *Emancipation's Diaspora: Race and Reconstruction in the Upper Midwest* (Chapel Hill: University of North Carolina Press, 2009), 106.

5 Interview of Edna Spencer by the author, 12 February 2007.

6 U.S. Bureau of the Census, Manuscript census schedules, Worcester County, Massachusetts, 1870, 1880, 1900.

7 Thomas L. Doughton, ed., "People of Color at Worcester: Part 3, Deaths, 1891–1930," unpublished supplement, 43. Special thanks to Thomas Doughton for sharing this information with me.

8 Massachusetts Manuscript Census, Worcester County, 1855; *Worcester Almanac, Directory, and Business Advertiser*, 1854; Nick Salvatore, *We All Got History: The Memory Books of Amos Webber* (New York: Times Books, 1996), 98; *Worcester Almanac, Directory, and Business Advertiser*, 1859, 1860; *Worcester City Directory*, 1870, 1880.

9 U.S. Bureau of the Census, Manuscript census schedules, Worcester County, Massachusetts, 1880.

10 E. Franklin Frazier, quoted in Farah Jasmine Griffin, *"Who Set You Flowin'?": The African American Migration Narrative* (New York: Oxford University Press, 1996), 107. Griffin describes the campaign of Chicago's Urban League to assimilate southern migrants who came north during the Great Migration, whom they found embarrassing, going so far as to distribute a pamphlet that encouraged migrants to pay attention to their personal appearance, to "refrain from wearing dust caps, . . . house clothing, and bedroom shoes for out doors," and "to reject their Southern mannerisms" (104). Elizabeth Pleck concluded that southern migrants to Boston resided in separate neighborhoods in part because of hostility from older residents and because they isolated themselves. See Pleck, *Black Migration and Poverty: Boston, 1865–1900* (New York: Academic Press, 1979), 75–77.

11 Between 1862 and 1880, 99 marriages involving a southern-born resident of Worcester took place. A total of 59 (60 percent) involved a southern-born person marrying a northern-born individual; 40 marriages (40 percent) occurred between southern-born persons. Between 1881 and 1890, 44 marriages took place in Worcester, 31 (70.5 percent) of them "mixed" (i.e., between a northerner and a southerner) and 13 (29.5 percent) between southern-born persons. Overall, between 1862 and 1890, 143 marriages involving southerners occurred, 63 percent of them "mixed" and 37 percent of them between southerners. See Thomas L. Doughton, ed., *Births, Deaths, Marriages of People of Color: Worcester, Massachusetts, 1849–1890* (Worcester: Nipnet Press, 1990); and Pleck, *Black Migration and Poverty*, 75.

12 "Among the Colored Churches," *The Watchman*, 12 April 1900.

13 "Corner-Stone Laying," *Worcester Evening Gazette*, 22 June 1891; *Minutes of the Worcester Baptist Association, Held with the Greeneville Baptist Church, Leicester, Mass., October 7 and 8, 1885* (Worcester: Henry A. Howland, 1885), 4.

14 "A New Baptist Church," *Worcester Evening Gazette*, 25 February 1885; Minutes, Pleasant Street Baptist Church, Worcester, Massachusetts, 4 August 1871, in possession of Pleasant Street Baptist Church; James Grossman, *Land of Hope: Chicago, Black Southerners, and the Great Migration* (Chicago: University of Chicago Press, 1989), 158. Boston's southern migrants also established their own separate church in 1871 called Ebenezer Baptist Church. See Pleck, *Black Migration and Poverty*, 80–82.

15 U.S. Bureau of the Census, Manuscript census schedules, Worcester County, Massachusetts, 1880 and 1900; Doughton, ed., *Births, Deaths, Marriages*.

16 U.S. Bureau of the Census, Manuscript census schedules, Worcester County, Massachusetts, 1880 and 1900; Doughton, ed., *Births, Deaths, Marriages*. Of the 22 members whose ages could be documented through the 1880 and 1900 manuscript censuses and Worcester birth, death, and marriage records, 14 were in their twenties and thirties, 2 were in their forties, 4 were in their fifties, and 2 were in their sixties. Of the 15 members whose occupations could be identified, 4 worked in skilled positions, 3 worked in semiskilled occupations, and 8 worked in unskilled positions.

17 U.S. Bureau of the Census, Manuscript census schedules, Worcester County, Massachusetts, 1880; Schwalm, *Emancipation's Diaspora*, 138–43.

18 U.S. Bureau of the Census, Manuscript census schedules, Worcester County, Massachusetts, 1880. Nick Salvatore notes that "the great majority" of the city's unskilled workforce, as well as the skilled workforce, was made up of northern-born blacks. He adds that since 39 percent of service workers were northern-born, "white families in the city apparently favored northern-born blacks in such positions." But given the fact that southern-born blacks made up roughly a third of the population, they are represented almost equally with their northern-born counterparts in each occupational category. See Salvatore, *We All Got History*, 256.

19 "Mt. Olive Corner Stone Laid," *Worcester Telegram*, 23 June 1891; "Worcester Whittlings," *Boston Guardian*, 14 February 1903; "Worcester," *Boston Advocate*, 8 January 1887.

20 "Local Matters," *Worcester Evening Gazette*, 1 May 1871, 23 May 1878.

21 Grossman, *Land of Hope*, 157. Historians have written extensively on the role of the immigrant church in sustaining ethnic culture. See, for example, Robert C. Ostgren, *A Community Transplanted: The Trans-Atlantic Experience of a Swedish Immigrant Settlement in the Upper Middle West, 1835–1915* (Madison: University of Wisconsin Press, 1988), 211–12.

22 Grossman, *Land of Hope*, 158–59.

23 "Obituary Report, Hiram Conway, D.D.," *Massachusetts Baptist Yearbook*, 1921, 151, American Baptist–Samuel Colgate Historical Library, American Baptist Historical Society, Rochester, NY; "Senior Pastor of This City Dead," *Worcester Evening Post*, 11 December 1920; "Baptist Council," *Worcester Daily Spy*, 25 March 1887.

24 "Of Interest to Church People," *Worcester Telegram*, 30 March 1887; "Mt. Olive Baptist Church," *Worcester Evening Gazette*, 30 March 1887.

25 "In New House of Worship," *Worcester Telegram*, 24 October 1891.

26 *Minutes of the Worcester Baptist Association*, 1886, 18.

27 "In New House of Worship," *Worcester Telegram*, 24 October 1891.

28 Grossman, *Land of Hope*, 160; "Worcester," *Boston Advocate*, 7 August 1886, 21 August 1886.

29 "Emancipation Celebration," *Worcester Daily Spy*, 2 January 1867; *Worcester Daily Spy*, 29 July 1871.

30 "Race Freed from Bondage," *Worcester Telegram*, 2 January 1891. (I am indebted to Al Southwick for passing along this clipping.)

31 Quotation from Corrine Bostic, *Go Onward and Upward! An Interpretive Biography of the Life of Miss Sarah Ella Wilson* (Worcester: Commonwealth Press, 1974), 49; "Funeral of Robert Morse," *North Brookfield Journal*, no date, and "Robert Morse Goes to Answer the Last Call," *Worcester Telegram*, 30 May 1912, in Association of Colored Peoples Papers, Worcester Historical Museum, Worcester, MA.

32 Salvatore, *We All Got History*, 161, 207, 229, 255; "Worcester," *Boston Advocate*, 27 November 1886.

33 Salvatore, *We All Got History*, 161, 207, 229; "Worcester," *Boston Advocate*, 13 February and 27 February 1886. Salvatore (*We All Got History*, 279) notes that despite Webber's initial concerns, he eventually joined the new club himself.

34 See, for example, *Boston Advocate*, 8 January 1887, 27 November 1886.

35 See, for example, *Boston Advocate*, 16 October 1886, 10 July 1886; and *Worcester Daily Spy*, 2 August 1872.

36 George H. Ward Post, No. 10, Grand Army of the Republic Records, Massachusetts Military Museum and Archive, Worcester, MA; Franklin D. Tappan, *The Passing of the Grand Army of the Republic* (Worcester: Commonwealth Press, 1939), 23–25; Donald R. Shaffer, *After the Glory: The Struggles of Black Civil War Veterans* (Lawrence: University of Kansas Press, 2004), 7; Stuart McConnell, *Glorious Contentment: The Grand Army of the Republic, 1865–1900* (Chapel Hill: University of North Carolina Press, 1992), 71. Of the three posts McConnell researched extensively — Philadelphia's Post 2, Post 13 in Brockton, Massachusetts, and Post 68 in Chippewa Falls, Wisconsin — only Brockton counted a single black member.

37 George H. Ward Post, No. 10, Grand Army of the Republic Records, Massachusetts Military Museum and Archive, Worcester, MA; Tappan, *Passing of the Grand Army of the Republic*, 23–25.

38 George H. Ward Post, No. 10, Grand Army of the Republic Records, Massachusetts Military Museum and Archive, Worcester, MA; Tappan, *Passing of the Grand Army of the Republic*, 23–25; *Roster of George H. Ward Post, No. 10, Department of Massachusetts, Grand Army of the Republic* (Worcester, 1888, 1896).

39 McConnell, *Glorious Contentment*, xiv; Shaffer, *After the Glory*, 157; Salvatore, *We All Got History*, 257.

40 Salvatore, *We All Got History*, 280–81; resolutions quoted in ibid., 291.

41 Franklin P. Rice, ed., *Dictionary of Worcester and Its Vicinity*, 2nd ed. (Worcester: F. S. Blanchard and Company, 1893), 24.

42 For more on the shift in national sentiment regarding African American rights, see Eric Foner, *Reconstruction: America's Unfinished Revolution, 1863–1877* (New York: Harper and Row, 1988). For an excellent examination of Civil War memory, see Blight, *Race and Reunion*.

43 Roy Rosenzweig, *Eight Hours for What We Will: Workers and Leisure in an Industrial City, 1870–1920* (New York: Cambridge University Press, 1983), 12; Timothy J. Meagher, *Inventing Irish America: Generation, Class, and Ethnic Identity in a New England City, 1880–1928* (Notre Dame, IN: University of Notre Dame Press, 2001), 20, 45; *Twelfth Census of the United States, Special Reports: Occupations* (Washington: Government Printing Office, 1904), 760–63; Rose Zeller, "Changes in Ethnic Composition and Character of Worcester's Population" (Ph.D. diss., Clark University, 1940), 142. Focusing on the city's white workers, Meagher (*Inventing Irish America*, 51) argues that the Irish were "at the bottom" of the city's socioeconomic ladder, but census data shows that blacks had much less access to industrial jobs than even people of Irish descent.

44 U.S. Bureau of the Census, Manuscript census schedules, Worcester County, Massachusetts, 1900. Property ownership in the county was better, with 25 percent of black households owning their own homes. Most, however, were northern-born, many with deep roots in Worcester County, such as the Hemenway family. Only six southern migrant households owned their own homes. These included Civil War–era migrants Robert Morse and William Waters of North Brookfield, Virginians who migrated there with surgeon Dr. Warren Tyler.

45 *Report of Massachusetts Bureau of Statistics of Labor, Thirteenth Annual Report* (Boston, 1882), 469; Timothy J. Meagher, "The Lord Is Not Dead: Cultural and Social Change Among the Irish in Worcester, Massachusetts" (Ph.D. diss., Brown University, 1982), 160.

46 *Twelfth Census of the United States: Occupations*, 760–63.

47 Meagher, "The Lord Is Not Dead," 161; *Twelfth Census of the United States: Occupations*, 760–63.

48 *Report of the Massachusetts Bureau of Statistics*, 79–80; Meagher, "The Lord Is Not Dead," 376.

49 John Bodnar, Michael Weber, and Roger Simon, "Migration, Kinship, and Urban Adjustment: Blacks and Poles in Pittsburgh, 1900–1930," *Journal of American History* 66 (September 1979): 554, 549. Blacks in Worcester, like their counterparts across the country, seem to have been significantly undercounted in the U.S. census. Many long-standing residents of the city mentioned in press reports simply never appear in the census. In 1900, state senate candidate David Walsh claimed that there were 2,500 black citizens in the city. Given the high stakes of turn-of-the-century politics, it seems likely that local politicians had an accurate count of the voting population. For Walsh's comments, see *Worcester Telegram*, 4 November 1901.

50 Meagher, *Inventing Irish America*, 45; "Color Line in Worcester," *Worcester Sunday Telegram*, 29 April 1888. I am indebted to Al Southwick for passing a clipping about this incident along to me.

51 "Color Line in Worcester," *Worcester Sunday Telegram*, 29 April 1888.

52 *Minutes of the Worcester Baptist Association, 1894* (Worcester: The Association, 1894), 18.

53 "They Have Two Good Homes Now," *Worcester Sunday Telegram*, 22 July 1900; *Constitution and By-Laws of the Women's Progressive Club of Worcester, Mass.*, reprinted in Stanley Holmes Gutridge, *For God and Humanity: A Documentary History of How Twelve Women in 1898 Served the Community and Emerged as the Association of Colored Peoples* (Worcester: published by the author, 2004), 1A–B; Michelle Reidel, "'In the True Spirit': Black Women's Organizations in Worcester, Massachusetts, 1900–1920" (unpublished seminar paper, Clark University, 1992).

54 Deborah Gray White, *Too Heavy a Load: Black Women in Defense of Themselves* (New York: W. W. Norton, 1999), 27–28.

55 "They Have Two Good Homes Now," *Worcester Sunday Telegram*, 22 July 1900; "Lucy Stone Club Buys Webber Estate," *Worcester Evening Post*, 19 July 1900.

56 "Modern Day War of the Roses Breaks Out in Worcester," *Worcester Evening Post*, 25 July 1900; "The Have Two Good Homes Now," *Worcester Sunday Telegram*, 22 July 1900; "Lucy Stone Club Buys Webber Estate," *Worcester Evening Post*, 19 July 1900.

57 "Northeastern Federation of Club Women Opens Convention," *Worcester Evening Post*, 11 August 1904; "Federation Ends Its Convention," *Worcester Evening Post*, 13 August 1904.

58 I generated the names of twenty-eight political activists by examining local newspaper reports from 1896 to 1900. See also U.S. Bureau of the Census, Manuscript census schedules, Worcester County, Massachusetts, 1870, 1880, 1900.

59 Blight, *Race and Reunion*, 300–337. Elizabeth Pleck found southern migrants emerging as leaders in Boston city politics, concluding, "More than any other sphere of black community life, Southerners dominated here." But, in contrast to Worcester, "few traces of southern background appeared in the concerns of these politicians" (Pleck, *Black Migration and Poverty*, 84).

60 McConnell, *Glorious Contentment*, xiv; Salvatore, *We All Got History*, 257.

61 Salvatore, *We All Got History*, 297.

62 Bess Beatty, *A Revolution Gone Backward: The Black Response to National Politics, 1876–1896* (Westport, CT: Greenwood Press, 1987), 29, 58.

63 "They Will Have Two Candidates," *Worcester Telegram*, 18 November 1896.

64 "Campaign Rallies — A Colored Winslow Rally," *Worcester Daily Spy*, 5 December 1896; "They Will Have Two Candidates," *Worcester Telegram*, 18 November 1896.

65 "They Will Have Two Candidates," *Worcester Telegram*, 18 November 1896.

66 Ibid.

67 "Colored Voters Meet," *Worcester Daily Spy*, 18 November 1896.

68 "Republicans Storm the Town!," *Worcester Telegram*, 20 November 1896.

69 "Colored Men Are Indignant," *Worcester Telegram*, 25 November 1896.

70 Ibid.; "It Condemns Inman's Methods," *Worcester Telegram*, 2 December 1896.

71 "Sprague a Winner," *Worcester Daily Spy*, 9 December 1896.

72 "Colored Voters," *Worcester Daily Spy*, 17 November 1897.

73 Beatty, *Revolution Gone Backward*, 153, 175.

74 Ibid., 174–75; Douglass quoted in George Fredrickson, *Black Liberation: A Comparative History of Black Ideologies in the United States* (New York: Oxford University Press, 1995), 30.

75 "A Rousing Rally," *Worcester Daily Spy*, 23 October 1900.

76 Ibid.

77 Ibid.

78 Ibid.

79 Ibid.

80 "Jumbo a Disturber," *Worcester Daily Spy*, 1 November 1900; "Democrats to Colored Men," *Worcester Telegram*, 1 November 1900.

81 "Jumbo a Disturber," *Worcester Daily Spy*, 1 November 1900. The *Spy* identified the man who referred to himself as "Jumbo, the African Dodger" as Johnson. The *Telegram* noted only that "a colored man" dressed "in a shabby suit" challenged Plummer.

82 Ibid.

83 "Appeal to Colored Voters for Washburn," *Worcester Daily Spy*, 5 November 1900.

84 "Stand by the Negro's Friend," *Worcester Telegram*, 5 November 1900; "Colored Man's Duty," *Worcester Daily Spy*, 5 November 1900.

85 "Stand by the Negro's Friend," *Worcester Telegram*, 5 November 1900; "Colored Man's Duty," *Worcester Daily Spy*, 5 November 1900.

86 "A Colored Man Reproaches Fellow Citizens," *Worcester Daily Spy*, 30 October 1900.

87 Ibid.

88 "Worcester Newsy Notes," *Boston Guardian*, 20 December 1902; Alan Damarjian, "A Struggle for Recognition: Black Voters in Worcester, Massachusetts" (unpublished seminar paper, Clark University, 1994), 9–11.

89 "Colored Voters Meet," *Worcester Daily Spy*, 18 November 1896.

90 "Wolcotts Have a Rally," *Worcester Telegram*, 2 November 1901; "To Colored Voters," *Worcester Telegram*, 4 November 1901; "D. G. Gaines Speaks," *Worcester Telegram*, 18 November 1901.

91 *Worcester Telegram*, 4 November 1901.

92 Ibid.

93 "Colored Man Knows Friends," *Worcester Telegram*, 9 December 1901.

94 "D. G. Gaines Speaks," *Worcester Telegram*, 18 November 1901.

95 "First Gun for Mayor!," *Worcester Daily Spy*, 10 December 1902.

96 "Fletcher's Landslide!," *Worcester Daily Spy*, 10 December 1902; "Fletcher by Increased Plurality," *Worcester Daily Spy*, 11 December 1902; Damarjian, "Struggle for Recognition," 30.

97 "Fletcher by Increased Plurality," *Worcester Daily Spy*, 11 December 1902.

98 Damarjian, "Struggle for Recognition," 31; "C. E. Scott Dies; Was 22 Years in City Council," *Worcester Evening Gazette*, 11 October 1938; "Black Trailblazer Sat on Council Long Ago," *Worcester Telegram and Gazette*, 17 November 1997.

99 Bethany Veney, *The Narrative of Bethany Veney, A Slave Woman* (Boston: George H. Ellis, 1889); Isaac Mason, *Life of Isaac Mason as a Slave* (Worcester: n.p., 1893); Allen Parker, *Recollections of Slavery Times* (Worcester: Charles Burbank and Company, 1895).

100 B. Eugene McCarthy and Thomas L. Doughton, eds., *From Bondage to Belonging: The Worcester Slave Narratives* (Amherst: University of Massachusetts Press, 2007), xxiv–xxv. A fourth narrative, Jacob Stroyer's *Sketches of My Life in the South*, appeared in 1879. Stroyer was a South Carolina slave who came to Worcester in 1870 and was educated in the city's evening schools and Worcester Academy. He left the city in 1879 and then served as a minister in Salem, Massachusetts.

101 "Aunt Betsy Is Taken by Death," *Worcester Evening Gazette*, 16 November 1915; "Aunt Betsy Veney Dies in 104th Year," *Worcester Telegram*, 16 November 1915; "Born in Slavery, Dies a Leader," *Worcester Telegram*, 27 August 1898; "Isaac Mason Buried," *Worcester Telegram*, 30 August 1898; "Old 'Pop' Parker Is Forever Free," *Worcester Evening Post*, 18 June 1906. Bethany Veney's narrative includes three letters from clergymen, including one from Rev. V. A. Cooper, who served for a time as Veney's pastor in Worcester. Senator George Frisbie Hoar contributed an opening statement to Isaac Mason's narrative attesting to Mason's character and the veracity of his story.

102 Veney, *Narrative of Bethany Veney*, 6; Parker, *Recollections of Slavery Times*, 6.

103 Mason, *Life of Isaac Mason*, 8.

104 *Thirteenth Census of the United States Taken in the Year 1910, Vol. II, Population* (Washington: Government Printing Office, 1913), 879; *Fourteenth Census of the United States, 1920, Vol. II, Population* (Washington: Government Printing Office, 1922), 445–47; *Sixteenth Census of the United States, 1940, Population, Second Series* (Washington: Government Printing Office, 1943); County and City Data Books, ⟨http://fisher.lib.virginia.edu/collections/stats/ccdb/⟩; Ella L. Vinal, "The Status of the Worcester Negro" (M.A. thesis, Clark University, 1929), 11–15, 16, 27–31, 34, 61–62; Meagher, *Inventing Irish America*, 46.

105 Vinal, "Status of the Worcester Negro," 61–62.

EPILOGUE

1 William S. McFeely, *Sapelo's People: A Long Walk Into Freedom* (New York: W. W. Norton, 1994), 125.

2 Interview of Edna Spencer by the author, Worcester, MA, 12 February 2007; Edna Spencer, "What Color Is the Wind?" (M.A. thesis, Clark University, 1985), 58, 61.

3 Spencer interview.

4 Ibid.

5 Ibid.

6 Ibid.; author email correspondence with Edna Spencer, 12 February 2009.
7 "John Street Baptist Church Marks 115th," *Worcester Telegram and Gazette*, 14 June 1999; "Fighter in His Own Way," *Worcester Sunday Telegram*, 29 March 1964; "NAACP Plans to Picket Stores Here," *Worcester Telegram*, 16 October 1963.
8 Spencer interview.

Bibliography

PRIMARY SOURCES

Manuscripts

American Antiquarian Society, Worcester, Massachusetts
  Chase Family Papers
  Civil War Collection
  Edward Earle Papers
  Green Family Papers
  Haven Family Papers
  Horace James Papers
American Missionary Association Archives, Amistad Research Center,
    New Orleans, Louisiana
  North Carolina Letters, 1863–67 (microfilm)
Massachusetts Historical Society, Boston, Massachusetts
  George Frisbie Hoar Papers
  Horace James Papers
Massachusetts Military Museum and Archive, Worcester, Massachusetts
  Adjutant General's Correspondence, January–February 1863
  George H. Ward Post, No. 10, Grand Army of the Republic Records
National Archives, Washington, DC
  Isaiah Allen Civil War Pension File
  Freedman's Savings and Trust Records, New Bern
  Andrew Mero Civil War Pension File
  Allen Parker Civil War Pension File
  Records of the Bureau of Refugees, Freedmen, and Abandoned
    Lands, Record Group 105
Southern Historical Collection, University of North Carolina,
    Chapel Hill
  New Bern Occupation Papers
Worcester Historical Museum, Worcester, Massachusetts
  Association of Colored Peoples Papers

Newspapers, Periodicals, and Directories

Boston Advocate, 1886–87

Boston Guardian, 1902, 1904

The Congregationalist, 1862–65

Freedman's Journal, 1865

The Freedmen's Advocate, 1864–65

The Freedmen's Record, 1865–67

The Liberator, 1850–65

Massachusetts Baptist Yearbook, 1921

Massachusetts Spy, 1859

National Aegis, 1854

The National Freedman, 1865–66

New York Times, 1862–63

North Brookfield Journal, 1912

North Carolina Daily Times, 1862–65

The Watchman, 1900

Worcester Almanac, Directory, and Business Advertiser, 1854, 1859–64

Worcester City Directory, 1865–1910

Worcester Daily Spy, 1850, 1854, 1861–1901

Worcester Daily Transcript, 1854

Worcester Evening Gazette, 1869, 1871, 1878, 1885, 1887, 1890–1901

Worcester Evening Post, 1900, 1904, 1906, 1920, 1938

Worcester Telegram, 1887, 1891–1901, 1933, 1955

City and County Records

Vital Statistics, City of Worcester, Marriage Records

Worcester County Probate Records, Worcester County, Massachusetts, Courthouse

Worcester County Registry of Deeds, Worcester County, Massachusetts, Courthouse

Census and Survey Materials

Massachusetts Manuscript Census, Worcester County, 1855 and 1865.

Report of Massachusetts Bureau of Statistics of Labor, Thirteenth Annual Report. Boston, 1882.

U.S. Bureau of the Census, Manuscript Census Schedules, Craven County, North Carolina, 1870.

U.S Bureau of the Census, Manuscript Census Schedules, Middlesex County, Massachusetts, 1860.

U.S Bureau of the Census, Manuscript Census Schedules, Worcester County, Massachusetts, 1850.

U.S Bureau of the Census, Manuscript Census Schedules, Worcester County, Massachusetts, 1860.

U.S Bureau of the Census, Manuscript Census Schedules, Worcester County, Massachusetts, 1870.

U.S Bureau of the Census, Manuscript Census Schedules, Worcester County, Massachusetts, 1880.

U.S Bureau of the Census, Manuscript Census Schedules, Worcester County, Massachusetts, 1900.

Eighth Census of the United States: Manufactures of the United States in 1860. Washington: Government Printing Office, 1865.

Ninth Census of the United States: The Statistics of the Population of the United States. Washington: Government Printing Office, 1872.

Ninth Census of the United States: The Statistics of Wealth and Industry of the United States, Volume III. Washington: Government Printing Office, 1872.

Eleventh Census of the United States: Schedules Enumerating Union Veterans and Widows of Union Veterans of the Civil War, 1890.

Twelfth Census of the United States: Special Reports: Occupations. Washington: Government Printing Office, 1904.

Thirteenth Census of the United States Taken in the Year 1910, Vol. II, Population. Washington: Government Printing Office, 1913.

Fourteenth Census of the United States, 1920, Vol. II, Population. Washington: Government Printing Office, 1922.

Sixteenth Census of the United States, 1940, Population, Second Series. Washington: Government Printing Office, 1943.

Interviews

Interview of Stanley Gutridge by the author, 12 July 2006, Worcester, Massachusetts

Interview of Edna Spencer by the author, 12 February 2007, Worcester, Massachusetts

Published Primary Sources

"An Act to Suppress Insurrection, to Punish Treason, to Seize and Confiscate the Property of Rebels, and for Other Purposes." *U.S. Statutes at Large, Treaties, and Proclamations of the United States of America.* Vol. 12. Boston, 1863.

Brown, Frederick G., William O. DuPuis, and Norman H. French, eds. *Boylston, Massachusetts, in the Civil War: The Letters Home of Pvt. John W. Partridge with Biographical Sketches of Other Boylston Soldiers.* Bowie, MD: Heritage Books, Inc., 1995.

Burnside, Ambrose E. *The Burnside Expedition.* Providence: N. Bangs Williams and Company, 1882.

Colyer, Vincent. *Report of the Services Rendered by the Freed People to the United States Army, in North Carolina.* New York: Vincent Colyer, 1864.

Curtis, W. A. "A Journal of Reminiscences of the War." *Our Living and Our Dead* 2, no. 3 (May 1875).

Day, David L. *My Diary of Rambles with the Twenty-fifth Massachusetts Volunteer Infantry.* Milford, MA: n.p., 1883.

Denny, J. Waldo. *Wearing the Blue in the Twenty-fifth Massachusetts Volunteer Infantry.* Worcester: Putnam and David, 1870.

Derby, W. P. *Bearing Arms in the Twenty-seventh Massachusetts Regiment of Volunteers Infantry during the Civil War, 1861–65.* Boston: Wright and Patterson, 1883.

Doughton, Thomas L., ed. *Births, Deaths, Marriages of People of Color: Worcester, Massachusetts, 1849–1890.* Worcester: Nipnet Press, 1990.

Draper, William F. *Recollections of a Varied Career.* Boston: Little, Brown, and Company, 1908.

Emmerton, James A. *A Record of the Twenty-third Regiment Massachusetts Volunteer Infantry during the Civil War, 1861–65.* Boston: William Ware and Company, 1886.

Ford, Andrew E. *The Story of the Fifteenth Regiment: Massachusetts Volunteer Infantry in the Civil War, 1861–64.* Clinton, MA: W. J. Coulter, 1898.

Hawkins, The Rev. William G. *Lunsford Lane; or, Another Helper from North Carolina.* Boston: Crosby and Nichols, 1863.

Higginson, Thomas Wentworth. *Cheerful Yesterdays*. Boston: Houghton, Mifflin and Company, 1898.

———. *Massachusetts in Mourning! A Sermon, Preached in Worcester, on June 4, 1854*. Boston: James Munroe and Company, 1854.

———, ed. "Preface." In *Harvard Memorial Biographies*. Vol. 1. Cambridge, MA: Sever and Francis, 1866.

Hill, Alonzo. *A Discourse Preached in Worcester, October 5, 1862, on Lieutenant Thomas Jefferson Spurr, Fifteenth Massachusetts Volunteers*. Boston: J. Wilson, 1862.

History of the Excursion of the Fifteenth Massachusetts Regiment and Its Friends to the Battlefields of Gettysburg, Antietam, Ball's Bluff and the City of Washington, DC, September 14–20, 1900. Worcester: O. B. Wood, 1901.

Hoar, George Frisbie. *Autobiography of Seventy Years*. Vol. 1. New York: Scribner's, 1903.

James, Horace. *Annual Report of the Superintendent of Negro Affairs in North Carolina, 1864*. Boston: W. F. Brown and Company, 1865.

———. *An Oration Delivered in Newbern, North Carolina, Before the Twenty-fifth Regiment, Massachusetts Volunteers, July 4, 1862*. Boston: Brown and Company, 1862.

———. *Our Duties to the Slave: A Sermon Preached Before the Original Congregational Church and Society in Wrentham, Massachusetts on Thanksgiving Day, November 26, 1846*. Boston: Richardson and Filmer, 1847.

———. *Trial before a Special Military Commission, Convened by Direction of Andrew Johnson, President of the United States, in Sept., 1866*. Washington: n.p.

Lane, Lunsford. *The Narrative of Lunsford Lane, Formerly of Raleigh, North Carolina*. 2nd ed. Boston: J. G. Torrey, 1842.

Mason, Isaac. *Life of Isaac Mason as a Slave*. Worcester: n.p., 1893.

Minutes of the Worcester Baptist Association, Held with the Greeneville Baptist Church, Leicester, Mass, October 7 and 8, 1885. Worcester: Henry A. Howland, 1885.

Minutes of the Worcester Baptist Association, 1886. Worcester: Henry A. Howland, 1886.

Minutes of the Worcester Baptist Association, 1894. Worcester: The Association, 1894.

Parker, Allen. *Recollections of Slavery Times*. Worcester: Charles Burbank and Company, 1895.

Powers, George W. *The Story of the Thirty-eighth Regiment of Massachusetts Volunteers*. Cambridge, MA: Dakin and Metcalf, 1866.

Putnam, Samuel H. *The Story of Company A, Twenty-fifth Regiment, Massachusetts Volunteers, in the War of the Rebellion*. Worcester: Putnam, David, and Company, 1886.

Rawick, George, ed. *The American Slave: A Composite Autobiography*. Vols. 14 and 15, North Carolina Narratives, Parts 1 and 2. Westport, CT: Greenwood Publishing Company, 1972.

Rice, Franklin, ed. *Dictionary of Worcester and Its Vicinity*. 2nd ed. Worcester: F. S. Blanchard and Company, 1893.

———. *The Worcester of 1898: Fifty Years as a City*. Worcester: F. S. Blanchard Company, 1899.

Roberts, Mrs. Frederick. "The Aftermath." *Carolina and the Southern Cross* (February 1914): 4.

———. "Historical Incidents." *Carolina and the Southern Cross* (April 1914): 10–12.

Roe, A. S. "Twenty Years of Harvard Street." *Proceedings of the Worcester Society of Antiquity*. Vol. 47. Worcester: Worcester Society of Antiquity, 1897.

———. *Worcester Classical and English High School: A Record of Forty-seven Years*. Worcester: published by the author, 1892.

Roster of George H. Ward Post, No. 10, Department of Massachusetts, Grand Army of the Republic. Worcester, 1888 and 1896.

Sprague, A. B. R. "Burnside's Expedition to North Carolina: The Capture of Roanoke Island." *Proceedings of the Worcester Society of Antiquity for the New Year, 1907*. Vol. 23. Worcester: Worcester Society of Antiquity, 1908.

Stanly, Edward. *A Military Governor Among Abolitionists*. New York: n.p., 1865.

Swint, Henry L., ed. *Dear Ones at Home: Letters from Contraband Camps*. Nashville: Vanderbilt University Press, 1966.

Tappan, Franklin D. *The Passing of the Grand Army of the Republic*. Worcester: Commonwealth Press, 1939.

Taylor, Susie King. *A Black Woman's Civil War Memoirs: Reminiscences of My Life in Camp with the 33rd U.S. Colored Troops, Late 1st South Carolina Volunteers*. Edited by Patricia Romero. New York: Markus Weiner, 1988.

Thayer, Eli. *A History of the Kansas Crusade: Its Friends and Its Foes*. New York: Harper and Brothers, 1889.

———. *The New England Emigrant Aid Company*. Worcester: Franklin P. Rice, 1887.

Veney, Bethany. *The Narrative of Bethany Veney, A Slave Woman*. Boston: George H. Ellis, 1889.

The War of the Rebellion: A Compilation of the Official Records of the Union and Confederate Armies. Series 1, Vol. 9. Washington: Government Printing Office, 1883.

Willis, Henry A. *The Fifty-third Regiment, Massachusetts Volunteers*. Fitchburg, MA: Blanchard and Brown, 1889.

SECONDARY SOURCES

Barrett, John G. *The Civil War in North Carolina*. Chapel Hill: University of North Carolina Press, 1963.

Beatty, Bess. *A Revolution Gone Backward: The Black Response to National Politics, 1876–1896*. Westport, CT: Greenwood Press, 1987.

Berlin, Ira, Barbara J. Fields, Thavolia Glymph, Joseph P. Reidy, and Leslie Rowland. *Freedom: A Documentary History of Emancipation, 1861–67: The Destruction of Slavery*. Series 1, Vol. 1. New York: Cambridge University Press, 1985.

Blight, David W. *Race and Reunion: The Civil War in American Memory*. Cambridge, MA: Belknap Press of Harvard University Press, 2001.

Bodnar, John, Michael Weber, and Roger Simon. "Migration, Kinship, and Urban Adjustment: Blacks and Poles in Pittsburgh, 1900–1930." *Journal of American History* 66 (September 1979): 548–65.

Bostic, Corrine. *Go Onward and Upward! An Interpretive Biography of the Life of Miss Sarah Ella Wilson*. Worcester: Commonwealth Press, 1974.

Boucher, Diane M. "The Howard Industrial School for Colored Women and Children." Unpublished seminar paper, Clark University, 2008.

Brooke, John L. *The Heart of the Commonwealth: Society and Political Culture in Worcester County, Massachusetts, 1713–1861*. New York: Cambridge University Press, 1989.

Broussard, Albert. *Black San Francisco: The Struggle for Racial Equality in the West, 1900–1954*. Lawrence: University of Kansas Press, 1993.

Brown, Norman D. *Edward Stanly: Whiggery's Tarheel "Conqueror."* University: University of Alabama Press, 1975.

Chasan, Joshua. "Civilizing Worcester: The Creation of Institutional and Cultural Order, Worcester, Massachusetts, 1848–1876." Ph.D. diss., University of Pittsburgh, 1974.

Click, Patricia C. *Time Full of Trial: The Roanoke Island Freedmen's Colony, 1862–1867*. Chapel Hill: University of North Carolina Press, 2001.

Cohen, William C. *At Freedom's Edge: Black Mobility and the Southern White Quest for Racial Control, 1861–1915*. Baton Rouge: Louisiana State University Press, 1991.

Cushing, John D. "The Cushing Court and the Abolition of Slavery in Massachusetts: More Notes on the Quock Walker Case." *American Journal of Legal History* 5 (April 1961): 118–44.

Damarjian, Alan. "A Struggle for Recognition: Black Voters in Worcester, Massachusetts." Unpublished seminar paper, Clark University, 1994.

Davis, Elizabeth Lindsay. *Lifting as They Climb*. New York: G. K. Hall, 1996.

Doughton, Thomas L. "Unseen Neighbors: Native Americans of Central Massachusetts, A People Who Had 'Vanished.'" In *After King Philip's War: Presence and Persistence in Indian New England*, edited by Colin G. Calloway, 207–30. Hanover, NH: University Press of New England, 1997.

Ellis, Mark E., and Linda V. Hart. "The Church Across the Street." *Quaboag Plantation, Special Commemorative Issue*, 1987.

Faulkner, Carol. *Women's Radical Reconstruction: The Freedmen's Aid Movement*. Philadelphia: University of Pennsylvania Press, 2004.

Foner, Eric. *Reconstruction: America's Unfinished Revolution, 1863–1877*. New York: Harper and Row, 1988.

Frank, Joseph Allan. *With Ballot and Bayonet: The Political Socialization of American Civil War Soldiers*. Athens: University of Georgia Press, 1998.

Fredrickson, George M. *The Black Image in the White Mind: The Debate on African-American Character and Destiny*. New York: Harper and Row, 1971.

———. *Black Liberation: A Comparative History of Black Ideologies in the United States*. New York: Oxford University Press, 1995.

Griffin, Farah Jasmine. *"Who Set You to Flowin'?": The African American Migration Narrative*. New York: Oxford University Press, 1996.

Grossman, James. *Land of Hope: Chicago, Black Southerners, and the Great Migration*. Chicago: University of Chicago Press, 1989.

Gutridge, Stanley Holmes. *For God and Humanity: A Documentary History of How Twelve Women in 1898 Served the Community and Emerged as the Association of Colored Peoples*. Worcester: published by the author, 2004.

Harris, William C. "Lincoln and Wartime Reconstruction in North Carolina, 1861–1863." *North Carolina Historical Review* 63 (1986): 149–68.

Harrison, Robert. "Welfare and Employment Policies of the Freedmen's Bureau in the District of Columbia." *Journal of Southern History* 72 (February 2006): 75–110.

Henri, Florette. *Black Migration: Movement North, 1900–1920.* Garden City, NY: Anchor Press, 1975.

Horton, James Oliver. *Free People of Color: Inside the African American Community.* Washington: Smithsonian Institution, 1993.

Horton, James Oliver, and Lois E. Horton. *Black Bostonians: Family Life and Community Struggle in the Antebellum North.* New York: Holmes and Meier, 1979.

Horton, Lois Elaine. "The Development of Federal Social Policy for Blacks in Washington, D.C., After Emancipation." Ph.D. diss., Brandeis University, 1977.

Hurd, D. Hamilton. *History of Worcester County: With Biographical Sketches of Its Pioneers and Prominent Men.* Vol. 2. Philadelphia: J. W. Lewis and Company, 1889.

Johnson, Michael P. "Out of Egypt: The Migration of Former Slaves to the Midwest during the 1860s in Comparative Perspective." In *Crossing Boundaries: Comparative History of Black People in Diaspora*, edited by Darlene Clark Hine and Jacqueline McLeod, 223–45. Bloomington: Indiana University Press, 1999.

Jones, Jacqueline. *American Work: Four Centuries of Black and White Labor.* New York: W. W. Norton, 1998.

Jones, Maxine D. "The American Missionary Association and the Beaufort, North Carolina, School Controversy, 1866–67." *Phylon* 48 (2nd Quarter 1987): 103–11.

King, Miriam L., and Dianna L. Magnuson. "Perspectives on Historical U.S. Census Undercounts." *Social Science History* 19 (Winter 1995): 455–66.

Kiser, Clyde Vernon. *Sea Island to City: A Study of St. Helena Islanders in Harlem and Other Urban Centers.* New York: Columbia University Press, 1932.

Lawes, Carolyn. *Women and Reform in a New England Community, 1815–1860.* Lexington: University Press of Kentucky, 2000.

Lemke, Sieglinde. Introduction to *Lifting as They Climb*, by Elizabeth L. Davis. New York: G. K. Hall, 1996.

Lofton, Williston H. "Northern Labor and the Negro during the Civil War." *Journal of Negro History* 34 (July 1949): 251–73.

Marvin, Abijah B. *History of Worcester in the War of Rebellion.* Cleveland: A. H. Clark, 1880.

McCarthy, B. Eugene, and Thomas L. Doughton, eds. *From Bondage to Belonging: The Worcester Slave Narratives.* Amherst: University of Massachusetts Press, 2007.

McConnell, Stuart. *Glorious Contentment: The Grand Army of the Republic, 1865–1900.* Chapel Hill: University of North Carolina Press, 1992.

McFeely, William S. *Sapelo's People: A Long Walk Into Freedom.* New York: W. W. Norton, 1994.

McPherson, James M. *Battle Cry of Freedom: The Civil War Era.* New York: Ballantine Books, 1988.

———. *For Cause and Comrades: Why Men Fought in the Civil War.* New York: Oxford University Press, 1997.

Meagher, Timothy J. *Inventing Irish America: Generation, Class, and Ethnic Identity in a New England City, 1880–1928*. Notre Dame, IN: University of Notre Dame Press, 2001.

———. "The Lord Is Not Dead: Cultural and Social Change Among the Irish in Worcester, Massachusetts." Ph.D. diss., Brown University, 1982.

Melish, Joanne Pope. *Disowning Slavery: Gradual Emancipation and "Race" in New England, 1780–1860*. Ithaca: Cornell University Press, 1998.

Mitchell, Reid. *The Vacant Chair: The Northern Soldier Leaves Home*. New York: Oxford University Press, 1993.

Mobley, Joe A. *James City: A Black Community in North Carolina, 1863–1900*. Raleigh: North Carolina Department of Cultural Resources, Division of Archives and History, 1981.

Mooney, James Eugene. "Antislavery in Worcester County, Massachusetts: A Case Study." Ph.D. diss., Clark University, 1971.

Munroe, James Phinney. *A Life of Francis Amasa Walker*. New York: Henry Holt and Company, 1923.

Nutt, Charles. *History of Worcester and Its People*. Vols. 1 and 2. New York: Lewis Historical Publishing Company, 1919.

Osofsky, Gilbert. *Harlem: The Making of a Ghetto, Negro New York, 1890–1930*. New York: Harper and Row, 1966.

Ostgren, Robert C. *A Community Transplanted: The Trans-Atlantic Experience of a Swedish Immigrant Settlement in the Upper Middle West, 1835–1915*. Madison: University of Wisconsin Press, 1988.

Painter, Nell Irvin. *Exodusters: Black Migration to Kansas After Reconstruction*. New York: Knopf, 1977.

Pleck, Elizabeth Hafkin. *Black Migration and Poverty: Boston, 1865–1900*. New York: Academic Press, 1979.

Powell, William S., ed. *Dictionary of North Carolina Biography*. Vol. 4. Chapel Hill: University of North Carolina Press, 1991.

Reid, Richard. "Raising the African Brigade: Early Black Recruitment in Civil War North Carolina." *North Carolina Historical Review* 70 (July 1993): 250–87.

Reidel, Michelle. "'In the True Spirit': Black Women's Organizations in Worcester, Massachusetts, 1900–1920." Unpublished seminar paper, Clark University, 1992.

Reilly, Stephen Edward. "Reconstruction Through Regeneration: Horace James's Work with the Blacks for Social Reform in North Carolina, 1862–1867." Ph.D. diss., Duke University, 1983.

Ripley, C. Peter. *Slaves and Freedmen in Civil War Louisiana*. Baton Rouge: Louisiana State University Press, 1976.

Rose, Willie Lee. *Rehearsal for Reunion: The Port Royal Experiment*. New York: Oxford University Press, 1964.

Rosenzweig, Roy. *Eight Hours for What We Will: Workers and Leisure in an Industrial City, 1870–1920*. New York: Cambridge University Press, 1983.

Salvatore, Nick. *We All Got History: The Memory Books of Amos Webber*. New York: Times Books, 1996.

Scheiner, Seth. *Negro Mecca: A History of the Negro in New York City, 1865–1920*. New York: New York University Press, 1965.

Schwalm, Leslie A. *Emancipation's Diaspora: Race and Reconstruction in the Upper Midwest*. Chapel Hill: University of North Carolina Press, 2009.

——. *A Hard Fight for We: Women's Transition from Slavery to Freedom in South Carolina*. Urbana: University of Illinois Press, 1997.

——. "'Overrun with Free Negroes': Emancipation and Wartime Migration in the Upper Midwest." *Civil War History* 50 (2004): 145–74.

Sears, Stephen. *Landscape Turned Red: The Battle of Antietam*. New Haven: Ticknor and Fields, 1983.

Shaffer, Donald R. *After the Glory: The Struggles of Black Civil War Veterans*. Lawrence: University of Kansas Press, 2004.

Spencer, Edna. "What Color Is the Wind?" M.A. thesis, Clark University, 1985.

Steckel, Richard. "The Quality of Census Data for Historical Inquiry: A Research Agenda." *Social Science History* 15 (Winter 1991): 579–99.

Taylor, Quintard. *The Forging of a Black Community: Seattle's Central District from 1870 through the Civil Rights Era*. Seattle: University of Washington Press, 1994.

Temple, Josiah. *History of North Brookfield*. N.p., 1887.

Thomas, Emily Frances. "'To Make Another New England of the Whole South': Massachusetts Freedpeople's Teachers, 1862–1900." M.A. thesis, Clark University, 1998.

Trotter, Joe William. "Black Migration in Historical Perspective: A Review of the Literature." In *The Great Migration in Historical Perspective: New Dimensions of Race, Class, and Gender*, edited by Joe William Trotter, 1–21. Bloomington: Indiana University Press, 1991.

Tyler, The Rev. Albert. "The Butman Riot." *Worcester Society of Antiquity Publications* 1 (1879): 85–89.

Vinal, Ella L. "The Status of the Worcester Negro." M.A. thesis, Clark University, 1929.

Voegeli, V. Jacque. *Free But Not Equal: The Midwest and the Negro during the Civil War*. Chicago: University of Chicago Press, 1967.

——. "A Rejected Alternative: Union Policy and the Relocation of Southern 'Contrabands' at the Dawn of Emancipation." *Journal of Southern History* 49 (November 2003): 765–90.

Von Frank, Albert. *The Trials of Anthony Burns: Freedom and Slavery in Emerson's Boston*. Cambridge, MA: Harvard University Press, 1998.

Watson, Alan D. *A History of New Bern and Craven County*. New Bern: Tryon Palace Commission, 1987.

White, Deborah Gray. *Too Heavy a Load: Black Women in Defense of Themselves*. New York: W. W. Norton, 1999.

Williams, Lillian Serece. *Strangers in the Land of Paradise: The Creation of African American Community, Buffalo, New York, 1900–1940*. Bloomington: Indiana University Press, 1999.

Williams, William H. *The Negro in the District of Columbia during Reconstruction*. Washington, DC: Howard University Studies in History, No. 5, 1924.

Zeller, Rose. "Changes in Ethnic Composition and Character of Worcester's Population." Ph.D. diss., Clark University, 1940.

Index

Abolitionists: on mass relocation of
contrabands, 54–55; of New England, 6;
passing of generation of, 4–5, 8, 132–33,
147; as patrons for postwar migrants,
106; on start of Civil War, 11–12, 13–14;
Union soldiers as, 34–37, 188 (n. 19)
— of Worcester: bonds between black
and white, 19; before Civil War, 2–3,
14–20; on Fugitive Slave Law, 16–19;
labor issues and, 184 (n. 7); as patrons
for postwar migrants, 106, 120, 125;
radicalism of, 14; on start of Civil War,
13–14, 15; in Union army, 24–26, 34–37;
women as, 60
Activism. *See* Political activism, postwar;
Social activism, by children of postwar
migrants
Adams, George, 111
Advertising, 93, 95, 119–20
African Brigade, 58, 100
Aid organizations, freedmen's, 60–65,
105–6
Allen, Albert, 108, 109
Allen, David Porter, 29–30, 97–98, 107–8,
198 (n. 26)
Allen, Isaiah: absence in census, 203
(n. 79); employment of, 29; escape
from slavery, 27, 187 (n. 1); migration
to Worcester, 98–101; as slave vs. free-
born, 198–99 (n. 28)
Alliances, black-white: in New Bern,
45–46; in Worcester, 52
Altruism, of soldiers, 188 (n. 19)

AMA. *See* American Missionary
Association
American Missionary Association
(AMA), 67, 68–69, 70, 75–76
AME Zion Church, 110, 116, 139, 142,
144–45
Anderson, William R., 158
Andrew, John, 7, 54, 100
Antietam, battle of, 99, 199 (n. 30)
Armstrong, Samuel, 124
Association for the Relief of Liberated
Slaves, 60

Baldwin, John Denison: on end of war,
88; on first battles, 23; on first contra-
bands in Worcester, 49; on Lincoln's
assassination, 90, 91; on 6th regiment,
22; on Stanly, 47; on start of war, 13
Ball's Bluff, battle of, 27
Baltimore: attack on 6th regiment in, 22
Barber, Thomas, 106
Barbers, 15, 16, 18, 51
Barbour, Mary, 28
Barker, Bazzell, 145
Barrett, William, 102
Barton, George, 53
Batcheller, Tyler, 98
Beals, H. S., 67, 70, 75, 76
Beals, Sarah, 74
Beaufort, 67, 70–72, 75, 79
Beckton, William George, 96, 154, 167
Beecher, Henry Ward, 46
Beecher, William H., 98

Bell, D. W., 163

"Benevolent sympathizers," 2, 5, 53, 132–33, 147, 172

Bethel AME Church, 139, 144

Bethune, Mary McLeod, 114

Bible, 40

Biddle, E. George, 110

Big Bethel, battle of, 23

Birth records, 89

Black codes, 83

Black community of Worcester: contrabands supported by, 48, 50–55; freedpeople supported by, 62–65, 72–73; on Fugitive Slave Law, 18–19; leaders in, 65, 146; multiracial, 51, 184–85 (n. 12), 191 (n. 7); New Bern connection with, 73; northern- vs. southern-born, 51, 134–36, 191 (n. 7); prewar, 15–20; on start of Civil War, 15, 20; in twentieth century, 171–77

— postwar, 130–73; challenges facing, 132–34, 138; churches of, 130–42; economic struggles in, 132–33, 138–39, 147–51; leaders in, 146; marriages in, 135–36, 206 (n. 11); memory of slavery in, 131–32, 134; members as patrons for migrants, 94–95, 106; political activism in, 133–34, 154–69; southern influence on, 129, 134, 175; treatment of, vs. during war, 134, 147, 174; voluntary organizations of, 142–47; women's club movement in, 152–54

Black convention movement, 20

Black Migration and Poverty (Pleck), 5

Black migration to Worcester. *See* Contrabands; Freedpeople; Postwar migrants to Worcester

Black population: of Massachusetts, 9, 172; multiracial, 184–85 (n. 12), 191 (n. 7); of North, after Civil War, 9; undercounting of, 119, 182 (n. 6), 209 (n. 49); of Washington, DC, 121–22; of Worcester County, 3–4, 7, 50–51, 88, 134, 179

— of Worcester: in 1850, 16; in 1860, 7, 50; in 1862, 88; in 1870, 7, 88; in 1880, 134; in 1890, 134; in 1900, 4, 134, 209 (n. 49); in 1900s, 171–72; census statistics on, 179–80; southern- vs. northern-born, 88–89, 134, 179–80, 197 (n. 2); undercounting of, 119, 182 (n. 6), 209 (n. 49)

Blackstone Canal, 12

Blight, David W., 131–32, 206 (n. 3)

Bodnar, John, 150–51

Boston: abolitionists of, 3, 14; black population of, 51, 182 (n. 6); churches of, 137, 207 (n. 14); contrabands' relocation to, 53; political activism in, 210 (n. 59); postwar migrants in, 124, 206 (n. 10); southern-born blacks in, 51, 136, 206 (n. 10); undercounting of blacks in, 119, 182 (n. 6), 202 (n. 79)

Boston Advocate, 142

Boston and Worcester Railroad, 12

Boston Educational Commission, 67, 68

Boston Guardian, 142

Boyden, M. Louise, 70–71

Bray, Nicholas, 44, 45, 46

Briggs, William T.: arrival in New Bern, 67; on black war refugees, 79; on challenges facing teachers, 69–70, 71, 72; Chase sisters and, 68, 194 (n. 43); on students' desire for knowledge, 74; as Superintendent of Colored Schools, 67

Brooke, John, 12

Brooks, Alice, 100

Brooks, Annie, 125, 126, 204–5 (n. 96)

Brooks, Cato, 96

Brooks, Elizabeth Carter, 114

Brooks, John H., 100, 199 (n. 34)

Brooks, Kitty, 204–5 (n. 96)

Brooks, Lewis, 100

Brown, A., 125

Brown, Charles, 149

Brown, Jennie, 126

Brown, John, 14, 15, 25

Brown, Sarah G., 68

Brown, William, 51, 52, 53, 149

Brown, Mrs. William, 73
Brown, William Wells, 20, 142
Browne, Mrs. E. J., 120
Brown v. Board of Education, 76
Bryan, Mary Norcutt, 79
Bryan, William Jennings, 160, 162, 164
Bryant, Christopher, 94, 148
Bryant, Eliza, 94
Bryant, Harriet, 94
Bryant, Julia Ann, 94, 197 (n. 13)
Bryant, Maria, 143
Bryant, Mary, 49–55; arrival in Worcester, 49–50; departure from Worcester, 95; employment of, 93, 197 (n. 12); after end of war, 93–95; and mass relocation of contrabands, 55; as patron for migrants, 94–95; residence of, 52, 93
Bryant, William, 49–55; arrival in Worcester, 49–50, 93; career of, 49, 50–54, 93–94; departure from Worcester, 95; after end of war, 93–95; and mass relocation of contrabands, 55; as patron for migrants, 94–95; residence of, 52, 93; in Union employment, 49, 50
Bull Run, battle of, 23
Bureau of Freedmen, Refugees and Abandoned Lands, 80
Burnap, Mary A., 66–67
Burns, Anthony, 14, 17–18, 184 (n. 7)
Burnside, Ambrose: on capture of New Bern, 33; contraband policy of, 37, 39; contrabands employed by, 37, 49, 50; Expedition of, 3, 30–32; and Stanly, 43
Busby, George Alfred: critics of, 165–66; political activism of, 156; as political candidate, 157–59, 166–69
Busby, Jennie Clough, 166
Butler, Benjamin, 29, 37, 155
Butman, Asa O., 17–19, 185 (n. 16)
Butman Riot, 18

California, 16
Candidates, black, in local elections, 157–59, 166–69

Canedy, Betsey L., 66–67
Carter, Harriette, 122
Censuses: ethnic and racial complexities ignored in, 184–85 (n. 12); on population of Worcester, 179–80; U.S., 9. *See also* Black population
Chain migration, establishment of, 2, 4, 89, 94
Chase, Anthony, 68
Chase, Lucy: arrival in Norfolk, 68; on employment of migrants, 121; postwar migrants linked to, 89, 104–5; relationship with students, 75; visits with Worcesterites in South, 68, 194 (n. 43)
Chase, Sarah: arrival in Norfolk, 68; as patron of migrants' children, 113; postwar migrants linked to, 89, 104–5, 113; visits with Worcesterites in South, 68, 194 (n. 43)
Chicago, churches of, 139–40, 141–42
Children: contraband, 39; of postwar migrants, 113–19, 147; postwar migration by, 103, 125
Christian Associations of New York and Brooklyn, 34
Churches, 130–42; relationships among, 142, 144–45; southern culture in, 131–32, 136–42, 175
Citizenship rights: for freedpeople, 82–83; postwar demand for, 92, 146–47; for veterans, 92, 146
Civil rights: failure during Reconstruction, 131; twentieth-century movement for, 177
— in Worcester: black political activists working for, 154–69; in Independence Day parade of 1865, 92; postwar demand for, 92–93; strategies for achieving, 133–34; in twentieth century, 177; for veterans, 92; white advocates of, 147
Civil Rights Bill of 1875, 155
Civil War: end of, 77–79, 88; first battles of, 23; memory of (*see* Memory of slavery and Civil War); public opinion

Dale Hospital, 91
Damon, J. F., 126, 128
Davis, Isaac, 13
Davis, Mrs. John, 60, 64
Davis, Toussaint L., 177
Davis, W. R., 161
Day, David L., 26, 187 (n. 39)
Death records, 89
DeBoise, Stacey A., 169
Democratic Party: on black migration, 54; black support for, 160–67
Denholm, McKay Company, 153
Denny, J. Waldo, 35–36, 104
Derby, W. P., 36, 37, 38
Devens, Charles, 23
Dictionary of Worcester and Its Vicinity (Rice), 147
Disfranchisement, 134, 142, 155, 161
Dix, John, 54
Dodd, Helen, 75
Domestic service: postwar migrants in, 103, 107, 119–20, 123, 128; women in, 119–20, 123, 128, 138, 200 (n. 42), 205 (n. 102)
Doughton, Thomas L., 170, 185 (n. 12)
Douglass, Frederick, 64, 75, 92–93, 132, 160
Draper, William F., 32–33
Dred Scott decision, 15, 127

Earle, Ann, 60, 64, 125, 204–5 (n. 96)
Earle, Edward, 125
Earle, Thomas, 35, 50
East Side–West Side picnics, 175–76
Economic depression of 1890s, 151
Economic struggles: of freedpeople, 84; in postwar black community, 132–33, 138–39, 147–51
Edmands, S. S., 98, 107–8
Education: of contrabands, 39–44, 56, 190 (n. 41); of freedpeople, 65–77, 89; of postwar migrants, 107–8, 123, 124, 128; of soldiers, 24
Edwards, Alfred, 146

Edwards, Daniel, 105, 154, 158
Edwards, Ella, 152
Edwards, Emma, 152
Edwards, Gertrude, 152
Edwards, Laura, 106
Elderly, homes for, 114, 152
Elections: black candidates in, 157–59, 166–69; black political activism in, 155–69
Elliot, Henry Clay, 160–61
Emancipation: announcement of, 57; in Massachusetts, 14, 184 (n. 6); memory of, 131–32, 147–48
Emancipation Days, 142–43, 176
Emancipation Proclamation: anniversaries of, 64, 77; announcement of, 57; annual celebrations of, 142–43, 156, 176; and mass relocation of contrabands, 54; purpose of war changed by, 57
Emancipation's Diaspora (Schwalm), 5–6, 183 (n. 11)
Emmerton, James, 38
Employment of contrabands, 37–38, 49, 50
Employment in Worcester: abolitionists and, 120, 125; before Civil War, 51; of contrabands, 49, 50; discrimination in, 148–51, 172, 177; in 1880 census profile, 138; Freedmen's Bureau and, 89, 119–28; in industry, 133, 138, 148–51; patrons of migrants and, 90, 120, 125; in twentieth century, 172, 176; wages for, 126

Faulkner, Carol, 5, 61, 64–65, 123, 204 (n. 96), 205 (n. 102)
15th Massachusetts Volunteer Infantry: at Antietam, 99, 199 (n. 30); at Ball's Bluff, 27; campaigns of, 3; casualties in, 27; education levels in, 24; establishment of, 23; first contact with slaves, 28–29; Poolesville camp of, 27, 28–29; postwar migrants linked to, 89, 96–101; slaves joining, 27–30; Worcesterites in, 23
51st Massachusetts Volunteer Infantry, 48, 89

Grand United Order of Odd Fellows, 143–44

Grant, U. S., 155

Great Migration: churches in, 139–40; vs. Civil War–era migration, 2; northern blacks' reaction to, 135, 206 (n. 10); studies of, 2; in Worcester, 171–72

Green, Elias, 125

Green, William, 31

Grey, Daniel, 125

Griffey, Josephine, 123

Griffin, Farah Jasmine, 206 (n. 10)

Griffing, Josephine, 205 (n. 96)

Grossman, James, 139–40, 141

Guides, contrabands working as, 38

Gutridge, Florida Wiggins, 115–19

Gutridge, Stanley, 115, 116, 118–19

Harper's Weekly, 57

Harrington, Samuel, 96

Harris, Sarah, 28

Harrison, Robert, 5

Hartwell, Samuel C., 102

Hatteras, Cape, 31

Haven, S. Foster, Jr., 99

Hawkins, William G., 63

Hayden, Lewis, 20, 53

Hemenway, Alexander, 137, 138

Higginson, Thomas Wentworth: abolitionism of, 14, 15; arrival in Worcester, 13; black alliance with, 52; in Burns incident, 14, 17–18, 185 (n. 16); on soldiers' lives, 26; on start of war, 12, 13–14, 15; on Worcester as Canada to slaves, 3, 20, 51

Highland Street (Worcester), 135, 136

Hill, Alonzo, 13, 100, 198 (n. 28)

Hill, Edward, 73

Historical memory. *See* Memory of slavery and Civil War

Hoar, George Frisbie: on Allen (Isaiah), 99, 100, 101; in Butman Riot, 18, 185 (n. 16); as civil rights advocate, 147;

Mason (Isaac) and, 53, 170, 212 (n. 101); on Walker family, 98

Holland, Jacob, 126

Home for Aged Colored People, 114

Hood, J. W., 84

Hopkins, Henry, 126

Hosmer, Susan, 66–67

Household of Ruth, 144

House of Representatives, U.S., 46–47

Howard, Charles, 122

Howard, Oliver, 71–72

Howard Industrial School, 124

Independence Day of 1865, 88, 91–93

Indignation meeting, 45–46

Industries: postwar, 133, 138, 148–51; prewar, 12–13; in twentieth century, 172

Inman, Albert H., 158, 159

Institutions, black, 142–47; fraternal, 143–45, 146; white financial support of, 133, 153; women's clubs, 113–15, 152–54

Irish immigrants: before Civil War, 13; as domestic workers, 120; in industrial jobs, 148, 150, 209 (n. 43); political activism of, 159; violence against blacks by, 127–28, 205 (n. 100)

Isolation, of postwar migrants, 128

Jackson, Aaron, 112, 148

Jackson, Andrew, 131

Jackson, Charlotte Veney, 111–12, 148

Jackson, Raymond, 168

James, Elizabeth, 70

James, Helen, 48, 59, 60, 65

James, Horace: abolitionism of, 25; on agency of freedpeople, 62; aid for freedpeople from, 57–60, 62; arrival in New Bern, 33; and black political organization, 83; in bonds between soldiers and contrabands, 30; on children of revolution, 58, 155, 174; church services by, 41; community values enforced by, 25, 41; death of, 86; in education of contrabands, 39–41,

43–44; in education of freedpeople, 65–68, 78; Emancipation Proclamation and, 57–58; evolution of views on slavery, 25; on first fruits of war, 1–2, 58, 174; at Freedman's Bureau, 80, 83, 86; fund-raising efforts of, 41, 48, 58–60; influence in New Bern, 3, 39–41; and Lane (Lunsford), 72–73; legacy of, 87; on meaning of war, 25–26; in relocation of contrabands to Worcester, 50; return to Massachusetts, 85–86; and Roanoke Island colony, 58–60, 79–81; selection as chaplain, 25; on Stanly's governorship, 47, 56; as Superintendent of Negro Affairs, 67; as Superintendent of the Poor, 56–58; teachers recruited by, 65–68, 69; in Trent River Settlement (James City), 81, 85, 101, 135; yellow fever and, 70

James City, 81, 85, 101, 135

Jankins, William: arrival in Worcester, 15–16, 51; in Burns incident, 17; death of, 156; political activism of, 156; pursuit of as fugitive, 16, 18–19, 185 (n. 16); recruitment of soldiers by, 146; support for Union, 15

Jenkins, George W., 77

Jennings, Thomas J., 39

Jewish immigrants, 135

Jim Crow: black political activism against, 155; in Worcester, 133, 152, 176–77

Johnson, Andrew, 80–81, 84–85, 86, 122

Johnson, Henry, 94, 139, 197 (n. 13)

Johnson, Julia Ann Bryant, 94, 139, 197 (n. 13)

Johnson, Michael P., 2, 5, 9, 107, 183 (n. 11)

Johnson, Robert H.: arrival in Worcester, 51; on dependence on patrons, 165; in employment of Bryants, 50, 51–52; as former slave, 51–52; political activism of, 154, 162–63, 165; residence of, 53

John Street (Mount Olive) Baptist Church, 130–42; in civil rights movement, 177; controversy over, 139–40;

establishment of, 130–31, 136–37, 139–41; financial support of, 133, 138–39, 141, 151; growth of, 140, 141; members of, 137–38, 141–42, 207 (n. 16); memory of slavery in, 141; pastors of, 140–41, 142, 177; political activism in, 163–64; southern culture in, 131–32, 136–42, 175; in twentieth century, 175, 177; white patrons of, 130–31, 132–33, 141, 165

Jones, Ellen M., 74–75

Jones, Henry, 96

Jones, Louise, 143

Jones, Raymond, 159

Joyner, Charles, 8

Kansas migration, 5, 14, 182 (n. 7)

Kansas-Nebraska Act of 1854, 14

Kennard, Sylvia, 153

Kennary, Patrick, 127–28

Kimball, John W., 102

Knights of Pythias, 144

Labor, slavery as issue of, 184 (n. 7)

Laborers, contrabands working as, 37–38

Lakeman, Sarah, 71

Landownership. *See* Property ownership

Lane, Lunsford, 62–64, 72–73, 95

Lane, Ned, 72–73

Larned, Daniel Reed, 44

Lassiter, Jesse, 84

Lee, Ann, 137

Lee, Ellen, 68

Lee, George W., 137

Lee, Minnie, 143

Lee, Robert E., 78

Lewis, John, 102

Lewis, Maria, 125–26

Libbey, J. L., 125, 127, 205 (n. 101)

Liel, Lacy, 95

Liel, Ruth, 95

Life of Isaac Mason as a Slave (Mason), 169–71

Lincoln, Abraham: assassination of, 90–91; call for volunteer soldiers, 12, 13;

contraband policy of, 29, 34; on goals of war, 28, 29, 34; on mass relocation of contrabands, 192 (n. 16); North Carolina black delegation to, 82; southerners' views of, 21; and Stanly's governorship, 43, 46–47; Unionist strategy of, 34, 43, 49, 56–57

Literacy classes. *See* Education

Littler, Thomas E., 102

Louisiana, postwar migrants from, 89, 96, 101–3

Lowell, Anna, 120, 124, 205 (n. 102)

Lucy Stone Club, 152–54

Lynchings, 142

Maine, black population of, 9, 183 (n. 11)

Manassas, battle of, 23

Manhood, of former slaves, 62, 64

Manning, David, 161–62

Manual labor school, 72–73

Manufacturing: postwar, 133, 138, 148–51; prewar, 12–13; in twentieth century, 172

Marble, Jerome, 117

Marriage: records of, 49, 89; of southern and northern blacks, 135–36, 206 (n. 11)

Maryland, postwar migrants from, 88, 89

Mason, Anna, 16, 52–53, 106, 192 (n. 13)

Mason, Isaac: arrival in Worcester, 16, 51, 53, 191–92 (n. 11); on benevolent sympathizers, 53, 147; career of, 16, 53, 170; church of, 139; death of, 156, 170; escape from slavery, 52–53, 171; on Fugitive Slave Law, 17, 171; in Independence Day parade of 1865, 92; narrative by, 169–71; as patron for postwar migrants, 106; political activism of, 156; property owned by, 52, 53; recruitment of soldiers by, 146; support for contrabands by, 52–54

Mason, James, 136

Massachusetts: black population of, 9, 172; concerns about migration in, 7, 54; emancipation of slaves in, 14, 184

(n. 6); freedpeople on liberty and, 75; proposed mass relocation of contrabands to, 54–55, 192 (n. 16); racial discrimination in, prewar, 19–20

Massachusetts Citizens Equal Rights Association, 156

Massachusetts Colored Veterans Association of Worcester, 146

Massachusetts Supreme Judicial Court, 14

Mass relocation: of contrabands, 54–55; of postwar migrants, 121–23

May, Mrs. Samuel, 121

McCarthy, B. Eugene, 170

McClellan, George B., 29, 97

McConnell, Stuart, 145, 146

McFeely, William, 174

McKinley, William, 160, 161–62, 164, 166

McPherson, James M., 188 (n. 19)

Meagher, Timothy J., 151, 172, 209 (n. 43)

Mechanics, 59

Media coverage. *See* Newspapers; *specific papers*

Melish, Joanne Pope, 6, 19, 184 (n. 6)

Memorial Day, 143

Memory of slavery and Civil War: in contemporary narratives, 169–71; in John Street Baptist Church, 141; patriotic, 131–32, 206 (n. 3); in political activism, 155, 172–73; in Republican Party, 147–48; in southern identity, 131–32, 134, 172; of veterans, 146

Mero, Andrew, 109–10

Mero, Charles Sumner, 109–10, 148

Mero, Jane Waples: church of, 139; family of, 109–10, 113; migration to Worcester, 96, 103; residence of, 109, 110, 112, 148; as servant, 103, 107, 109; status in community, 110

Mero, Susan, 110

Merriam, Anne P., 67, 78, 104, 194 (n. 43)

Middle class: postwar migrants employed by, 119–20; in Union army, 9, 24

Migrants: after war (*see* Postwar migrants to Worcester); during war (*see* Civil

Nipmuc Indians, 51
Norfolk, 68
North Brookfield, 22–23, 98, 108
North Brookfield Journal, 108, 201 (n. 54)
North Carolina: disfranchisement in, 161; postwar migrants from, 3–4, 88–89, 96, 134–35, 197 (n. 2); Stanly as military governor of, 43–47; Union victories in, 32; Worcester soldiers in, 3. *See also* New Bern
North Carolina Daily Times, 78, 81, 83–84
Northeastern Federation of Colored Women's Clubs, 153, 160
Northeastern Federation of Women's Clubs, 114
Northern states, voting rights in, before Civil War, 19
Northern whites: on aid for freedpeople, 61–62; concerns about migration, 7, 54; on Fugitive Slave Law, 16–17; racial assumptions of, 61–62; slaves' view of, as liberators, 34; on start of Civil War, 11–12

Old South Congregational Church, 25–26, 41
Opelousas Tommy, 102, 103

Parker, Allen: church of, 137, 142, 170; escape from slavery, 27, 94; in Grand Army of the Republic, 146, 170; migration to Worcester, 94–95; narrative by, 169–71
Partridge, John W., 33, 41, 42
Paternalism, 99
Patriotic memory, 131–32
Patrons: abolitionists as, 106, 120, 125; black Worcesterites as, 94–95, 106; for children of migrants, 113–19, 147; divisions over dependence on, 165–66; in employment of migrants, 90, 120, 125; importance of, 7, 90, 119, 128–29; of John Street Baptist Church, 130–31, 132–33, 141, 165; missionary teachers as,

104–5; motivations of, 107; passing of generation of, 2, 5, 53, 132–33, 147; political, 157, 159, 168–69; racialist notions of, 107; and residential patterns, 107–12; soldiers as, 96–104
Pearson, Sara, 71
Peckham, A. C., 68
Peninsular campaign, 29–30, 97
Perkins, Joseph, 105
Peters, Josephine, 124
Petersham, 60
Phelps, Emory, 146
Pickett, Major, 36
Pinchback, P. B. S., 161
Piper, Emily, 67
Pittsburgh, job discrimination in, 150–51
Plantations, model, 85–86
Pleasant Street Baptist Church, 137, 140, 142
Pleck, Elizabeth, 5, 119, 124, 136, 182 (nn. 6, 7), 202 (n. 79), 206 (n. 10), 210 (n. 59)
Plummer, Clifford H., 162–63
Polish immigrants, 150–51
Political activism, postwar, 154–69; lack of unity in, 160, 165–66; in local elections, 155–69; memory of slavery in, 155, 172–73; by New Bern freedpeople, 81–84; shift in leadership of, 133, 154–56; strategies of, 133–34, 156–57, 166; by veterans, 146
Political patronage, 157, 159, 168–69
Pond, B. W., 72, 73
Poolesville (Maryland), 27, 28–29
Population of Worcester, 12, 179. *See also* Black population
Port Royal, 60
Postwar migrants to Worcester, 88–129; adjustment to North, 112–13, 128; children of, 113–19, 147; churches of, 130–42; education of, 107–8, 128; after 1875, 103–4, 134; employment of, 89, 90, 119–28; Freedmen's Bureau and, 89, 119–28; gender of, 103, 200 (n. 42);

hostility toward, 127–28; isolation of, 128; legacy of, 171–77; from Louisiana, 89, 96, 101–3; from Maryland, 88, 89; missionary teachers' links to, 89, 95–96, 104–5; from North Carolina, 3–4, 88–89, 96, 134–35, 197 (n. 2); pace of arrival, 7; patrons of (*see* Patrons); permanence of, 119, 126, 131; residential patterns of, 106–12, 135, 148–49, 201 (n. 52); soldiers' links to, 1, 4, 89, 96–104; southern- vs. northern-born, 88–89, 134, 197 (n. 2); from Virginia, 3–4, 88–89, 96–101, 134–35, 197 (n. 2); wages of, 126

Potter, George, 157, 159

Poverty, black, 147, 182 (n. 7)

Presidential elections: of 1868, 155; of 1900, 160–66

Prisoners of war, 78

Progressive Club, 152–54

Property ownership: by former slaves, 52, 53; by postwar migrants, 106–12, 201 (n. 52); in 1900, 148–49; freedmen's land returned to southern whites, 80–81, 85; total rates in Worcester, 52, 53, 192 (n. 13); in twentieth century, 174–75

Providence (Rhode Island), 12

Public opinion: on Lincoln's assassination, 91; on purpose of Civil War, 11–12, 13; on start of Civil War, 11–12, 13–14

Putnam, Samuel, 39

Quakers, 55, 125

Racial discrimination: in elections, 158–61; in employment, 148–51, 172, 177; postwar, 148–51, 158–61; prewar, 19–20; in twentieth century, 172, 176–77

Racialist notions: in debate over aid for freedpeople, 61–62; in employment of migrants, 120; of migrants' patrons, 107; of missionary teachers, 71–72; romantic, 71, 195 (n. 52)

Racial oppression, migration attributed to, 10, 183 (n. 16)

Racial segregation. *See* Segregation

Radical abolitionism, 14

Raiford, Augustus, 148

Railroads, 12, 38

Raleigh, 1865 political convention in, 81–83

Randall, Carl F., 162

Recollections of Slavery Times (Parker), 169–71

Reconstruction: broken promises of, 2, 4–5, 8, 131, 174; debate over aid in, 61–62; harmful policies of, 84–87; property ownership in, 85; violence against blacks in, 85

Reconstruction (Foner), 10

Refugees. *See* War refugees

Relief organizations, freedmen's, 60–65, 105–6

Republican Party: black support for, 155–69; and civil rights, 147; establishment in Worcester, 14; and mass relocation of contrabands, 54; memory of slavery in, 147–48; southerners' views of, 21

Residential patterns: of postwar migrants, 106–12, 135, 148–49, 201 (n. 52); in twentieth century, 175–76, 177; of white households, 107

Rhode Island, black population of, 9, 183 (n. 11)

Rice, Franklin, 147, 148

Rice, George T., 53

Richardson, Merrill, 23, 24–25

Ringalls, W. R., 159

Ripley, Peter, 102

Roanoke Island: in Burnside Expedition, 31–32, 33; freedpeople relocated to, 58–60, 79–81; missionary teachers in, 69, 70

Roberts, Mrs. Frederick C., 42, 79

Rock, John S., 19

Roe, Alfred S., 116–18

Rogers, Hattie, 21

Roger Wolcott Club, 166–67
Rollins, Joseph, 151
Romantic racialism, 71, 195 (n. 52)
Roper, Alice, 66–67
Roper, Ella, 69, 75
Rose, Willie Lee, 183 (n. 15)

Salem Street Society, 24
Salisbury, Stephen, 153
Salvatore, Nick, 143–44, 146, 155–56, 207
    (n. 18)
Sapelo's People (McFeely), 174
Saunders, Elizabeth Morse, 108
Saunders, James, 108
Scheiner, Seth, 183 (n. 16)
Schools. *See* Education
Schwalm, Leslie A., 5–6, 9, 50, 97, 183
    (nn. 11, 15), 200 (n. 42), 203 (n. 81),
    205 (n. 100), 206 (n. 4)
Scott, Catherine, 154
Scott, Charles E., 154, 162, 165, 167, 169
Scott, Edward, 154
Scott, George, 146
Scott, Walter, 154
Scouts, 38
Sea Islands, 183 (n. 15)
Sears, Stephen, 199 (n. 30)
Seattle, 183 (n. 16)
2nd North Carolina Colored Infantry, 100
Segregation, racial: in education, 75–76;
    postwar laws on, 142; and postwar
    migration to Worcester, 134; prewar,
    19–20; in twentieth century, 176–77
Self-liberation, in Midwest migration, 6
Senate, U.S., 46
Separate but equal policy, 76
Servants: contrabands as, 37–38; migrant
    women as, 103, 200 (n. 42)
Shannon, Alonzo, 113
Shannon, George, 110
Sherman, William Tecumseh, 77–78
Simmons, Helen A., 105–6
Simon, Roger, 150–51
Sims, Anthony, 18

6th Massachusetts regiment, 22
Sketches of My Life in the South (Stroyer),
    212 (n. 100)
Slavery: end of (*see* Emancipation); as
    labor issue, 184 (n. 7); memory of (*see*
    Memory of slavery and Civil War);
    narratives on, 169–71; as reason for
    Civil War, 12, 13, 15, 25, 34, 57; Union
    soldiers' first encounters with, 34–39
Slaves: communication networks of, 21;
    emancipated (*see* Freedpeople); fugi-
    tive (*see* Contrabands); views on Civil
    War, 11, 21; in Worcester before Civil
    War, 3, 14, 15–19
Smith, Abby, 115
Smith, Elias, 44
Smith, Juliet B., 67
Smith, Louise Wiggins, 117
Smith, Martin, 117–18
Social activism, by children of postwar
    migrants, 113–15
Social interactions, after Civil War, 83
Social mobility, 148–51
Social workers, 118–19
Soldiers
—black: after emancipation, 58; first,
    15, 100, 197 (n. 9); fund-raising for
    families of, 58; lack of, at start of war,
    15; recruitment of, 92, 146, 197 (n. 9);
    as veterans, 92, 131, 145–46
—Union: antislavery sentiments of,
    34–37, 188 (n. 19); changes in views of
    slavery, 34–39; contrabands employed
    by, 37–38, 49; contrabands' loyalty to,
    36–37, 49; first encounters with slavery,
    34–39; Lincoln's call for, 12, 13; motiva-
    tions of, 25–26, 35, 188 (n. 19); slave res-
    cues by, 46; on southern whites, 36–37,
    56; Stanly's policies opposed by, 45–46,
    56; as teachers of contrabands, 39–41,
    43–44; violence between blacks and, 9,
    183 (n. 15). *See also specific regiments*
—Worcester: bonds created with south-
    ern blacks, 1, 4, 28, 30, 49, 89, 131; in